Foreword by Jack R. Taylor

Discovering the
KINGDOM

A Guide for Seeking First the Kingdom

Michael Gissibl

Cover Art by Jennifer Hunter Jones.
Connect with Jennifer's FaceBook page at "Glimpses of Glory Studio."
Her work can be purchased at www.glimpsesofglory.biz
or she can be contacted at jejones@integrity.com.

www.burkhartbooks.com
Bedford, Texas

Endorsements

Michael Gissibl has dedicated his life to "seek first the Kingdom of God," unlike few other men I have known. In his book *Discovering the Kingdom*, Michael shares many revelatory ways in which he has learned to walk in incredible relationship to the Father. Michael does not approach these as abstract ideas that he prescribes arbitrarily. Rather, he is a practitioner of these disciplines and shares from a place of personal experience. Michael is a loving husband and father, a faithful friend and a passionate follower of Jesus. I trust that you will be both challenged and inspired as you read.

Rob Sperti, Pastor in community,
Garden City Church, Milwaukee Wisconsin

When Papa Jack Taylor introduced me to Michael Gissibl, he had already put his approval on the man. When a spiritual father validates, the other sons must take the relationship of brotherhood seriously. I have found that Michael is very insightful with a clear understanding of the Kingdom and the King. He has made seeking the kingdom first his primary focus. As you look into the pages of this book, you will find a fresh and pure revelation of the kingdom. Michael brings clarity of Kingdom DNA and reveals how it filters down into the day to day life of a believer. I personally have found principles in this book that are showing me how to walk in the 5-fold ministry in the church with a better kingdom focus. I highly recommend this book and the man.

Charles L Coker, Senior Leader
Identity Church , Deltona Florida

In *Discovering the Kingdom*, Michael guides us in a rediscovery of what has been there all along, but what the Lord has been waiting for His church to truly prioritize and understand. At the Lord's command the church has been praying for over 2000 years that His kingdom would come and His will be done. This book is a tool and yet a charge to live and proclaim in confidence that our prayers have been and are being answered. This is a call to keep the main thing, the kingdom, as the main thing!

David White, Lead Pastor
The Gathering Church, Moravian Falls, NC

There will never be a more important topic than the Kingdom of God. All of God's people have one primary goal in life. We are to seek the Kingdom first. This book will help you discover the topic and launch you on the path needed to achieve that. I hope you will find it helpful and insightful.

Louis DeSiena, Senior Leader
Torch Bearers Church, Jacksonville, Florida

Michael Gissibl (pronounced like "kissable") has no doubt spent the time to recommend how to seek the Kingdom. His passion is evident in every page and his insight is not only informative, but inspiring. *Discovering the Kingdom* is a treatise on how the Kingdom operates and how we can discover our place in it. As the context for all that is, the Kingdom is the most noble and necessary pursuit of this life. Michael demonstrates how this message has been forgotten, the demand for its return, and the rewards for discovering it for ourselves. *Discovering the Kingdom* has the potential to change lives.

Tim P. Taylor, Founder/Publisher
Burkhart Books, Bedford, Texas

Dedication

This book is dedicated to the Church of Jesus Christ. May the content in this publication become material for Jesus to use in building His Church.

Angela,
May this book become
a solid foundation for
the building of the Kingdom
realm of Consciousness in
your personal experience.

Resting in Jesus,
M.S.

Acknowledgments

Nothing accomplished is done alone. This work is no different. Those who have contributed are too vast in number to share. There are, however, six, I would like to acknowledge and thank.

Myles Monroe, thank you for "Seeking first the Kingdom." It was your pursuit of the Kingdom that empowered you to become such an insightful and effective teacher. I spent the first ten years seeking the Kingdom through the reading and studying of your material. They imparted more to me than all other Kingdom teachings combined. There is no value I could place on what you gave me. I honor you by presenting this work as the fruit of your labors.

I want to thank Jack Taylor for beginning Sonslink, an organization of spiritual sons that gather regularly in Kingdom fellowship. It was at a meeting in late 2015 that I met, for the first time a group of people who understood, to one degree or another, the Kingdom. This was my first human contact with such people. The synergy that took place was energizing and transforming. For the first time, I understood what was taking place in John and Jesus' mothers as two Kingdom men united for the first time. What inspired me more than anything was spending time with Jack, a man who clearly had been caught, captured and consumed by the Kingdom. Witnessing such a man confirmed, validated and inspired my pursuit of the Kingdom. I would not be where I am today if it weren't for Jack Taylor and Sonslink.

I want to thank my wife for her patience with me as I struggled through 14 years of study on this subject. I am indebted to you Sweet Baby.

I want to thank Tim Taylor for his contributions to this manuscript. Co-laboring with him not only made this project possible but gave fuller expression of my heart.

I want to thank Jesus for granting me access into His marvelous Kingdom.

I want to thank Holy Spirit for co-laboring with me to establish "Your Kingdom come on earth as it is in Heaven."

Contents

Foreword

I write many forwards, prefaces, forewords, introductions, endorsements, and the like and I love it. I have a different kind of joy and anticipation for each of them. For all of them, I really am gripped by the message. I do not remember a book that sparked in me any more anticipation than this one. Allow me to present in order the reasons for this:

The man: **Michael Gissibl** (actually pronounced like "kissable"), is an intriguing Christian, an able writer, a deep thinker, and as near a modern mystic as anybody I know. Several years ago, he began to develop a taste for knowledge on the Kingdom of God. That knowledge soon became a life-shaping passion which brought him to one of our Sons' events, during which he became a spiritual son. Our passions met on this common theme and the rest is history. It is my delight to introduce to you the man who penned this splendid work.

The message: the contents on the following pages deal with the most important theme in the New Testament or, for that matter, the Old Testament, namely the Kingdom of God. Many books have been written on the subject and many more will follow, but this book will remain special among them for a number of reasons, the greatest of which, in my opinion, is the freshness with which the subject is presented which involves a challenge to the reader to make a life-long commitment to seek the Kingdom with instructions on how to do it.

The mission: contained in this volume is the unapologetic demand to make room for both the King and His Kingdom in your life. Michael is a man on a mission and he makes it plain in the pages to follow. Pay close attention to the instructions following each chapter and take heed to the requested assignments. When the reader is finished with this book the journey in Kingdom-seeking and finding will have begun. Next to the thrill of discovering the Kingdom of God and the collateral implications for one's own self is the pleasure of helping another do the same.

The meaning: Read the book you have opened with the excitement that would accompany a journey to an ancient land in search of buried treasure with map in hand. You will find in the days ahead potential information that will powerfully impact the remainder of your life.

Thanks, Michael, for a work well done!

Jack Taylor, President,
Dimensions Ministries
Melbourne, Florida

Preface

Repentance is the threshold we must walk through to experience the Kingdom. Without a change of mind it's not possible to see the Kingdom let alone fulfill our role of making it known on earth as it is in Heaven. This book was created as an instrument of repentance and is designed to deposit the foundation required for Kingdom living: knowledge and understanding of the Kingdom of Heaven.

Repentance is not a religious word, rather it's something we do all day every day. Each time a high school student enters a new classroom he is repenting. Every time we transition from one activity to another we must engage in repentance. When Jesus declared "repent for the Kingdom of Heaven is at hand" He was making available an opportunity to turn our thinking to the greatest idea mankind will ever be presented. He was giving us a chance to enter a way of thinking that would structure the brain in such a way as to change the essence and nature of the mind. The result being a fresh awareness of Heaven on earth.

Repentance means a change of mind. Conventionally speaking we refer to this change of mind as going from one care or interest to another. From one school of thought to another or one way of thinking to another. Additionally, we look at repentance as a change in the way we think. We might say repentance is going from thinking negatively towards a person to positive or moving from "sinful thoughts" to "grateful thoughts." These are good examples but I would like to expand our definition and bring a more complete picture of what Christ meant. When the body of Christ takes on the added components of repentance discussed in this chapter we will begin experiencing a new way of life that more closely lines up with the one God All Mighty intended for us.

Repentance is more than a change in thinking, it is a change in the brain's biological construct which enables new vision and awareness to be formed. Consider this: We think about 60,000 thoughts a day. 90% of those thoughts we rethink over and over and become programmed. This conforms the mind to a certain pattern which in turn wires our brain to see through the filter created by our conditioned and programmed thoughts. Your biology, neuro-circuitry, biological chemistry, hormonal expression, the genes you convey, and the reality you become aware of is all determined by both your conscious and sub-conscious thoughts. When you change the way you think, physical and chemical alterations take place. The only possible way for a human to see and experience the Kingdom on earth in a manner which the Lord intended is to change what you're thinking about to things discovered while seeking first the Kingdom. Unless we change the way we think from our present way to the Kingdom, we are stuck in the mire of this world's pattern which produces awareness limited to its reality. Perhaps Jesus' command to "seek first the Kingdom" has greater implications and repercussions than we could presently consider or imagine!

Volume one of DISCOVERING THE KINGDOM is a re-programming document designed to bring the reader into a change of mind in the direction of Christ's Kingdom. It was assembled with the intent of being a study guide. This book is a workbook for the reader to chew and digest information containing substance that will renew the mind in the direction of Christ-like transformation. The more we familiarize ourselves with Kingdom information the greater the change of mind becomes. Similarly, the more we seek first the Kingdom the more our thoughts align with the King and His Kingdom. My prayer for you is that, while you read this book as a vehicle through which you seek first the Kingdom, that Jesus open the eyes of your understanding and bring enlightenment of this most precious of gifts, the Kingdom of Heaven.

Introduction

Influencing Culture, Preaching the Kingdom, and Creating Reality

The church has been equipped with authority to determine culture within nations. We have been tasked with the privilege of molding society and establishing cultural norms in line with Heaven. Influencing the earth with Heaven's substance is the responsibility of the church. In light of this, let's see how we've done. There are an estimated 1.3 million full-time missionaries and 4.2 million full-time Christian workers worldwide. There are more churches in the US than at any time in history. Church membership in the US is about 147 million, worldwide 2.3 billion. There are more Christian radio and TV channels than at any time in history.

Clearly the church's gospel is being spread farther and wider than ever before but is it the gospel Jesus told us to spread? How well have we done in transforming lives and impacting culture with our gospel? Is the fruit of our gospel equal to that of Jesus and the disciples in the Book of Acts?

Despite the impressive statistics, the United States is deeply unhappy, unfulfilled and drowning in darkness. The numbers speak for themselves. We rank first in fear, stress, anger, divorce, obesity, and anti-depressant use. More US soldiers killed themselves in 2012 than were killed in combat. Americans spent 208 billion dollars on prescription drugs in 2013. Almost 25% of American women are taking anti-depressants, which is higher than anywhere else in the world. According to an article by David Kupelian, "one-third of the nation's employees suffer chronic debilitating stress and more than half of all 18-33 year-olds experience a level of stress that keeps them awake at night, including large numbers diagnosed with depression and anxiety disorder."

Tens of millions of Americans use alcohol or drugs to numb their pain. About 50 million Americans have a drinking problem and/or use drugs. More people have been diagnosed with mental disorders in America than anywhere else on the planet.

America is the most obese industrialized nation on earth. The US leads the world in eating disorder deaths. The number of Americans on food stamps grew from about 17 million in 2000 to more than 47 million in 2013.

America has the highest divorce rate in the world. America has the highest incarceration rate and the largest total prison population in the entire world by a very wide margin.

How is it that a country so devoted to spreading the "gospel" is so unhealthy? With the "Word of God" being preached so much, why aren't we representing accurately the God we worship?

How can this be? Why aren't we seeing more societal change? How is it so many Christians are having so little effect on culture? The disciples of Jesus in the first century were far less in number yet accomplished far more. How can this be? Isn't the Gospel of Jesus Christ the Power of God? We are a nation full of believers that devoutly listen to our church leaders proclaim the transforming power of Jesus. So why the "disconnect," and how do we "reconnect" to the power and influence of Jesus and His disciples? How can America be in such a rapid tailspin and yet at the same time have the all-powerful, loving, merciful God regularly preached to millions?

The answer is simple yet profound. The church is so close, and yet so far from the heart and message of Jesus Christ. The church has been preaching and teaching the Gospel about Jesus Christ and not the Gospel Jesus preached and commanded us to teach and preach. Jesus identified a specific gospel when He said:

And this gospel of the Kingdom will be preached in the whole world.
Matthew 24:14a

He also said, "I must preach the gospel of the Kingdom ... because this is why I was sent."
Luke 4:43

The church has preached many other gospels: healing, salvation, being born again, grace, the love of the Father, etc., but has left out the only gospel Jesus preached and asked us to preach. In doing so we have fragmented THE gospel of the Kingdom into its parts making it ineffective. The whole is not only greater than the sum of its parts, it contains substance altogether different from its parts. This simple yet profound distinction is the difference between seeing the Will of God manifesting on earth as it is in Heaven and that of experiencing a form of godliness absent of the power, purpose and plan of God (2 Timothy 3:5).

One Gospel establishes a governmental rule under Heaven that transforms hearts, minds, culture and nations. The other is merely a religion, with little difference from any other. The pursuit of one gospel awakens the realm of existence of God and His rulership while the other is a system of the blind leading the blind. The Apostle Paul, before his conversion, showed us the real enemy of the Kingdom, religion, as he killed those preaching the Kingdom. We must lay down our religious activities of pursuing the parts and take up the interest of the Kingdom. As we seek first the Kingdom, all these parts will be given to us with added substance!

Jesus' first public statement was the call to change the way you think—"repent"—because the way you think keeps you from seeing the Kingdom (Matthew 4:17). The kingdom of darkness operates out of ignorance. Its power comes from people's ignorance. God's people perish for lack of knowledge. If the lens bringing awareness of the Kingdom is information discovered while seeking the Kingdom, then blinding us is as easy as removing Kingdom information.

The god of this age has blinded the minds of unbelievers so that they cannot see the light of the gospel ...."

Corinthians 4:4a

Jesus rebuked the religious leaders of his day because they kept knowledge of His Kingdom from the people. They were keeping them in bondage to religion and from entering His Kingdom. Present day religion conditions the mind with the "parts" of the gospel while seeking first the Kingdom patterns the mind with substance from within the Kingdom. This is the only substance capable of producing Kingdom realities on earth.

Woe to you Pharisees, because you love the most important seats in the synagogues and greetings in the marketplaces. Woe to you, because you are like unmarked graves, which men walk over without knowing it." One of the experts in the law answered him, "Teacher when you say these things, you insult us also." Jesus replied, "And you experts in the law, woe to you, because you load people down with burdens they can hardly carry, and you yourselves will not lift one finger to Help them. Woe to you, because you build tombs for the prophets, and it was your forefathers who killed them. ⁴⁸So you testify that you approve of what your forefathers did; they killed the prophets, and you build their tombs. Because of this, God in his wisdom said, 'I will send them prophets and apostles, some of whom they will kill and others they will persecute.' Therefore, this generation will be held responsible for the blood of all the prophets that has been shed since the beginning of the world, from the blood of Abel to the blood of Zechariah, who was killed between the altar and the sanctuary. Yes, I tell you, this generation will be held responsible for it all. Woe to you experts in the law, because you have taken away the key to knowledge. You yourselves have not entered, and you have hindered those who were entering."

Luke 11:43-52

Jesus' rebuke rings through the centuries to our time. The leaders of the church today have done the same thing. By preaching our "gospel" of grace, salvation, being born again, etc., we have kept the multitudes from hearing the actual message that Jesus preached, which was the "gospel" of "The Kingdom." We have also kept the multitudes from seeing the substance that manifests from a life given over to the Kingdom. The leaders of the church have managed to lock up access to the Kingdom and the Keys of the Kingdom by keeping the knowledge of the Kingdom from the people. This is evidenced by the lack of influence the church has had in the world. The message of the Kingdom is being preached when the culture of the Kingdom manifests on earth. Restoring the Kingdom message to the Church will cause Her to mirror the fruits of Jesus' ministry and the ministry of the 1st-century Disciples. When the message of the Kingdom is restored to the church the impact and effect of the Kingdom will once again be brought to earth.

Jesus' gospel—"the gospel of the Kingdom"—is the whole, the current gospel being preached is its parts. We have substituted the whole for its parts. This has made our gospel as ineffective as a car attempting to be driven apart from its "wholeness." You can no more effectively drive a car by throwing parts together as you can preach "parts" of the gospel. The church needs the gospel of the Kingdom to be her top priority, then we will see the fruits of the parts evidenced in our hearts, cities, and nations. The whole has always been greater than the sum of its parts. Jesus did not bring us a religion. Instead, as it says in Isaiah, he brought a government:

For to us a child is born, to us a son is given, and the government will be on his shoulders. And he will be called Wonderful Counselor, Mighty God, Everlasting Father, Prince of Peace. Of the increase of his GOVERNMENT and peace, there will be no end. He will reign on David's throne and over his kingdom, establishing and upholding it with justice and righteousness from that time on and forever. The zeal of the Lord Almighty will accomplish this.

Isaiah 9:6-7

We must come out of the darkness and into the light of the knowledge of the gospel of the Kingdom. We must take off the robes of ignorance and clothe ourselves with understanding. We must do away with our ineffective religious activities and embrace Jesus' teaching. We must preach what He commanded us to preach—THE KINGDOM! The nature and essence of the Kingdom are discovered in the field of seeking first the Kingdom. The Church must begin seeking first the Kingdom before we start making known its nature.

This treatise looks closely at what Jesus taught and what he commanded us to teach. Consider this a textbook for Kingdom understanding with the intent of renewing the mind and planting foundational truths related to the Kingdom of Heaven. If embraced, with the right heart, Kingdom information will empower us to fulfill God's original intent for man. Knowledge and understanding of the Kingdom are the catalysts for seeing God's Kingdom come on earth as it is in Heaven. Knowledge and understanding of the Kingdom is the soil through which Kingdom revelation bursts forth. This book reveals keys and unlocks knowledge and understanding of the Kingdom. It's designed to be a tool to help fulfill Jesus' mandate for you to seek first the Kingdom.

The church has been preaching the Gospel about Jesus Christ. It has preached the parts of the good news of the Kingdom and not the Kingdom as a whole. This is the reason for our present condition of powerlessness and lack of influence. The tide that transforms nations will begin shifting once the church re-discovers the message of the gospel of the Kingdom and makes the decision to seek it above everything. The difference in substance between the information found while seeking first the Kingdom versus information found while seeking the parts are light-years away from one another. By comparing the life of Jesus with the present church we can discover an accurate picture to reflect upon and see clearly the distinction the two substances produce.

Preaching the Kingdom

Jesus never told the public about Himself. He never asked His followers to teach about Himself, He gave them one message, "the Kingdom of Heaven." Jesus never taught on healing. He simply gave His disciples power gifts to authenticate and validate the Kingdom message.

He never taught on baptism, He told us to baptize. He never taught on worship, He talked to one woman about it. He never taught on the resurrection. He mentioned it a couple of times. He never taught on how to build a thriving church. In fact, He told us He would build His Church. It's not our responsibility. We are to make students of His message—the Kingdom (Matthew 28:19). Jesus never even taught on being born again. It's only mentioned once in scripture to a single man in private late at night.

Jesus taught mostly on one subject and when He sent out His disciples He commanded them to preach the same subject (Matthew 10:7). That subject was the Kingdom.

The Gospels mention the word *kingdom* 130 times but the church only three. It appears that Jesus' favorite theme was, "The kingdom of Heaven is like ...." He was constantly talking about the Kingdom. Jesus even called Himself "a door" and referred to Himself as the *way* into the Kingdom (John 10:7-9). Entering through "the Door" takes us beyond the appearance of Jesus into the essence of who Jesus is, the Kingdom itself. Whenever Jesus spoke about the Kingdom He was talking about the nature and essence of who He is. The church must move past the appearance of Jesus, His presence, and begin discovering His essence, the Kingdom.

When you compare the influence Jesus had on earth versus the limited influence the church presently has, the discrepancy is eye-opening! We have been introducing people to a "door" and He introduced "a country" and brought us a government. Furthermore, Jesus confirmed His message with substance from the government He brought us, adding to the authenticity of His message. He then sent out His disciples with the same message and same substance. There is only one way to materialize this substance and that's seeking first the Kingdom of God and His righteousness. Becoming a serious student of the Kingdom is the narrow pathway to seeing, experiencing and demonstrating Jesus' Kingdom.

Jesus has called us to make "Disciples of all nations" with His message of the Kingdom. Meanwhile, we're struggling to invite our friends to visit our church with our message about Jesus. As beautiful as Jesus is—as wonderful as He has become to us—we must consider this to be a major problem in our theology. Until we discover the Jesus that is identical to His Kingdom, we will fail in our attempts to present accurately the essence and actuality of who He is. Jesus and the Kingdom are one in the same. The Jesus we are currently presenting is limited to what is perceived through His appearance. The Jesus discovered while seeking the Kingdom contains progressive revelation shedding light on the essence, nature and actuality of who He is. To limit our awareness of Jesus to His presence is to sacrifice wakefulness to His essence which is the Kingdom.

Another example follows: Jesus is a king. A king rules a country. In Jesus' case, it's the Kingdom of Heaven that He rules. Most countries have a Ministry of Tourism with the intent of attracting tourists. Which approach would be more successful: the one using their president as its primary marketing tool, or the one using the country's attractions and resources? Does the US attract visitors by putting the face of their president all over its marketing material? No, we use pictures of mountains, beaches, and scenic highways. We talk about our national parks, world-class restaurants, and economic stability and opportunity. We present the essence of our nation which becomes the magnet of attraction.

This is why Jesus never talked about Himself. He knew introducing His country and its benefits would be far more successful. His essence, the whole, would do what His presence, the part, could never do. Jesus said the preaching of the Kingdom of Heaven would be so successful in the harvest that all those who receive the message of the Kingdom would forsake everything to possess it—knowing everything they need is found in it.

The kingdom of Heaven is like treasure hidden in a field. When a man found it, he hid it again, and then in his joy went and sold all he had and bought that field. Again, the kingdom of Heaven is like a merchant looking for fine pearls. When he found one of great value, he went away and sold everything he had and bought it.

Matthew 13:44-46

Years ago, as I read this parable I saw the Kingdom's all sufficiency. Its total ability to provide every need of mankind had suddenly burst into my awareness. It was then I realized if the Kingdom was anything the Kingdom was everything.

Jesus claimed to be "The Door." His presence is the entrance to this fantastic existence. But we have managed to reduce this life of ours to worshiping a door. As beautiful as He is and as touching as He can be, we must acknowledge this fact and begin understanding what's behind it. The majority of the world does not have an intimate relationship with Jesus and, therefore, He is only a door to them. In effect, He said, "I am the doorway, I am the way. Enter through me and see." If all we needed was Jesus then He would have never given us a Kingdom (Luke 22:29), nor would He have told us to preach the Kingdom. We need the Kingdom as much as we need Jesus for the two are inseparable. Jesus, apart from the Kingdom is incomplete

Jesus told us plainly, "as you go preach the Kingdom of Heaven is at hand" (Matthew 10:7). He identified which gospel He wanted us to preach when He said:

And this gospel of the kingdom will be preached in the whole world as a testimony to all nations, and then the end will come.
Matthew 24:14

"And THIS gospel" is what gospel? The gospel "of the Kingdom will be preached in the whole world." Not the gospel of healing, salvation, baptism, being born again, or any of the other gospels the church has been preaching for 1900 years.

His is a very specific gospel, giving rise to a very unique substance on earth. It has very narrow focus: the gospel of the Kingdom. Here are some Biblical facts to consider before we begin seeking first the Kingdom. Let these facts become our root system of belief in the preeminent priority Jesus established for us: Seeking first the Kingdom of God and His righteousness.

1. John the Baptist's teaching, which paved the way for Jesus, was "Repent for the Kingdom of Heaven is near" (Matthew 3:2). This invitation and proclamation still remain available to us. It is precisely a decision to change our thinking and priorities to understanding the Kingdom that prepares the way of the King.
2. Jesus identified specifically why He came to earth. "I must proclaim

the good news of the Kingdom of God to the other towns also because that is why I was sent" (Luke 4:43b).

3. Jesus' first commissioning words to His disciples for their initial ministry were to "… preach the Kingdom of God and heal the sick" (Luke 9:2).

4. In Luke 10:9, the second commissioning of the 72, Jesus commanded them to preach the message of the Kingdom.

5. Jesus used the phrase "The Kingdom of Heaven is like" more than any other—13 times in Matthew alone. Jesus devoted more time to introducing the Kingdom than anything else.

6. Jesus made it clear that His followers top priority should be "Seek first his Kingdom …" (Matthew 6:33). In context, Jesus is saying that "seeking the Kingdom" is more important than earning a living. This is hard to grasp in western culture, nevertheless necessary to bring about the Kingdom. He implies that "all these things" could define life, therefore, Jesus was offering a different way of life. In His way, seeking first the Kingdom, "all these things" are given to us.

7. Jesus' last words during the last days of His life on earth were found in Acts 1. We see that "He appeared to them over a period of forty days and spoke about the kingdom of God"(Acts 1:3). For almost six weeks straight Jesus taught on the Kingdom of God.

8. Jesus told us the Kingdom of Heaven is so fulfilling and valuable that when we discover it, we leave everything behind to pursue it (Matthew 13:44-45).

9. We learn that Jesus delivered to us the Kingdom in Luke 22:29: "And I confer on you a Kingdom, just as my Father conferred one on me." "Confer" is a legal term meaning to grant and bestow upon or give to. Jesus legally gave us not a religion but the Kingdom.

10. Jesus' first public words were "THE PEOPLE WHO WERE SITTING IN DARKNESS SAW A GREAT LIGHT, AND THOSE WHO WERE SITTING IN THE LAND AND SHADOW OF DEATH, UPON THEM A LIGHT DAWNED."

From that time Jesus began to preach and say, "Repent, for the kingdom of Heaven is at hand."

Matthew 4:16-17

11. Later on, after sharing the parable about the message of the Kingdom, a foundational parable for all others, He exclaimed in Matthew 13:19:

Do you not understand this parable? How will you understand all the parables?

Apparently receiving correctly the message of the Kingdom is paramount to what Jesus taught the multitudes. We must begin pressing into this most significant of messages. We must commit our loyalty to what E. Stanley Jones called the Unshakable Kingdom and the Unchanging Person!

Here are two keys that will help us bring the message of the Kingdom alive in scripture and in practical everyday life.

1. **We can't see what we're not looking for.** Intently focus on looking for the Kingdom. Engage your Will towards and your affections on the pursuit of understanding the Kingdom. That's why Jesus commanded us to seek first the Kingdom. Seek first means to make it the top priority. We will be surprised how much scripture changes before our eyes when we commit to this. Be prepared to persevere and keep in mind as a woman in labor forgets her pain so too does the one seeking the Kingdom forget the troubles once it's unveiled.

2. **In order to see something, we must understand the thing we're attempting to see.** The more we commit ourselves to receiving knowledge of the Kingdom, the more it will be revealed. Repetition is good, for in it lies the key to a renewed mind. Sometimes it appears to be a waste of time but something profound takes place as we rehearse the knowledge of the Kingdom. God sheds light and brings understanding. Understanding is comprehension of information. It's grasping the information with progressively more awareness of the intrinsic nature of the information being studied. It's in these moments that breakthrough takes place. Revelation is plentiful as we brood over and soak in the knowledge of the Kingdom. My prayer is for the veil of ignorance to be lifted from the eyes of the church, enabling Her to see into the Kingdom of Heaven.

One more thing before we move on to gain insight of the Kingdom. Read the next section carefully with an open mind and imagine … just imagine what we could do if we truly believed what Jesus preached ….

Creating Reality

What if we were able to discover the ability to create reality? What if we had within ourselves the capacity to bring reality into existence? What if we have been creating reality and will continue for the rest of our lives? We are made in the image of our Creator; therefore, it is our nature to create. Ignorance and enslavement have kept us from creating a more desired reality than our present state of existence. This book is an introduction to the world of creativity according to God's design and purpose.

Quantum mechanics has discovered a principle called "superposition" which supposes two realities existing at once. Because our experience never views the two realities together, it begs the question: When does "superposition" end and what collapses this "dual reality" into one possibility or the other? The answer might surprise you: The observer's perception collapses the "superposition," leaving only the observers perception of which of the two realities is real. This may sound unreal, but in the quantum field, this is established science. I wonder if our Creator had quantum superposition in mind when he said: "be it unto you according to your belief"?

Let's consider "superposition" in relation to the kingdom of darkness and the Kingdom of Heaven. Suppose these two kingdoms existed at once. If the observer's perception collapsed the "superposition" what would be the determining factor of which reality remained? The observer's perception: his ability to see and become aware of one or the other Kingdom. That's what determines which kingdom is made real on earth. The kingdom who succeeds in molding a nation's perception is given the stage of reality in that nation. Man does not create thought; thought creates the man. It is the structures of influence erected by the kingdom of darkness and the Kingdom of light which create thought. What determines our thoughts, therefore, is which kingdom is influencing us. In order for the church to come under the influence of the Kingdom of Heaven, we must seek first the Kingdom. There is no higher obedience than to Jesus' command for us to make it our top priority to seek His Kingdom and righteousness.

Discovering the Kingdom is a book designed to empower you to perceive the Kingdom. Because the essence of information carries an influence that forms you into that which the information holds, the more information we receive on the Kingdom the greater the conformity to it. Information assembles formation within its content-producing conformity. Conformity brings an ability to perceive the essence of the information and the substance within the information. Consequently, this book is a study guide to lead us under the influence of the Kingdom of Heaven bringing about a change of mind that produces both individual and cultural transformation. The more we can see and become aware of the Kingdom of God the more we and Holy Spirit co-create its existence both within our personal lives and on earth.

This is one reason governments establish cultural norms. These norms create perception, which perpetuates the established reign of the particular kingdom by opening the eyes of societies to itself. A society's beliefs, customs, and way of life determine the nature of the kingdom by forming community or societal perception out of a conditioned pattern of thinking both in the conscious and sub-conscious mind.

The kingdom of darkness is presently ruling the nations because it has succeeded in entangling the collective perception of society into believing it is the only kingdom that exists, ensuring its perception is maintained as reality.

What if God's people re-discovered the Kingdom of Heaven? What if we became aware, once again, of the existence of the Kingdom of God on earth? Is it possible that if we can perceive the Kingdom of God, we can make known its reality on earth? Is it possible for us to see and become aware of the Kingdom of Heaven to the point we "collapse" the present reality of the kingdom of darkness and simultaneously "create" the reality of the Kingdom of Heaven on earth? Is this not the essence of the Lord's Prayer:

Our Father in Heaven, hallowed be your name, your kingdom come, your will be done, on earth as it is in Heaven.
Matthew 6:9-10

It is the earnest desire of this author that we all discover the reality of this prayer and see it demonstrated in our lives, churches, communities, nations, and the world.

Imagine with me, as we understand the Kingdom and become aware of its existence, we will change the world!

Michael Gissibl

A Glossary of Kingdom Terms

It is important in a discussion to clarify the meanings of words. We must be on the same page of definitions in order to properly understand one another when we make a statement. Words have meanings and knowing the proper meaning is imperative. For this reason, we begin our discussion of the Kingdom with a glossary of terms in order to define what we mean so that what we say will be understood and received.

A "term" is a word or phrase used to describe a thing or express a concept. Terms help bring a thing to life and aid the reader's ability to understand a subject. By identifying Kingdom terms we more closely align ourselves with the mind of Christ and position ourselves to receive the Kingdom. Deeply rooted in language is culture. The Kingdom of Heaven is like a foreign language. We must study the terms and learn the language in order to experience the culture. This chapter is a list of terms relating to the Kingdom of Heaven.

The Bible is not a religious book. It is a book about a King, His Kingdom, and His children. The more Kingdom terms we understand the more captive our thoughts become to the King's. The greater our thoughts become captured by Christ, the more we will awaken to the Kingdom. Seeking first the Kingdom has similar effects to marinating. As we soak in Kingdom information we extract the properties of the Kingdom until they become infused.

When we hear a word it invokes the mental concept that we've formed about the word over the course of our lives. Much of these concepts lie in our subconscious mind and dictate the way we perceive the word's meaning. For example, when I say the word "Bible" most people's concept is that of a religious book used by Christians. When I say the word "prayer," people's concept largely relates to talking to a Divine being who doesn't respond. These are conditioned responses resulting from wrong ideas formed as a result of patterned thinking, not in line with the mind of Christ.

Entire societies form concepts. Those living in the Kingdom have different concepts than religious Christians. Paul, in the book of Romans, narrowed transformation down to one idea, "renewing of the mind". Jesus began His ministry with the statement "repent", change our mind.

The more familiar we are with God's idea of a word the more we will become established in His Kingdom. We begin thinking Kingdommindedly by familiarizing ourselves with Kingdom terms and the ideas behind them. Benjamin Lee Whorf, one of the greatest linguists of all time, wrote a book entitled, *Language Thought and Reality*. In it, he documents a lifetime of research which showed a culture's language determined their thoughts which in turn created reality. Since governments form and pattern thought through language what better government to subject ourselves to than the one Jesus brought: the Kingdom of Heaven. As we discover the language of the Kingdom it will produce a pattern of thought that will bring awareness of the Kingdom once again.

Information places us in formation to its contents. As we receive information, we set in motion a process that begins forming us into its image. In other words, information is a container holding substance that conforms us into its likeness. Seeking first the Kingdom provides us with substance conforming us into the image and likeness of Christ and His Kingdom.

As we go through this list, pictures will emerge in our mind's eye identifying our understanding of the term. Lay aside old ways of thinking and make room for the new. As we read scripture take these concepts and apply the new understanding of them and watch the Bible change before our eyes. We can set our intentions on seeing the Kingdom by seeking first the Kingdom. We can ask Holy Spirit to open the eyes of our understanding. We can pray for the Spirit of wisdom and revelation to invade our thoughts with the knowledge of the King and His Kingdom. We can ask believing, and we shall receive!

Keep in mind the Kingdom is ever expanding. These terms are meant to be a springboard launching you into the Kingdom. As sight is given you are sure to enter the flow of life teeming with revelation. As you continue seeking the Kingdom know you are pursuing a government that has no end. It's as expansive as it is unshakable!

Ambassador - A public officer clothed with high diplomatic powers, commissioned by a government to transact the business of his government. An accredited person sent by a country as its official representative.

The Adamic Dominion Mandate - The command given to Adam and his seed to govern earth with Heaven's rulership.

The Bible - Not a religious book but a legal one—a constitution (the system of beliefs and laws by which a country is governed). A book written about a king, His kingdom, and royal family.

Citizen - From the Greek word, *polites* (politician). As a citizen of Heaven, we have been appointed to a legal office with the responsibility of representing our government. We have a legal and moral obligation to implement and uphold the Will and intent of our government. One who, under the laws of the country is a member of the political community, and owes allegiance and duties, while being entitled to the enjoyment of full civil rights. As citizens of Heaven, it's our responsibility to make manifest by faith and understanding the customs, culture and social norms of our government. It is furthermore the responsibility of Heaven's citizen's to have influence and impact by enacting the laws and principles of Heaven on earth.

Colonization - The extension of a kingdom's influence to a distant territory.

Colony - A territory under the authority and influence of a distant country. A group of pilgrims who settle in a distant territory but remain subject to and associated with (culturally tied to) the original country.

Culture - Glory/influence or reminiscence of a culture (the earth shall be filled with the culture of Heaven; "let your light so shine"—a reflection of the culture of Heaven in our homes, on our jobs, and in our lives (Habakkuk 2:14; Matthew 5:16). Our sphere of influence will reflect the culture of Heaven. The culture of Heaven is always established within the child of God first. Then we become equipped to establish it on earth.

Covenant - Legal term meaning a contract between two parties. The Bible is referred to as the Old and New covenant.

The Cross - An instrument used for crucifixion resulting in resurrection. In the Kingdom, only the resurrected participate. Therefore, the message of the cross is the power of God.

Disciple - A committed student of Jesus' teaching on the Kingdom.

Dominion - The power to rule, govern and exercise sovereign authority as royalty. We are given dominion to rule on earth to the degree Christ has dominion in our lives.

Faith – A system of belief based on convictions to what is truth.

The Fall - Adam's sin initiated separation from God. His disobedience was the declaration of independence of earth, from Heaven, through rebellion, culminating in the loss of position to govern the earth.

Father - Source.

Glory - The glory of kingdoms is influence. All kingdoms get their glory from influence. The impact of the king's culture on a territory is his glory.

God - The sovereign and reigning King of the universe, Heaven, and earth.

God's Will - The mind of God regarding a thing.

Government - Authoritative direction through structures of influence. Direction and control exercised over citizens. The continuous exercise of authority over individuals and society.

Heaven - A country from another realm, accessible on earth and destined to once again become the system of rulership. Able to be entered and lived out now.

Lord - Denotes ownership—a person exercising absolute ownership rights. In the Kingdom, we own nothing and have access to everything at the Lord's discretion.

Keys of the Kingdom - The principles by which the Kingdom operates.

Kingdom - A system of government Jesus came to restore—the impact and influence of a king on territory. A nation governed by a king. The king is the ultimate power in a kingdom. The principle goal of a kingdom is influence. Kingdom is the form of government Isaiah prophesied would be on Jesus' shoulders in Isaiah 9:6.

The Kingdom of God - God's first community on earth.

The Kingdom on Earth - The territory called earth, owned by the Creator, yet to be conformed to the law, authority and dominion of the Creator.

The Kingdom of Heaven - The governed territory of God, an entire sphere fully under God's authority, and conforming to the law and order of the King of Heaven. Refers to God's headquarters. The Kingdom of Heaven is where God is. The Kingdom of God is the impact of that place on a territory.

Knowledge - Information (see Understanding and Wisdom).

Prayer - Earthly license for Heavenly influence. A legal transaction between a government and its citizens. Prayer begins in Heaven, flows to a human and goes back to Heaven culminating in Heaven's release back down to earth. The water cycle model (Isaiah 55:10).

Regulated by Another Government - Our unique position of holding dual citizenship lets us determine by whom we will be governed—the Kingdom of Heaven and its laws or the systems, principles, and laws of this world.

Righteousness - Position of right standing with Heaven enabling us to have official power and authority to make legal decisions and judgments on earth. This is a governmental term not religious.

Revelation - An unveiling, uncovering or revealing. In the Kingdom revelation is made available in knowledge and understanding. All truth in the Kingdom flows out of the Spirit of revelation. It can be difficult to differentiate knowledge, understanding, and revelation. As long as we are seeking first the Kingdom, no matter what we choose to call the information we're receiving, we can rest assured it's producing lasting fruit.

Seek - To pursue, study, explore, make an effort to understand, learn, consider, desire to know, have a passion for and be diligently dedicated. We are commanded to seek the Kingdom—pursue, study, attempt to understand and desire to know the impact and influence of Jesus and His structure of influence (His Kingdom).

Sovereign - A person, body or state in which independent and supreme authority is vested. Few Americans have any experience with the fact that a king is the ultimate power in a kingdom. The king is "sovereign." His word becomes law within his governed territory.

Understanding - The progressive unfolding of information or increased awareness and comprehension of substance within information. Inherent within understanding is revelation. The more understanding you receive the more revelation is made available. Although you can receive revelation separate from understanding, you can't receive understanding without revelation. Knowledge without transforming itself into understanding erects itself as pride in the heart of man. However when knowledge and understanding that comes out of seeking first the Kingdom is received, a door opens for the Lord to bring Kingdom revelation. This Kingdom revelation is the substance Jesus uses to build His Church and establish His culture and influence first in us, then through us.

Wisdom - Applying information once its essence has been made aware to us. As new information is received, it's important to remain committed to reviewing the information. Whenever the message of the Kingdom is preached, Satan himself comes to snatch the information from us (Matthew 13:1-23). Why? Because he does not want Kingdom knowledge to become understood for fear of it being applied. Knowledge without understanding produces pride. Let patience do its work by transforming information into understanding.

Then we will be able to equip, empower, and discharge information God's way.

 NOTE: You may want to return to this chapter as you read to recall the definitions. Use this material as a textbook. Take in the information with the intent of re-patterning your thoughts and renewing your mind into the conformity of the mind of Christ. Put on the mindset of a student going to school in the classroom of the Kingdom of God.

Chapter One

Seek First

The design of Satan is to keep humanity ignorant. This ignorance is isolated and centered on one teaching, the Kingdom. Ignorance of the Kingdom of God is the only tool the enemy possesses that gives him influence to suppress the manifestation of the Kingdom of Heaven on earth. This power has enabled him to maintain the systems of rulership erected under his guidance, enslaving humanity for millennia. To maintain his rule, he has worked hard to prevent the teaching of "The Kingdom of Heaven."

This one teaching is clearly Jesus' most important message.

It's the reason He came to earth (Luke 4:43).

It's the first thing He mentioned in public ministry (Mark 1:15).

It's the last thing He spoke of on earth (Acts 1:3).

This one teaching consumed Jesus' life and ministry and is what He claimed to be "the gospel." The *good news* is the teaching about the Kingdom (Matthew 24:14). Each time we make a decision to receive information regarding the Kingdom we become a recipient of Jesus' gospel. As a result substance is added to our lives bringing about transformation into the likeness of Christ and His Kingdom.

The central issue facing the present church is found in 2 Corinthians 4:4:

The god of this age has blinded the minds of unbelievers, so that they cannot see the light of the gospel ....

Satan has kept us from seeing the knowledge of the Kingdom and Christ's influence through it. The antidote to all the world's problems is found in the knowledge and understanding of this glorious gospel, for in it contains the keys to the influence of Christ's reign on the earth. Seeking first the Kingdom grows and develops a lens through which we become aware of the Kingdom. The more vision of the Kingdom that comes into focus the more our sight becomes overtaken by Kingdom awareness.

So do not worry, saying, "What shall we eat?" or "What shall we drink?" or "What shall we wear?" For the pagans run after all these things, and your Heavenly Father knows that you need them. But seek first his kingdom and his righteousness, and all these things will be given to you as well.

Matthew 6:31-33

As a follower of Christ do you ever worry? Do you ever fret about the things you need in life? Jesus referred to such a person as a "pagan." His Kingdom is so fulfilling it frees your mind from all thought and fixes your entire being in the Kingdom. I invite you to consider incorporating the antidote to worry and the pursuit of all things.

Jesus identified the top priority for all who choose to follow him. The phrase "seek first" means "make it your top priority." Jesus left no doubt where a follower of His ought to be devoting his time and energy. Those committed to making the pursuit of the Kingdom their supreme loyalty will discover a way of life that transcends anything conceived in the mind of man.

This is no different than college students. When they decide on a major, once they have completed their core classes, they "seek first" their area of study. This ensures their capacity to fulfill future job responsibilities. The longer they engage in seeking first their area of study the greater awareness they receive. Graduate school makes this even more evident. For students, all time, energy, and study are concentrated on their specific field of study. In order to become qualified, you must "seek first" your area of study. There are no followers in upper-level college courses, only devoted disciples actively seeking first their course of study.

The steady accumulation of information relating to our priority ensures we will be empowered in a manner conformed with the information. Kingdom substance makes its way into our identity ultimately conforming us into the image of Christ. Bearing His nature and likeness, we become representatives of Heaven on earth much like Jesus and the early disciples.

A great challenge in life is the daily demand of establishing priorities. There are many things competing for our time. Life was not designed to be complicated. The key to simplifying our lives is prioritization.

Prioritization protects us from doing things that misuse our time. We will devote ourselves to what we have chosen to be our top priorities.

Jesus is telling us to make a decision to place pursuing His Kingdom at the top. In Matthew 6, Jesus promises that if we commit to this discipline, He will provide what we need. Built into the act of seeking first the Kingdom is provision from Heaven. A provision that goes beyond imagination and carries with it a particular kind of substance and nature only found in the Kingdom.

Jesus took everything we need and placed it in His Kingdom. He took all of humanity's God-ordained wants and desires and centrally located them in His Kingdom. This beautiful Kingdom is so fulfilling that when we find it, we lay down everything, and at any cost—give ourselves over to it (Matthew 13:44-45). The irony is the more we discover the Kingdom, the less "cost" there is to exchange what we have for it. The only cost in pursuing the Kingdom is in our initial pursuit because we think we have to give up things. Once we've been caught, captured, and consumed by the Kingdom there is only gain! The richest source of eternal treasure is found while seeking first the Kingdom.

Organization of our priorities is essential. Once we set and organize them, it's important to discipline ourselves to maintain the order. "Self-Discipline" means "self-imposed restrictions." Identifying the correct priorities in life is the key to a fruitful and fulfilled life. In addition to establishing priorities, organizing them, and having self-discipline, we must know we have the right priorities. As a follower of Jesus, it's important to identify and keep in mind what He established as the top priority.

A crucial principle to keep in mind is the initial testing phase. As we pursue the Kingdom, Satan will attempt to derail our efforts. We need to use this opportunity to examine our commitment level. If our resolve is resolute we will persevere through it and God will add Kingdom substance to us. If our resolve is wavy and unstable, we need to ask Holy Spirit to rise up in us and empower us. Ask for revelation. This is a great source of empowerment during times of weakness. Rest assured all who hunger and thrust after Jesus' priority find themselves in position to experience satisfaction. Don't be surprised by the trials and hardships but rather in humility anticipate being satisfied!

Jesus set apart the right priority for all humans. It says in Matthew 6:33, "Seek first His Kingdom and His righteousness." "First" means "Top Priority." Everything else is second. Jesus is telling us He wants us to consume our energy and time in these two things, making them preeminent. A "kingdom" is a "king's government." All disciples of Jesus are commanded to seek His government like a political science major seeks understanding their systems of government.

If we are to "seek first His Kingdom and His righteousness," our top priority, therefore, is pursuing information and education of Heaven's government and its influence in all areas of our lives.

At home, at work, with our spouses and kids, in our relationships, in our bodies, during our prayer time, in our churches, and all other areas of life.

Everywhere, all the time, consuming ourselves with the pursuit of understanding this idea of God's governmental rulership. These are God's priorities for all mankind. Seek the governmental influence of God and seek to be in right standing with His government, the Kingdom of Heaven. When we do this, EVERYTHING else Jesus said will be added to us. The more revelation we receive about the Kingdom and righteousness the more natural it becomes to make it our top priority.

 Q/A: What is the highest priority of the disciple of Jesus?

Understanding is more important than knowledge. But wisdom is most prized. The wisest man to ever live was Solomon. He was asked by God, "what do you want?" Solomon answered "Wisdom" (1 Kings 3:5-15).

- Knowledge is information. The Bible being the richest storehouse and a sure foundation of knowledge.

- Understanding is the comprehension of knowledge. It's where the substance within knowledge becomes available and accessible. To grasp or take in what is contained within knowledge requires we take upon ourselves the discipline of revisiting the information long enough to allow its content to form in us. Patience and perseverance are keys to receiving understanding. You are being trans-formed in formation with the information being received.

- Wisdom is the application of knowledge. It's a course of action birthed from information (knowledge) that is understood. The greatest activity in the Kingdom is walking in wisdom. Information that is understood resulting in Divine empowerment to act is precisely that. For example, Jesus said in John 5:19:

    ... the Son can do nothing by himself; he can do only what he sees his Father doing ...

Jesus acquired knowledge, understood it and applied it perfectly.

The knowledge we are to seek first is of the Kingdom. All information received while seeking first the Kingdom is designed to conform and transform us into its image. The Bible is the constitution of the Kingdom. Therefore, our foundation of truth is the Bible. Although the Bible contains absolute truth, not all truth is equal in impact and substance. By mandating us to seek first the Kingdom, Jesus was pointing us in the direction of more far-reaching and consequential truth. When an all wise King declares a subject to be top priority we can be assured the information is of utmost importance.

Once we receive knowledge, understanding must be added. This is a necessary work done by the Holy Spirit as we meditate on and revisit the knowledge. Knowledge without understanding produces pride.

First, we get information. That information can only produce fruit for God's Kingdom if we understand it then apply it. Wisdom is supreme because we can have knowledge and understanding and still not apply it. Obstacles such as worry, fear, the pursuit of things, faulty ways of thinking, lack of self-discipline, and wrong priorities inhibit us from walking in wisdom.

Understanding destroys frustration and opens the door for wisdom. A parable is a style of teaching used to conceal the truth until the listener is ready to receive it. The purpose of a parable is not to tell the truth but hide it. A parable is used due to the following principle: **nothing is ours until we discover it.**

> *The disciples came to him and asked, "Why do you speak to the people in parables?" He replied, "The knowledge of the secrets of the kingdom of Heaven has been given to you, but not to them. Whoever has will be given more, and he will have an abundance. Whoever does not have, even what he has will be taken from him. This is why I speak to them in parables: Though seeing, they do not see; though hearing, they do not hear or understand. In them is fulfilled the prophecy of Isaiah: You will be ever hearing but never understanding; you will be ever seeing but never perceiving. For this people's heart has become calloused; they hardly hear with their ears, and they have closed their eyes. Otherwise, they might see with their eyes, hear with their ears, understand with their hearts and turn, and I would heal them. But blessed are your eyes because they see, and your ears because they hear. For I tell you the truth, many prophets and righteous men longed to see what you see but did not see it, and to hear what you hear but did not hear it."*
>
> Matthew 13:10-17

Jesus spoke to the multitudes in parables, but the knowledge of the secrets of the Kingdom of Heaven was given to those students who sacrificed. They are those who have given up houses, forsook boats, and businesses for the sake of seeking first the Kingdom. Those who left a comfortable lifestyle to become a student of Jesus' teaching received the secrets. In other words, the followers of Christ who make Him their top priority listen to Him, and they understand Him. When they hear Him say "make it your top priority to seek My Kingdom," they do so. The result is the secrets of the Kingdom are entrusted to them. A way of life made available to only those seeking first the Kingdom opens up and is received with joy and thanksgiving. Are you ready to put all your eggs in one basket?

> *"For I know the plans I have for you," declares the Lord, "plans to prosper you and not to harm you, plans to give you hope and a future. Then you will call upon me and come and pray to me, and I will listen*

to you. You will seek me and find me when you seek me with all your heart."

Jeremiah 29:11-14

A disciple is one who chooses to seek first His teacher's thoughts. A disciple is intentionally focused on his teacher's way of thinking in order to make known his Will. A teacher's great desire is to impart his mind to his students. Likewise, a student's ultimate pursuit is capturing the mind of his teacher. There is an important distinction between Jesus' Kingdom teaching style and teachers in this world. In the Kingdom, the Teacher does not determine the lesson, the student does. Jesus would say "Your interest determines my subject." As the disciples demonstrated at the Last Supper, we are all under different revelation levels.

I have much more to say to you, more than you can now bear.

John 16:12

The key to receiving the secrets of the Kingdom is proving our interest level by making the Kingdom our top priority. Make the pursuit of the Kingdom first in our lives and the Kingdom secrets will be opened to us.

Everything we need is in the Kingdom. Everything we're searching for is in one place, the Kingdom. When we find the Kingdom we stop striving. In effect, "Come to me," Jesus says, "and I will give you rest." Jesus is telling us that He has everything we need and want if we would just come to Him. He is the doorway into the Kingdom. As we come to Him, we will not only discover Him in the Kingdom, we will discover the Kingdom in Him.

The kingdom of Heaven is like treasure hidden in a field. When a man found it, he hid it again, and then in his joy went and sold all he had and bought that field. Again, the kingdom of Heaven is like a merchant looking for fine pearls. When he found one of great value, he went away and sold everything he had and bought it.

Matthew 13:44-46

Jesus uses two different stories to communicate the same message. Humanity will search and search until it finds the Kingdom. When

41

someone discovers it he effortlessly exchanges something lesser for something greater! It's important to note that the man, when he found the treasure, bought the field in order to obtain the treasure. The treasure is the Kingdom. The field is seeking first the Kingdom. Therefore, in order to find the Kingdom, we must buy into the mindset of seeking first the Kingdom. We will always see what we seek.

Throughout history, man's search was never for a religion. It was for a better world. Humans are looking for the answer to meaning, purpose, and a better system of governance. Man has been using religion to try to find this. The fulfillment of purpose and meaning can only be found in the Kingdom. Christianity must come to grips with this and stop selling a religion. Why did Jesus choose men from the business community to entrust His Kingdom message and power to? Why not leaders from the religious community? Because Jesus knew what Saul, an educated religious leader, demonstrated: The enemy of the Kingdom is the religious establishment. "Meanwhile, Saul was still breathing out murderous threats against the Lord's disciples" (Acts 9:1).

Beware of the religious spirit as the Kingdom is rising!!

The greatest obstacle mankind faces is blindness to the Kingdom. Ignorance is the foundation of the kingdom of darkness. Everything Satan has built on earth came as a result of mankind's blindness to God's Kingdom.

Once a man sees the Kingdom his life changes forever and the kingdom of darkness suffers loss. Note that the only time in the New Covenant we see Satan himself working is in an attempt to snatch a seed from the heart of man. And what might that seed be? The seed of the message of the Kingdom. All other satanic attacks are his workers, demons, and evil spirits. This fact alone sheds light on the impact and influence seeking first the Kingdom must have against the kingdom of darkness. I pray we see with greater intensity why God's priority for us is to seek His Kingdom and righteousness.

Q/A: In order to discover the Kingdom what must you do?

What are some practical ways to participate in the activity of seeking first the Kingdom?

The Bible is where we seek first the Kingdom. Sound biblical teaching is the foundation of seeking the Kingdom. The Church has made everything else a priority and left the Kingdom out altogether. Entire denominations have made "born again" their priority. Other denominations prioritize speaking in tongues, healing, worship, repentance, the Bible, evangelism, community, and communion. All these have their place and are important but not at the expense of making the Kingdom less than our top priority. The whole is greater than the sum of its parts. The whole is also different from the sum of its parts. The whole contains substance, has a nature and essence different than the sum of its parts. The substance received from seeking first the Kingdom is essential to the Will of God on earth. The Kingdom is the only foundation to build upon. Everything else is unstable sand. In His wisdom, Jesus knew if we would seek first His Kingdom everything else would take care of itself.

Seeking first anything other than the Kingdom is like refusing a fully furnished home because you are choosing only a few accessories. It's like rejecting a car and accepting parts of it. Nowhere is it possible to bring into existence the whole of something by picking and choosing parts of it.

Therefore I tell you, do not worry about your life, what you will eat or drink; or about your body, what you will wear. Is not life more important than food, and the body more important than clothes? Look at the birds of the air; they do not sow or reap or store away in barns, and yet your Heavenly Father feeds them. Are you not much more valuable than they? Who of you by worrying can add a single hour to his life? And why do you worry about clothes? See how the lilies of the field grow. They do not labor or spin. Yet I tell you that not even Solomon in all his splendor was dressed like one of these. If that is how God clothes the grass of the field, which is here today and tomorrow is thrown into the fire, will he not much more clothe you, O you of little faith? So do not worry, saying, "What shall we eat?" or "What shall we drink?" or "What shall we wear?" For the pagans run after all these things, and your Heavenly Father knows that you need them. But seek first his kingdom and his righteousness, and all these things will be given to you as well. Therefore do not worry about tomorrow, for tomorrow will worry about itself. Each day has enough trouble of its own.

Matthew 6:25-34

Consider where Jesus told us not to focus our thinking and where He wants our focus and attention directed. Consider the condition of "adding things" to our lives as we seek first the Kingdom. Our priorities should not be things but a place and a position.

Q/A: What are your priorities in life? In your relationship with God, what is your priority?

Q/A: What are some practical steps you can take to begin shifting your mind off "things" and onto the Kingdom?

Blessed are those who hunger and thirst for righteousness, for they will be filled.

Matthew 5:6

In the same way we seek the Kingdom, we need to thirst for right positioning (righteousness) within the Kingdom. We can never experience the Kingdom without being placed in Heaven on earth. The greater our understanding of this positioning within the Kingdom the greater our awareness of the Kingdom and more expansive our demonstrative and expressive capacity becomes.

Thirst is a natural experience that creates a craving to go after the satisfying of our thirst. This is what needs to happen to us spiritually. We need to become so desperate for right positioning with God's government it's like a thirst. No human ever casually responds to thirst. The longer we go without fluids the more obsessed we become. Additionally, the healthier we are the more water we need.

If we want to be positioned badly enough, Jesus is saying He will position us. But we need to want it like a thirst. We lost the Kingdom message about 1900 years ago. Only top priority pursuers of it will rediscover it. Only those who hunger and thirst for it will be satisfied (Matthew 5:6).

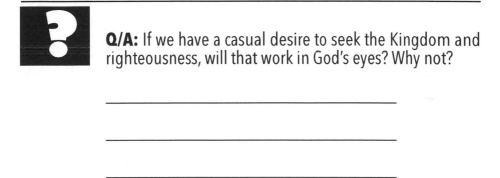

Q/A: If we have a casual desire to seek the Kingdom and righteousness, will that work in God's eyes? Why not?

_____

_____

_____

The way we are given things is through right positioning with our government not running after them. Under this world we are taught to take, in the Kingdom we learn to receive. There are only receivers in the Kingdom, no takers.

As they were walking along the road, a man said to him, "I will follow you wherever you go." Jesus replied, "Foxes have dens and birds have nests, but the Son of Man has no place to lay his head."

Luke 9:57-58

Jesus knew this man was looking for things, so He let the man know: "I have nothing for you. You don't follow me to get things." In this passage, Jesus destroys religion that's motivated by getting things. Let seeking first the Kingdom, therefore, become a tool that transforms us by shifting our thinking away from things and onto information that grows and develops the renewed mind.

 Q/A: Are you following Jesus to get blessed or to know Him and His Kingdom?

If we were honest with ourselves we would say "to get blessed". This is a natural answer but one that needs to be addressed. Take a minute and confess your fault to God asking Him to empower you, through the Holy Spirit to change your thinking. Remember, there are many gospels but only one Jesus preached: the gospel of the Kingdom. Each "gospel" produces after its kind but only one gospel opens to us Kingdom sight and fulfills the Lord's prayer!

Aristotle discovered a key to synergy when he proclaimed "The whole is greater than the sum of its parts." Jesus gave us the key to spreading His culture and influence on earth: Seek the "whole" which is the Kingdom. When we do this we come under the Lord's control of the "parts" and He distributes them in a synergistic way according to His infinite wisdom and power. The answer to more joy in our lives is not to seek joy which is a "part" of the whole; it's to seek the "whole" which is the Kingdom. The answer to "provision" is not to work harder or find a better job; it's to seek the "whole" and trust the Provider to provide. Out of the whole comes the parts but the parts, separate from the whole are not a part of the whole—the way God designed them to be. They take on a different nature and contain an essence independent from the whole. The only means of collapsing the kingdom of the parts (the kingdom of darkness) is to seek first the Kingdom of the whole long enough to see its existence firmly rooted within us.

Synergy is the creation of a whole that is greater than the simple sum of its parts. Seeking first the Kingdom of God places us in synergy with the King. By virtue of its wholeness, the Kingdom ensures superior results with superior substance. Furthermore, because the whole has an independent existence from its parts, we can never discover the Kingdom by pursuing its parts. We can come in contact with certain parts of the Kingdom's cultural norms and even experience the presence of the King, but that's not the same as entering and experiencing the Kingdom. Additionally, the expression of the King is vastly different in the Kingdom than anywhere else. "If I ascend to heaven, you are there! If I make my bed in Sheol, you are there!" (Psalm 139:8). Far better to ascend and abide in the whole than make your bed in the parts.

A further principle discovered at the Berlin school of Experimental Psychology asserts when the human mind forms a percept (the end result of becoming aware of or knowing), the whole has a separate reality of its own, independent of its parts. This is a mirrored principle to the Kingdom. The attributes found in the Kingdom were never designed to stand on their own. No cultural norm found in the Kingdom was designed to be understood outside of the whole. Its reality is not the same. Perhaps this helps explain the promises in the Bible and their lack of existence today. By seeking first the whole we bring into view a different reality. A reality where God resides. Where His culture and social norms are put on display. This awareness of His reality empowers us to bring into existence another dimension: the Kingdom of Heaven on earth. A dimension whose appearance and essence is completely other than our present awareness. A dimension designed to become a template for all creation. Instead of attempting to pull in parts of the Kingdoms culture into our existence, it's time we begin seeking the whole.

 Consider this: A stereogram is a 3D image hidden within another picture. To see the 3D image you must commit to intently looking upon the picture. As you do the 3D image comes into view. The same principle applies to the Kingdom: As you commit to intently looking at the Kingdom, in due time the Kingdom will appear. The key is making it your priority and having patience.

Remember, the whole is not only greater than its parts, it has an independent existence from its parts and is synergistically superior in every way.

Consider this: *Emergence* is the process of becoming visible after being hidden. The emergence of the Kingdom can only be realized and actualized by pursuing the whole. That's why Jesus commanded us to seek the whole—the Kingdom—not its parts. An example of this is found in a picture which portrays a Dalmatian dog sniffing the ground in the shade of an overhanging tree. The dog is not recognized by first identifying its parts (feet, ears, nose, tail, etc.), and then inferring the dog from those component parts. Instead, the dog appears as a whole, all at once. The same principle of emergence applies to the Kingdom. The Kingdom will not come into view for us until we stop focusing on the parts (salvation, joy, peace, forgiveness, etc.) and begin focusing on, as our top priority, the whole. When our center of attention becomes the Kingdom, a river of revelation begins flowing to us, expanding our understanding and awareness of the Lord's ever-expanding, eternal Kingdom.

When we pursue a part of the Kingdom outside of the pursuit of the whole, we encounter a different state or reality of the part. It's the same part in two different states of existence each possessing its unique effect according to its source. "Love," for example, apart from the whole of the Kingdom takes on a different manifestation than Kingdom love. Kingdom love springs forth from the whole, whereas "love," the "part," is void of the Kingdom "whole." Both forms of love can come from God but contain a different essence. This principle applies to all parts found in the Kingdom. Possessing the parts within the whole ensures the highest form of the Will of God being expressed on earth. This form is what's required to collapse present culture while at the same time growing Heaven's.

Application: What do you need to change to make seeking the Kingdom your highest priority? Are you willing to change? Make the commitment today to seek the Kingdom first and ask the Holy Spirit to remind you when you step off course! While seeking the Kingdom, anticipate revelation of the Kingdom.

Your name   Date

Chapter Two

Righteousness

Throughout His earthly ministry, Jesus told us to do many things. In one instance He established His top priority for us. His phrase "seek first" in Matthew 6:33 makes it clear what's most important. A priority is something regarded as more important than another. Jesus tells us the most important priority in life is to seek His Kingdom and righteousness.

? **Q/A**: What does it mean to "seek?"

_____

_____

What benefits come out of seeking?

_____

_____

"Seek" means to search for—to look for; to set our intention and affection in one direction. It implies "to look for by inquiring, investigating and exploring with great intent, focus, and purpose."

Seeking is the act of gathering knowledge and understanding. Because the Kingdom is invisible during the initial pursuit, only understanding with the intent of becoming conformed to the substance discovered in the information will satisfy our search. Therefore, when seeking the Kingdom we are looking for knowledge first, then understanding of the knowledge. This process opens awareness to the realm of the Kingdom, allowing us to experience a new way of living.

Knowledge is information. Understanding is the realization of the content contained within the information. This is a key to entering and experiencing the Kingdom. The largest storehouse of revelation on earth is knowledge and understanding of the Kingdom. To pursue knowledge and understanding of the Kingdom positions us to receive Heaven's release of revelation to us.

The greatest source of Kingdom knowledge is found in God's Word.

As we study His word, meditating and marinating in it, He promises to reveal His Kingdom to us. Ask, seek and knock (Matthew 7:7).

Nothing is more important than seeking His Kingdom and righteousness. The most important information on earth is discovered as we seek to understand these two terms. Its value is measured in how futile all other things become once understanding of the Kingdom and righteousness is open to us. The purpose of this section is to learn what righteousness is and what it is not. In doing so, we will understand why righteousness was made such a high value for us.

 Q/A: What is the priority? What did Jesus tell us needs to be our top priority?

_____

_____

The Kingdom, His righteousness, is the number one priority. Biblical righteousness carries two definitions:

1. Righteousness is a governmental term identifying a person's right standing with his/her country. It is not a religious word but a word from the courts of law meaning right standing or positioning with the government. To be in right standing and relationship with authority is to be righteous. Righteousness, under this definition, is not an act but a position. It is a legal and lawful position empowering a citizen with rights handed down by their government. The demand of righteousness is the fulfillment of the laws, requirements and regulations of a country. In God's country, the demand is perfection. If you want to be in right standing in the Kingdom of Heaven you must be perfect.

2. Righteousness is also a state of moral perfection required by God

to be in right relationship with Him and His country, Heaven. Deuteronomy 6:25 says, "And if we are careful to obey all this law before the LORD our God, as he has commanded us, that will be our righteousness." Perfect obedience to God's laws is righteousness. James 2:10 says: "For whoever keeps the whole law and yet stumbles at just one point is guilty of breaking all of it." What God is telling us is if we obey Him perfectly all the time we will have right standing with Him and His government. Then His laws, customs, culture, social norms: all His ways will find legal access on earth through man.

Jesus came to fulfill ALL the Law

Do not think that I have come to abolish the Law or the Prophets; I have not come to abolish them but to fulfill them. I tell you the truth, until Heaven and earth disappear, not the smallest letter, not the least stroke of a pen, will by any means disappear from the Law until everything is accomplished. Anyone who breaks one of the least of these commandments and teaches others to do the same will be called least in the kingdom of Heaven, but whoever practices and teaches these commands will be called great in the kingdom of Heaven. For I tell you that unless your righteousness surpasses that of the Pharisees and the teachers of the law, you will certainly not enter the kingdom of Heaven.

Matthew 5:17-20

A close look at Jesus' life will find Him fulfilling the law perfectly.

- Eight days after his birth he is taken to the temple to be circumcised just as the law required (Luke 2:21).

- Forty days after his birth Mary went to the temple for a purification rite because the law required it (Luke 2:22).

- When Jesus was 12 we find him in the temple during the Passover feast. Why? Because the law demanded each man present himself before the Lord during the feast of Passover (Luke 2:42). The Jews consider a boy to become a man at age 12. It was probably Jesus' Bar Mitzvah.

- After this, the Bible tells us Jesus continued in obedience to his parents (Luke 2:51). Why would the Bible tell us this? Because the law requires a child to obey his parents and it was giving witness to how Jesus was fulfilling ALL righteousness. Step by step Jesus was fully obeying the demands of a holy and perfect God.

- In Matthew 3:13-17, Jesus came to John to be baptized but John said he didn't want to baptize him. John felt he needed to be baptized. Jesus told him, "John, you don't understand, I need to be baptized by you in order to fulfill the laws of My government (ALL righteousness). I have an assignment you are not aware of. It's important you baptize me." So John baptized Jesus.

- No one could ever convict Jesus of sinning (John 8:46), He fulfilled the law completely.

 Q/A: How did Jesus know his father ALWAYS heard him (John 11:41-42)?

_____

_____

It was because of His righteousness. Since Jesus was perfect He had right standing with the authority of the Kingdom of Heaven. Because He had right standing with authority He knew His prayers were heard. Jesus succeeded in making known the Kingdom on earth as it is in Heaven because of righteousness and His understanding of it. Righteousness became the conduit through which Heaven's culture and influence was displayed and demonstrated through the Son of man.

During the days of Jesus' life on earth, he offered up prayers and petitions with loud cries and tears to the one who could save him from death, and he was heard because of his reverent submission. Although he was a son, he learned obedience from what he suffered and, once made perfect, he became the source of eternal salvation for all who obey him and was designated by God to be high priest in the order of Melchizedek.

Hebrews 5:7-10

The Bible also tells us Jesus was heard because of his reverent submission (Hebrews 5:7-10). "Reverent submission" is a synonym for "total obedience."

Jesus' ministry was so successful because of His right standing with the government of Heaven. He succeeded in bringing Heaven on earth because He was a law-abiding citizen legally capable of executing His dominion rights on earth.

But about the Son, he says, "Your throne, O God, will last forever and ever, and righteousness will be the scepter of your kingdom.

Hebrews 1:8

A "scepter" is a staff a king uses to formalize his decisions. This verse tells us God's decision-making process is always determined by the concepts of righteousness. Everything God will do to us and through us is because of righteousness. Additionally, a scepter represented a king's authority.

In this verse replace the word "scepter" with the word "authority." How does the verse read now? Authority that comes from righteousness is the authority of our government. The authority Jesus regularly displayed on earth was a result of His righteousness. Jesus' righteousness activated Heaven's power to Him and through Him. The key for us experiencing this authority trapped in righteousness is seeking first knowledge and understanding of righteousness. Almighty God is the one who set the requirements: Total righteousness, perfection. Jesus fulfilled God's demands. He completed all God's requirements.

Jesus said,

"It is finished." With that, he bowed his head and gave up his spirit.

John 19:30

The Gift of Righteousness

Jesus has the legal right to freely give His righteousness away. Only now it is a righteousness apart from the effort of keeping the law. It is a righteousness that is by faith.

Now we know that whatever the law says, it says to those who are under the law, so that every mouth may be silenced and the whole world held accountable to God. Therefore no one will be declared righteous in his sight by observing the law; rather, through the law we become conscious of sin. But now a righteousness from God, apart from law, has been made known, to which the Law and the Prophets testify. This righteousness from God comes through faith in Jesus Christ to all who believe. There is no difference, for all have sinned and fall short of the glory of God, and are justified freely by his grace through the redemption that came by Christ Jesus.

Romans 3:19-24

This is a righteousness that is completely accepted by our Father.

I delight greatly in the Lord; my soul rejoices in my God. For he has clothed me with garments of salvation and arrayed me in a robe of righteousness.

Isaiah 61:10

Jesus obeyed in my place to obtain righteousness for me. Jesus obeyed all of God's law and gave His obedience to us.

For if, by the trespass of the one man, death reigned through that one man, how much more will those who receive God's abundant provision of grace and of the gift of righteousness reign in life through the one man, Jesus Christ. Consequently, just as the result of one trespass was condemnation for all men, so also the result of one act of righteousness was justification that brings life for all men. For just as through the disobedience of the one man the many were made sinners, so also through the obedience of the one man the many will be made righteous.

Romans 5:17-19

Jesus' obedience has made us accepted (Ephesians.1:6) and given us boldness and access into a relationship that has potential to bring Heaven on earth.

In him and through faith in him we may approach God with freedom and confidence.

Ephesians 3:11

Therefore, since we have a great high priest who has gone through the Heavens, Jesus, the Son of God, let us hold firmly to the faith we profess. For we do not have a high priest who is unable to sympathize with our weaknesses, but we have one who has been tempted in every way, just as we are—yet was without sin. Let us then approach the throne of grace with confidence, so that we may receive mercy and find grace to help us in our time of need.

Hebrews 4:14-16

This access is to "the throne;" the highest position in government, the place where the King sets laws, considers petitions and grants favor and authority. As representatives of the Kingdom no longer living for ourselves, we approach the throne to receive mercy and find grace to empower us to fulfill our mandate: To establish Heaven on earth. We no longer approach the throne for "things" but rather to enact the Will of God on earth through a co-laboring relationship.

So Jesus took our sins upon Himself (1 Peter 2:24), and gave us His righteousness placing us in right relationship with the Father and His government. Now there is righteousness apart from moral perfection. It is a righteousness that is granted upon belief (faith) in Christ's work on our behalf. There is now righteousness apart from the effort of obeying the law (Philippians 3:9). Jesus received all of our sin and we received all of His righteousness, positioning us as co-laborers with Christ. Receiving this gift, it becomes important we press into understanding our new identity. In order to see the fruits of righteousness we must grow and develop in our understanding of this precious gift. To become a doer of the word and not just a hearer requires you commit to becoming a student of both the message of the Kingdom and the message of righteousness.

Q/A: In light of receiving righteousness by faith, how does our Father look upon us? What are His thoughts and feelings towards you?

The answer is:

- How our Father feels about Jesus, He feels about you.
- The Father calls you beloved and is well pleased with you (Matthew.3:17).
- You are looked upon by the Father as holy, in the likeness of nature with Jesus (Hebrews 10:10, 13-14).
- The Father sees you perfected, complete without lack in anything.
- The Father sees you the same way He sees Jesus.

... for those who are led by the Spirit of God are sons of God. For you did not receive a spirit that makes you a slave again to fear, but you received the Spirit of sonship. And by him, we cry, "Abba, Father." The Spirit himself testifies with our spirit that we are God's children. Now if we are children, then we are heirs— heirs of God and co-heirs with Christ, if indeed we share in his sufferings in order that we may also share in his glory.

Romans 8:14-17

The free gift of Jesus' righteousness has positioned us before God rightly, empowering us with citizen rights and an ideal relationship with the King of kings. This one act on Jesus' part has set the stage for us to partake in the re-establishing of Heaven on earth. We now have a legal connection with the government of Heaven through our citizenship there. We have been given legal jurisdiction over the earth, allowing us to possess the land everywhere our foot treads. We have been qualified to partake in an inheritance found in the Kingdom (Colossians 1:12-13). The inheritance is the Kingdom and all it contains (Matthew 25:34). What a work Jesus did on our behalf!! Apart from the righteousness of Jesus, humanity is doomed to eternal separation from God the Father. With Jesus' righteousness, all things are possible.

There is, however, a process we must go through in order to begin experiencing our inheritance. Once the Holy Spirit convinces us of righteousness through faith (John 16:8), there is a putting on of this righteousness (Ephesians 4:23-24), which involves active participation on our part. We need to study what it means to be a citizen, politician, and ambassador. We must familiarize ourselves with concepts depicting relationship with government. As we do revelation will open to us awareness of our identity as Kingdom representatives. This wakefulness in our identity empowers us to fulfill our mandate of covering the earth with the culture and influence of Heaven.

1. Seek first understanding of right standing with our King and government. Remember, understanding is the process of things contained in knowledge being revealed to us. This requires becoming a student willing to learn about the Kingdom and righteousness, two sides of the same coin. As we continue our diligent pursuit, transformation begins as our mind is renewed.

2. Recondition our way of thinking from sin consciousness to righteousness consciousness through the renewing of our mind (Romans 12:2). If we commit to renewing our minds, we will discover a new identity awaiting us.

3. No longer look at scripture as a religious book. Rather read it as a constitution. A document from Heaven with blueprints for Heavenly living on earth, the ultimate fruit of righteousness.

The same righteousness that empowered Jesus to deny Himself and pick up His cross daily has been given to us. The same righteousness that commissioned Jesus to only do what He saw His Father doing empowers us to do likewise. The same righteousness that enabled Jesus to heal the sick has been given to us. The same righteousness that gave Jesus authority over the wind, food, and gravity is the same righteousness that has been given to us by faith. The same righteousness that moved Heaven to perform on Jesus' behalf throughout His life has been imputed to us. The same righteousness in Jesus that caused the laws of earth to be subject to higher laws, the laws of Heaven is the same righteousness in us. The same righteousness that manifested a servant's heart throughout Jesus' ministry has emboldened us. We have been made the righteousness of God in Christ (2 Corinthians 5:21). The same righteousness Jesus established through works He has given to us by simply believing (Romans 3:22). This belief, once established in our minds and hearts, becomes the mechanism for transformation into manifesting the divine nature as sons of God. May we be found in the secret place hungering and thirsting for righteousness!

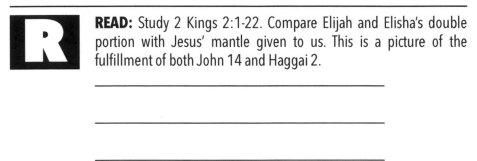

READ: Study 2 Kings 2:1-22. Compare Elijah and Elisha's double portion with Jesus' mantle given to us. This is a picture of the fulfillment of both John 14 and Haggai 2.

_____

_____

_____

I tell you the truth, anyone who has faith in me will do what I have been doing. He will do even greater things than these because I am going to the Father. And I will do whatever you ask in my name so that the Son may bring glory to the Father. You may ask me for anything in my name, and I will do it.

John 14:12-14

"The glory of this present house will be greater than the glory of the former house" says the Lord Almighty. "And in this place I will grant peace," declares the Lord Almighty.

Haggai 2:9

A key to righteousness is putting on Jesus' righteousness by faith. The simple act of accepting and receiving this free gift by faith sets a thorough and dramatic change in motion. It positions us to see with different eyes, hear with a new set of ears and conceive with a different mind. Understanding righteousness places within our line of vision a lens that brings into existence the Kingdom of Heaven, resulting in transformation.

We do, however, speak a message of wisdom among the mature, but not the wisdom of this age or of the rulers of this age, who are coming to nothing. No, we declare God's wisdom, a mystery that has been hidden and that God destined for our glory before time began. None of the rulers of this age understood it, for if they had, they would not have crucified the Lord of glory. However, as it is written: "What no eye has seen, what no ear has heard, and what no human mind has conceived the things God has prepared for those who love him." These are the things God has revealed to us by his Spirit.

1 Corinthians 2:6-10

We enter into this new life in Christ by changing our way of thinking from "self-consciousness" or "sin consciousness" to "righteousness consciousness." Put another way, we retrain and re-pattern our minds to focus not on our sin nature and what we do wrong, but on Jesus' perfection, subsequent forgiveness and the provision that comes through and is discovered in the righteousness given to us.

For if, by the trespass of the one man, death reigned through that one man, how much more will those who receive God's abundant provision of grace and of the gift of righteousness reign in life through the one man, Jesus Christ.

Romans 5:17

Be patient; carrying and manifesting the fruit of righteousness takes time. An apple tree takes about three years before it produces apples. Keep in mind, the first two years it's still an apple tree. The longer you remain dedicated to seeking first the Kingdom and righteousness the greater and swifter the transformation.

As sons and daughters of the living God our purpose on earth is to reign. Representing the Kingdom of Heaven on earth through dominion is a God ordained purpose for humanity. Ruling is in our DNA and became the mission of Jesus as He "only did what He saw His Father doing." Righteousness is God's gift to man, empowering us for reigning in this life (Genesis 1:26-31).

Jesus said the "prince of this world is coming and he is unable to hold me back" (John 14:30). This reality was a result of Jesus fulfilling all righteousness, therefore, He was given supreme authority to do business on behalf of His government, the government He brought (Isaiah 9:6).

Once the Holy Spirit convinces us of righteousness, we need to let Him convince us the devil is condemned (John 16:8-10) and that means he no longer has any hold on us. We are free to execute the Will of our Father the King. No matter how you feel or what the circumstances, you are hidden in Christ. His authority is yours. His righteousness is yours. His freedom to be about our Fathers business is ours. Whom the Son sets free is free indeed!

Put on the new man, which after God is created in righteousness and true holiness.

Ephesians 4:24

Because the human heart is easily condemned, Paul instructs us to put on the breastplate of righteousness.

Finally, be strong in the Lord and in his mighty power. Put on the full armor of God so that you can take your stand against the devil's schemes. For our struggle is not against flesh and blood, but against the rulers, against the authorities, against the powers of this dark world and against the spiritual forces of evil in the Heavenly realms. Therefore put on the full armor of God, so that when the day of evil comes, you may be able to stand your ground, and after you have done everything, to stand. Stand firm then, with the belt of truth buckled around your waist, with the breastplate of righteousness in place, and with your feet fitted with the readiness that comes from the gospel of peace. In addition to all this, take up the shield of faith, with which you can extinguish all the flaming arrows of the evil one. Take the helmet of salvation and the sword of the Spirit, which is the word of God. And pray in the Spirit on all occasions with all kinds of prayers and requests. With this in mind, be alert and always keep on praying for all the saints.

Ephesians 6:10-18

Q/A: Why is the prayer of a righteous man powerful and effective (James 5:16)?

His prayer is effective because he is rightly aligned with his government: allowing for legal movement on earth by Heaven.

When God told Moses to tell them "I Am that I am sent you," He was expressing to the Israelites, "I Am whatever you need sent you" (Exodus 3:14). God made a covenant with His people. Total righteousness was the requirement. The result would be that "I Am what you need" would be there for all those living in the covenant of righteousness. Total obedience brings us into an ever expanding place where God becomes our answer for everything.

Legal righteousness opens Heaven on earth and permits the influence of God to become established. The glory (influence) comes through righteousness by faith. The longer we remain committed to seeking first the Kingdom of God and His righteousness the more we will be led into activity with transformational effects.

Now if the ministry that brought death, which was engraved in letters on stone, came with glory, so that the Israelites could not look steadily at the face of Moses because of its glory, fading though it was, will not the ministry of the Spirit be even more glorious? If the ministry that condemns men is glorious, how much more glorious is the ministry that brings righteousness! For what was glorious has no glory now in comparison with the surpassing glory. And if what was fading away came with glory, how much greater is the glory of that which lasts! Therefore, since we have such a hope, we are very bold. We are not like Moses, who would put a veil over his face to keep the Israelites from gazing at it while the radiance was fading away. But their minds were made dull, for to this day the same veil remains when the old covenant is read. It has not been removed because only in Christ is it taken away. Even to this day when Moses is read, a veil covers their hearts. But whenever anyone turns to the Lord, the veil is taken away. Now the Lord is the Spirit, and where the Spirit of the Lord is, there is freedom. And we, who with unveiled faces all reflect the Lord's glory, are being transformed into his likeness with ever-increasing glory, which comes from the Lord, who is the Spirit.

2 Corinthians 3:7-18

You Heavens above, rain down righteousness;
let the clouds shower it down.
Let the earth open wide,
let salvation spring up,
let righteousness grow with it;
I, the Lord, have created it.

Isaiah 45:8

Application:

Declare over yourself, "I AM RIGHTEOUS IN CHRIST!" Make it a habit to confess your righteousness until it becomes woven into the fabric of your identity. Commit to walk in "right" relationship with the Father through the Son by the Holy Spirit today! Put to death sin consciousness and replace it with righteousness consciousness.

Your name   Date

Chapter Three

Colonization

Black's Law Dictionary defines "colony" as "a dependent political community, consisting of a number of citizens of the same country who have emigrated from a mother country and who remain subject to the mother country." It goes on to say, "Territory attached to another nation known as "the mother country" with legal, political, and economic ties."

Colonization is "the duplication of a country in a foreign place." The Garden of Eden was the expression of God's idea of colonization: duplicating Heaven on earth. The culmination of this grand idea taking place once the whole earth is filled with the culture and governing influence of Heaven.

Colonization is like franchising in that a model is duplicated. A thought put into existence begins spreading. Nobody has done this better than McDonald's. Founded in 1948 with one restaurant, by 1965 there was more than 700. Today it's the greatest restaurant empire in history. They are found in 118 countries worldwide, serve 68 million customers each day and have over 35,000 restaurants.

God's original idea was to extend His invisible Kingdom to the visible earth. That idea has not changed. In Genesis 1:26, we see God delegating authority to man with the intent of establishing dominion on earth. That word "dominion" carries the same concept and function as "kingdom." This Kingdom is to be a reflection, an exact representation or model of the Kingdom where God rules, the Kingdom of Heaven.

God wanted to establish a colony on earth, a territory where He could duplicate the attributes and distinctions of Heaven. Up until 1 Samuel 8:6, He tried to find a people willing to let Him rule. His intent was more than leading; it was colonizing (filling the entire territory of earth with His influence). Habakkuk 2:14 speaks of a knowledge of the glory of the Lord filling the earth. The word "glory" primarily refers to influence. Habakkuk saw a day when specific information would produce such influence it would spread throughout the entire earth. This information is the knowledge and understanding of the Kingdom from God's perspective and the means to its colonial spread. Habakkuk's prophecy sheds light on the magnitude of transformation

Paul spoke about would come as a result of taking in new information ("be transformed by the renewing of your mind" Romans 12:2).

God invented colonization (Genesis. 1:26) and said it was very good (v.31). God's goal was to influence earth with Heaven's culture. Make the territory earth, like the Kingdom of Heaven.

> *This, then, is how you should pray: "Our Father in Heaven, hallowed be your name, your kingdom come, your will be done on earth as it is in Heaven."*
>
> Matthew 6:9-10

God wanted to influence the earth from Heaven through His children. The capacity for Him to have such an effect hinges on our understanding His Kingdom model of influence. God wanted to impact the earth with His own family values using His family. The more we discover our identity in the Kingdom the more we will become familiar with our roles as royal children, ambassadors, and citizens. God wanted to colonize the territory of earth with the nation of Heaven. Heaven is a literal country in another realm; ("Our father who is IN Heaven").

In the first message Jesus preached, He established His mission which is a statement of colonization. From that time on, Jesus began to preach:

> *Repent, for the kingdom of Heaven is at hand.*
>
> Matthew 4:17 (NASB)

In Matthew 6:9 we see the Lord's Prayer is a prayer of colonization. "Your Kingdom come, your Will be done on earth as it is in Heaven" requires the act of colonization. Whenever a country wants to duplicate itself in another territory it's called "colonization." The Bahamas, Jamaica, and Barbados were islands colonized by the kingdom of Britain. Haiti, Guadeloupe, and Martinique were colonized by the kingdom of France. Cuba, the Dominican Republic, Columbia, and Venezuela were colonized by the kingdom of Spain.

When one visits these colonies, he sees they look just like the kingdom they represent. In the Bahamas, they drive on the left side of the road just like in Britain. They drink tea, not coffee, because as it is in Britain, so it became in the Bahamas. Through the process of Britain entering the

Bahamas with the intent of establishing itself in the territory, the Bahamas became just like Britain.

Jesus' mission was and is to make earth just like Heaven. A close study of the gospels and book of Acts reveals countless accounts where colonization took place. Everywhere Jesus went He brought with Him the effects of His government. Every time He sent out His disciples the same effects took place. As soon as the church once again begins raising up disciples and sending them out with the message of the Kingdom, then we will witness the effects of the government of Heaven on earth again.

In 1962, the Bahamas rose up and declared independence from Britain. By 1964, the British Parliament authorized the islands to self-govern and in the same year, a new constitution granting the Bahamas independence was given by their former colonial overlords. In the same way, Adam and Eve declared independence from the Kingdom of Heaven when they disobeyed God in Genesis 3. The result was separation from the home country. All relationships, protection, and benefits were severed. All the blessings of Kingdom culture, social norms, and living were lost in one act. The systems of government placed on earth by Heaven were overtaken and a new ruler was given the right to implement his system. The influence of Heaven was lost and its rival power was put in position to expand its capacity to have effect on the character, development and structure of both individuals and society.

Sin separated humanity from the King and His Kingdom. As a result, the kingdom of darkness began its thrust of colonization. All manner of evil followed as mindsets and conditioned patterns of thought were established under the rule of Satan's kingdom. The attributes of Heaven, once predominant on earth, were exchanged with the culture and lifestyle of the kingdom of darkness. Generation after generation, we see the effects of our independence from the rule of Heaven on earth.

Our part of North America was colonized by Britain. Our founders became oppressed and in 1775 began the struggle to come out from under oppression. It took until 1781, after much suffering on both sides, before we became free. Freedom began with a change of mind and culminated with perseverance and steadfastness rooted in the mindset that brought about the transformation.

The whole world is under the oppressive influence of the kingdom of darkness. Only a decision to come out from under this dark kingdom and begin seeking first Christ's Kingdom will empower us to re-discover God's Will, purpose, and plan for our lives. Transformation begins by changing the way we think. As long as a nation remains in ignorance of God's ways, the kingdom of darkness rules. The moment a remnant within a nation rises out of ignorance, empowerment begins. All earthly governments presently fall under the control of the kingdom of darkness (ignorance). Someday, the kingdom of this world will become the Kingdom of our God (Revelation 11:15). It is the church's responsibility, the remnant, under the Great Commission, to go and make disciples of all nations. In doing so, we become living stones for Christ to begin building His church, equipping us with the keys of the Kingdom and empowering us to fulfill the colonization of earth with Heaven. It only takes a small community of believers whose soil contains Kingdom seed for God to awaken a never-ending expansion and expression of the Kingdom of Heaven. May God use you to pioneer such a community as you commit to seeking first His Kingdom and His righteousness.

Then Jesus came to them and said, "All authority in Heaven and on earth has been given to me. Therefore go and make disciples of all nations, baptizing them in the name of the Father and of the Son and of the Holy Spirit, and teaching them to obey everything I have commanded you. And surely I am with you always, to the very end of the age."
Matthew 28:18-20

Colonization Reviewed

Jesus only told us to seek two things. The Kingdom of God and His righteousness. Everything else He promised to add to us.

Kingdoms colonize in order to extend their power and influence. As representatives of Heaven, it is our responsibility to seek God for knowledge and understanding of His Kingdom and how He wants to extend its influence and authority both in our hearts and onto the earth. "For the earth will be filled with the knowledge of the glory of the Lord as the waters cover the sea" (Habakkuk 2:14). The sooner God's people enter into seeking first the Kingdom the more we will see Habakkuk's prophesy coming to pass.

It is important to understand God made us legal creatures not emotional. We have emotions but they ought not to govern us, truth does. Society has formed us to be largely emotional. We must see this and become willing to change. By committing to seek first understanding of the Kingdom we take the first step. In our relationship with King Jesus, there is time for emotional and intimate communion as well as approaching Him as a legal representative of His country. Learning to communicate both ways is an essential part of our maturing into the royal sons and daughters He created us to be. We will have an eternity to embrace the Lord emotionally but only a blink of an eye to stand as a legal representative for the cause of our King.

Colonization is a blessing or a curse depending who is doing the colonizing. If the colonizer is an evil kingdom than oppression and bondage will result. If we have Heaven's Kingdom, then love, righteousness, joy, peace and freedom prevails. As the Kingdom message emerges, those given over to it will become the vessels used by the Lord to fill the earth with the culture of Heaven.

All kingdoms want to expand. All kingdoms desire to gain territory. It's evident the kingdom of darkness presently has overwhelming influence on earth. God wants to take back that influence through His people. "The highest Heavens belong to the LORD, but the earth he has given to mankind" (Psalm 115:16).

The more territory kingdoms have the more glory they possess. There was a time in the late 1800's when the saying was, "The sun never sets on the British Empire." This was because their empire had colonies on every ocean and every continent except Antarctica. There will come a day when the earth will say "the sun never sets on the Kingdom of Heaven." God has entrusted the church with the responsibility of colonizing the earth, therefore, the timeline is largely in our hands.

The first territory necessary for God to possess is our hearts. The Kingdom of God always begins within us. The continual spread of His influence over our mind, Will, emotions, senses and all other areas of an individual's life makes it possible for that influence to spread outward. The Kingdom moves from the micro to the macro, from inward to outward. Many will try to bring the Kingdom to earth and will fail. They will discover they were really building their own kingdom. Why? Because they did not allow the Holy Spirit to first build Christ's

Kingdom inwardly. If you are not intimately familiar with the Kingdom of God within and you believe you're building the outward Kingdom, you are deceived. What you are likely building is rooted in the kingdom of darkness. We cannot exaggerate the urgency of seeking first the Kingdom but we can't mistake that urgency with an "urgency" of the Kingdoms expression on earth. The former is our responsibility; the latter is the Lord's. We must settle into our role so God can move in His.

Once, having been asked by the Pharisees when the kingdom of God would come, Jesus replied, "The kingdom of God does not come with your careful observation, nor will people say, 'Here it is,' or 'There it is,' because the kingdom of God is within you."

Luke 17:20-21

As we become transformed into the image of Christ we become trustworthy and begin acquiring the keys of the Kingdom. Central to the colonization of the Kingdom is keeping our attention on inner Kingdom development. Allowing the King to reign in all areas of our personal life is paramount. Those looking for the outward Kingdom before the inward is established will need to resort to emotional hype, sensationalism, and witchcraft. Thinking they are building the Kingdom on earth, they will eventually realize they were erecting their own.

The more keys we possess, the more Holy Spirit is empowered to take back territory on earth as it is in Heaven. In pursuit of the Kingdom, keep in mind God's attention is fixed on His Kingdom within us flourishing first.

Application: Receive your appointment as an Ambassador of Heaven to the colony of earth. Begin to walk in your authority as a representative of Heaven. Mark this day as the day the prayer of your life became, **"Thy Kingdom come, Thy will be done on earth as it is heaven!"**

Your name   Date

Chapter Four

Citizenship

As individuals who have been born twice (naturally and spiritually) we are legally recognized by two countries. This is called "dual citizenship." The moment we are born our natural government put a claim on us as its citizen. It gave us rights, empowering us to live up to the quality of life offered by the country. It also gave us responsibilities that help maintain the country's culture, ideas, and social norms.

When we are "born again," Heaven places the same claim on us. We are given the same precious rights and responsibilities, only they came from a different country—Heaven. Once we become born again or more accurately translated "born from above" we are given access to explore the country of Heaven.

The moment we are born from above we are presented a choice we never knew existed—to live under the governing systems, responsibilities, and rights of a natural country or spiritual Kingdom. All of us, due to ignorance, have been subjected to our natural government's way of living. Once again, as in the days of Jesus, God is making us aware of the open citizenship enrollment into His country. This requires, above all, understanding. An informed decision can only be made once choices are presented and understood.

Governments inherently possess, exert and exercise tremendous authority and influence. They not only establish and maintain the parameters for expressing life outwardly but have sobering amounts of influence on the inward life, namely our thoughts. We will discuss this in more detail later. For now, rest assured our decision as to which government to submit to has major life determining effects. Due to man's fallen nature, we have been subjected to the influence of earthly government. Our thoughts have been conditioned and taught in accordance with the image of the kingdom of darkness's influence over earthly governments.

Any human seeking citizenship must first study the constitution. Before anyone is given the ability to freely function in the country, he needs to pass a test showing his understanding of the country's way of thinking. Similarly, we must understand the mind of our King before we begin functioning as a Kingdom citizen on earth. The act of pursuing understanding of a constitution is the means through which a government conforms its citizens. Giving ourselves over to the principles and laws of the constitution ensures conformity within the structure of the government. The study of a country's fundamental principles by which it governs its citizens will cause the principles themselves to become part of our identity. As we begin studying Heaven's constitution we take on its very nature by bringing to life the Kingdom of Heaven within us. A key to not being conformed to this world is becoming an active participant in the study of our citizenship in Heaven. In doing so, we will be transformed by the renewing of our minds, which will result in a transfer of our being from one government influence to another. Jesus identified the pathway to such an activity—seeking first the Kingdom. A transformation in appearance and nature of both the individual first, then his or her sphere of influence awaits those committed to Jesus' top priority for mankind: seeking His Kingdom.

As a natural citizen growing up, we were taught our rights. Once we understood them, they empowered us to live with maximum freedom under the government. We enjoy the benefits of citizenship to the degree we understand the laws and rights it presents. For example, in Driver's Education, we are taught how to drive. When we become of age and pass the test, we experience our right to drive and all benefits that come with receiving a license to drive. The government then issues us a form of identification—our Driver's License.

We applied for and received another form of ID, a passport from our natural country. Using it, we experienced the benefits of unlimited travel. In America, we have the right to live in peace without the police entering our homes. These are all rights afforded to us by the Constitution. The Constitution empowers us so long as we're aware of its rights. If a right is denied, it's our responsibility to claim that right. If need be, we can petition the government to rule on our behalf. If the right is denied, we are entitled to legal counsel who will present our case before a judge. We even have the right to bring in a witness if need be. But if we don't know our rights they can be taken from us and we will be powerless to get them back. Being a citizen of Heaven (Philippians 3:20) is no different.

Q/A: What is a key to bringing Heaven to earth?

A key to bringing Heaven to earth is understanding our rights and responsibilities as a citizen of Heaven. When Paul declared you to be a citizen of Heaven, he was identifying you as a legal person. Citizens under earthly governments are conditioned to be emotional people. Only the rulers and lawmakers understand their identity as legal people. Understanding this fact empowers you to fulfill your greatest mandate for King Jesus, bringing His Government on earth as it is in Heaven.

Devoting ourselves to the study of the Bible with the proper perspective will empower us to live a "Kingdom Citizen" lifestyle. To the disciples of Jesus, the Bible is not a religious book but the Constitution of Heaven. The Bible is the established plan, purpose, and Will of our King regarding His country. It is written to His citizens who also happen to be His children. All authority on earth comes from our understanding and relationship to this most precious of all documents, the law of God.

As you discover your citizenship in Heaven it is natural for you to receive your rights and privileges under a selfish pretense. We must be aware as we come in contact with this self-centeredness, reminding ourselves that all rights in the Kingdom are to be used for the purpose of the Will of the King. Our rights, like all gifts, are designed to be offerings given back to the Giver for His use. Cultivating an eternal perspective will help equip us with the ability to store up treasure in Heaven rather than on earth.

The most productive way of understanding the value of the Bible is to begin in the book of Matthew. As we study this first of four gospels, we focus our intentions on looking for the Kingdom. When we see the Kingdom mentioned, look closely at what's being said. How important was the Kingdom to Jesus' ministry and how often did He teach on the subject? Fruitful citizens of the Kingdom make it their top priority to seek it. If we make it the priority that Jesus did, the Bible will be transformed before our eyes. It will no longer be a religious book, but will become a relational guide, leading us to exercise all the rights, responsibilities, and powers we have as citizens of the Kingdom.

Receiving and holding onto knowledge, understanding, and wisdom about the Kingdom is the way to move from citizenship under an oppressive earthly government to a liberating Heavenly one. This one act of seeking information about the Kingdom removes the cataracts from our spiritual eyes and empowers us to see into the superior realm of Heaven. Additionally, understanding empowers us to begin enacting Heaven's laws, principles and system of rulership on earth. In the same way a politician establishes and upholds government influence through understanding and implementation of law, so too does the citizen of Heaven. In fact, almost half of the members of congress are lawyers. This fact validates the importance of both acquiring understanding and becoming a legal person in order to establish and maintain government influence.

As we grow in understanding of our rights and responsibilities as citizens of Heaven, we should not be surprised by the trials that come our way. A key to maintaining confidence through these trials is understanding that as a legal citizen of Heaven we have been born into the greatest "righteous racket" in history. Our Father is the judge, the Holy Spirit is our counsel, and Jesus is our witness. The whole system is rigged in our favor! Knowing this, we can be patient in tribulation and in constant contact with our Heavenly government just like the Apostle Paul was (Romans 12:12). As we begin understanding the authority we have been given, it is important we acquire wisdom. Keep in mind Jesus learned obedience from what he suffered. Let our suffering become a tool used to teach us as well, knowing a student is not above his teacher.

 Q/A: What makes thoughts?

Neuroscience has discovered it is thought that makes man; man does not create his thoughts. If this is true then what makes thoughts? Governments. The structures set up by governments have such influence over man they create thought. It's no wonder Jesus commanded us to seek first His government, He knew "as a man thinks, so is he" (Proverbs 23:7). In light of this, how important is it to place our supreme loyalty under the direction of the government Jesus brought us? And what will this transformation look like as we allow the government of Heaven to condition and pattern our thoughts? A key to receiving the mind of Christ is coming under His government, the Kingdom of Heaven. The key to coming under the Kingdom of Heaven is making it your top priority to understand it.

How Systems Work

There are six primary systems working together to form government and culture. They are healthcare, economics, education, government, religion/spirituality, and media/entertainment. Here are six rudimentary and foundational examples of how a system conditions our thinking and behavior under earthly government:

1. *Healthcare*— The maintenance and improvement of physical and mental health. When we are sick, we are conditioned to focus on the symptoms and go to the doctor. We obtain a diagnosis and prescription to treat our symptoms.

2. *Economics*—The branch of knowledge concerned with the production, consumption, and transfer of wealth. The means to a successful life is money. We make money by going to work. The more we work, the more money we make, the better our lives. Or so we are conditioned to think under the earthly economic system. The economy, under most earthly governments, is our greatest source.

3. *Education*— The process of receiving or giving systematic instruction resulting in an enlightening experience. The world's system of education presents its own philosophy and ideas that shape family values and condition our thinking. In most cases the educational system is at odds with the Kingdom of Heaven. Since education is the process and activity of receiving information it's important to broaden our definition to include all activity involved in receiving information: School, TV, social media, church, and interpersonal relationships all contain the essence of education and are legitimate

platforms for shaping our thinking.

4. *Government*—Authoritative direction. The continuous exercise of authority over individuals and society. The system of government has its own modus operandi. In America, democracy, (I understand we were founded as a republic but no longer do we function as such), and free market capitalism is the paradigm through which we form government and culture.

5. *Religion*—In Christianity, Jesus is the religious leader. We go to a building usually once a week, give a little money, listen to someone talk about a religious book called the Bible, say a prayer and go on with life. Most church members have been conditioned as followers of Jesus to seek things from Him or the institutional church itself.

6. *Media*—The plural form of the word medium meaning an intervening agency, means, or instrument. The main means of mass communication (especially television, radio, newspapers, and the Internet) regarded collectively. Through what is spoken and what we see, the media is perhaps the greatest mind molder used for good or evil. Under earthly governments media is used largely to serve the government's agenda. What our government is allowing over the airwaves reveals the heart condition of those in power.

The country of Heaven uses the same systems to govern its citizens only via different means. These means come to life as the church transitions its identity out of the world's system into the Kingdom through the renewing of the mind. A belief system forged in the Kingdoms crucible eventually produces substance only found in Heaven.

1. *Healthcare*—When we are sick, Heaven's constitution conditions us to focus on the King's healing power. We are told to call the Elders of the church, lay hands on the sick, and they will be made well (James 5:14). We have the right and responsibility to petition our King for healing (Psalm103:3). The Kingdom mindset carries substance on our words and in our touch that creates healing out of sickness: "they WILL be made well!" Additionally, we must begin understanding

how to properly care for our bodies, for they are temples of the Holy Spirit (1 Corinthians 6:19). Kingdom healthcare is preventative in nature but requires understanding and action.

2. *Economics*—As a citizen of Heaven instead of pursuing "life" (food, shelter, clothing, safety, love and belonging) Jesus promises to "add all these things" to us freely as we seek first His Kingdom and righteousness (Matthew 6:33). Living life as a citizen of an earthly government, our source is the economy. This is not so as a citizen of Heaven. King Jesus is our source. In Heaven "commonwealth" is the economic means. Commonwealth is when the King chooses to make His wealth common to all citizens, swearing to be their source of need and provision. We will study this later in detail.

3. *Education*—Jesus made education in His country very easy when He said, "make the top priority in your life to seek My Kingdom and My righteousness. As a citizen of Heaven, everything we need and want is contained in these two subjects (Matthew 13:44). Jesus desires all citizens under Heaven to be highly educated in these areas. The educational system of Heaven is the most exhilarating adventure the human heart will ever encounter. This ever expanding Kingdom enlarges the boundaries of exploration and observation to the point you will enter eternal life proclaiming "my eye has not seen, nor ear heard what God has prepared for me!" God has placed eternity in our hearts already (Ecclesiastes 3:11). Seeking first the Kingdom of God and His righteousness is the primary means of uncapping realization and observation of this marvelous state of existence. Eternal life was meant to be lived NOW!

4. *Government*—Heaven's government is the opposite of a democracy (rule by majority). In a kingdom, the king rules. A democracy implies ownership. In a kingdom the king owns everything. In a democracy, citizens vote for leaders. In a kingdom the king appoints leaders. As we move from being governed by this world system to Heaven's, a major indication of transformation is receiving the thoughts of Christ. We have the mind of Christ but presently His thoughts are not ours. Out of ignorance we have chosen to be governed by

a system other than the Kingdom of Heaven. Coming under the government of Christ's Kingdom ensures a continual metamorphosis within the mind of man. This culminates in an infusion of Christ's thoughts into the mind of man which begins the renewing of the mind process. This conversion leads to transformation: conforming to the image of Christ.

5. *Religion*—Under the government of Heaven, the Church is not a religious gathering place but a group of called-out ones, establishing the Will of their King in a specific territory. Every citizen of Heaven is appointed the position of a politician with the responsibility of enacting law on behalf of the King. In the Kingdom followers of Jesus have become disciples of Jesus by choosing to seek first the Kingdom instead of seeking things.

6. *Media*—The country of Heaven's media is pure, lovely, edifying, and Christ-centered. It assists in the renewing of the mind process and plays a role in maintaining a steady flow of thoughts originating from the Kingdom of God within us.

While transforming earthly systems into Heaven's systems, we are under the jurisdiction of the Kingdom. We have the right and responsibility to petition our government in times of injustice. We need to be careful not to become presumptuous, failing to observe the limits of what is permitted. Possessing authority on earth demands wisdom and a daily dying to self. Without these character traits we are sure to fall into the snare of building our own kingdoms.

Heaven's government exercises authority over us at all times. When the laws of Heaven's country are violated on earth, we have the responsibility to petition our government to correct the wrong. *The earth is the Lord's and the fullness of it* (Psalms 24:1). All of creation is waiting in expectation for us to take back ownership and rulership of earth on behalf of the rightful owner, Jesus the King (Romans 8:19). As we petition in faith and understanding, the Kingdom within us responds and makes the corrections. This is an important distinction. It is God that works in us, not ourselves.

We don't want to let our zeal become carnal in our attempts to "overthrow" earthly rulership. We don't overthrow anything. As we come into agreement with Heaven through the renewing of our minds, the earthly systems collapse and the domain of Christ is established. It is the effects of the Kingdom on earth that will bring awareness to the Kingdom itself. This awareness is what begins the process of the collapse of earthly rulership and the building of the Kingdom on earth.

 Q/A: How did the Apostle Paul understand Citizenship?

Paul understood citizenship. He understood his unique position of dual citizenship. As a citizen of Heaven, he activated and implemented God's healthcare plan by supernaturally healing the sick. In Acts 19, Paul brought a cultural transformation of the city of Ephesus through the preaching and demonstration of the Gospel of the Kingdom. "Paul entered the synagogue and spoke boldly there for three months, arguing persuasively about the kingdom of God ... God did extraordinary miracles through Paul" (Verses 8,11). He carried with him the distinct expression of his citizenship in Heaven by demonstrating his country's attributes everywhere he went. He demonstrated that preaching the gospel of the Kingdom invites extraordinary miracles to validate the Kingdom's existence. In effect, he became uniquely one with his King and country.

One day in Jerusalem, Paul was about to be beaten when he acted on his legal rights as a Roman citizen not to be flogged without legal due process. The authorities became afraid when he placed a demand on his right. They refused to beat him.

The crowd listened to Paul until he said this. Then they raised their voices and shouted, "Rid the earth of him! He's not fit to live!" As they were shouting and throwing off their cloaks and flinging dust into the air, the commander ordered Paul to be taken into the barracks. He directed that he be flogged and questioned in order to find out why the people were shouting at him like this. As they stretched him out to flog him, Paul said to the centurion standing there, "Is it legal for you

> *to flog a Roman citizen who hasn't even been found guilty?" When the centurion heard this, he went to the commander and reported it. "What are you going to do?" he asked. "This man is a Roman citizen." The commander went to Paul and asked, "Tell me, are you a Roman citizen?" "Yes, I am," he answered. Then the commander said, "I had to pay a big price for my citizenship." "But I was born a citizen," Paul replied. Those who were about to question him withdrew immediately. The commander himself was alarmed when he realized that he had put Paul, a Roman citizen, in chains.*

Acts 22:22-29

 Q/A: How does the Kingdom culture mold us?

_____

_____

Paul, knowing his rights as a citizen of Rome, gave him authority to enforce those rights. In like manner, knowing God's healthcare plan within the Kingdom of Heaven empowered him to manifest the power of the Kingdom of Heaven on earth. Similarly, knowing Jesus' desire to colonize the earth with the culture of Heaven empowered Paul to transform an entire city. Without knowledge and understanding he would not have experienced the benefits of his earthly rights or Heavenly power.

As a citizen of a natural country, we live under systems of rulership that mold the minds of society and determine how industry functions. Industry controls the flow of information and molds the minds of society. Take economics, for example. This model in America dictates how we make a living and gather for ourselves basic needs and wants.

"Life" under this system is defined as the pursuit of basic needs (food, shelter, clothing, safety, etc.). In America, we go to work and get a paycheck. We use that money to live. If we have money left over, we do with it what we want. The world economic model is one of pursuing the fulfillment of our needs through work. Its foundational premise is gathering things for ourselves to better ourselves and our loved ones. This world system is based on the concept of "ownership."

Q/A: How does the Kingdom economic model work?

The Kingdom economic model is the opposite. We own nothing but have access to everything. In the country of Heaven, we are stewards of the King's resources. The word "Lord" means "owner."

Jesus is Lord of ALL.

When we become a citizen of His country He swears to provide our needs. He makes it His responsibility to provide for His citizens. God's Kingdom does not contain the concept of ownership. Everything is the King's. He is the owner of ALL! To most, this is a major change in the way you think. Nevertheless, it is necessary to bring about transformation.

David declared, "The earth is the LORD's, and everything in it, the world, and all who live in it" (Psalms 24:1). One revelation of the Lordship of Jesus Christ will change your perception of life and silence fear, stress and anxiety forever.

> *Therefore take no thought, saying, What shall we eat? or, What shall we drink? or, Wherewithal shall we be clothed? (For after all these things do the Gentiles seek:) for your Heavenly Father knoweth that ye have need of all these things. But seek ye first the kingdom of God, and his righteousness; and all these things shall be added unto you. Take therefore no thought for the morrow: for the morrow shall take thought for the things of itself. Sufficient unto the day is the evil thereof."*
>
> Matthew 6:31-34 (KJV)

Citizenship Summarized

Jesus is redefining "life." He's extending an invitation to transfer and position our allegiance to the King and His Kingdom. He's saying, in effect, "You no longer need to pursue your needs. I will provide them for you. There is one thing I ask of you. Seek to understand my Kingdom and righteousness. When you do this I will teach you my ways, empower you to live the life I designed for you, and all things needed for your well-being will be supplied to you."

Under the world system, "life" consists of the pursuit of fulfilling our needs. In His Kingdom God provides for our needs as we seek the Kingdom which becomes our life. Jesus said "I have food to eat that you know nothing about" (John 4:32). The realization of His provision is discovered as we step out in faith and take upon ourselves His top priority for us: seeking the Kingdom.

As a citizen of the country of Heaven, we have rights and responsibilities. The following is a list that compares and contrasts our dual citizenship. A close look at the differences will help bring an understanding of the outworkings of the two systems. As we go through this list again, consider two questions:

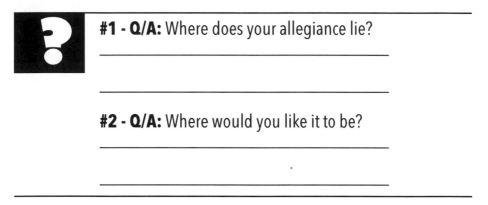

#1 - Q/A: Where does your allegiance lie?

_____

_____

#2 - Q/A: Where would you like it to be?

_____

_____

Jesus' ministry model was essentially to open the eyes of humanity to both systems of rulership and invite whosoever wanted to come under His Kingdom model. We must establish our primary citizenship in Heaven. As Moses led the people out from under Pharaoh's system, so too does God want to lead us out from under this world's system. The Promised Land awaits the "whosoever wills." The kingdom of ignorance (darkness) no longer has a hold on us as the Kingdom of light (knowledge) shines brighter and brighter.

COMPARING AND CONTRASTING OUR DUAL CITIZENSHIP

THE WORLD	THE KINGDOM
The church is a religious organization following a religious leader. Those a part of this organization are rooted in seeking things more so than seeking the Kingdom. As Paul demonstrated before his conversion, it is the religious who most oppose the Kingdom and resist its increase.	The *church* is a group of politicians with a legal right and responsibility to establish the King's Will on earth. The Greek word for citizen is *polites*. The English word "politician" is derived from the Greek word *polites*. As a citizen of Heaven, we have been appointed to a legal office with the responsibility of implementing and upholding the laws, social norms and culture of our government. We have a legal and moral obligation to implement and uphold the Will and intent of our government. Because Heaven is the superior system of rulership on earth, we are chief among all political representatives. Petition our government whenever and wherever Heaven's culture and social norms are not the governing influence. We have the legal right to establish our government's Will.
In the *Economic system* we work to live (we work to make money to pay for our needs). The patterned mindset is ownership.	We seek the Kingdom and the King provides our needs. He is our source vs. the economic system being our source.
Healthcare—you pay to have a service that, in most cases, no longer has your interest of health in mind.	We petition our government and make a constitutional claim (Psalm 103:3; Jeremiah 30:17; James 5:14; Exodus 15:26, 23:25; Acts 10:38). The Great Physician is our doctor of choice.

THE WORLD	THE KINGDOM
Education within the church—we learn about Jesus and the things He did. We are taught about all gospels except the Kingdom.	In the *Kingdom learning system,* we learn what Jesus told us to learn—the Kingdom of Heaven. We also preach what Jesus taught us to preach, which is the Kingdom.
*Prayer is t*alking to God, asking for things.	Prayer is the act of an ambassador bringing the Will of his government to earth on the King's behalf. In the Kingdom, prayer is the act of establishing the Will of Heaven on earth through petition, proclamation, or intercession. Prayer is the earthly license for Heavenly activity. The discipline of listening is key to establishing a fruitful prayer life.

Q/A: Where is real freedom found?

When Jesus told us to "seek first the Kingdom," He understood we all would be under dual citizenship. He was telling us to, "Make sure your allegiance is to My Kingdom." He was presenting us with an opportunity to step into a divine lifestyle. He was directing us down the road that leads to an existence on earth as it is in Heaven.

Freedom is found under the Kingdom of Heaven's government but slavery is found under the governments of the world. Our citizenship in Heaven has a far greater value than any other country's rights and privileges. A Christian is a religious person but a citizen is a legal human. A Christian looks at the Bible as a devotional book despite it being the law of God, a legal book. The Bible, to a citizen of Heaven, is the constitution of Heaven. A religious person petitions God with their emotions. A legal person petitions God with the law and with truth. A religious person asks and even begs God for things. A Kingdom citizen establishes legal precedence for God to act on earth through prayer, proclamation, and petition.

Making a decision to enter the Kingdom of Heaven is commendable, however, there is a condition required. In order to experience the Kingdom, we must make it our top priority to seek after it.

We must seek Kingdom understanding as if we were a doctoral student pursuing a Ph.D., not like someone in a buffet line. We need to be laser-focused in our devotion, not giving ourselves to a multitude of things.

> *Get wisdom, get understanding; do not forget my words or swerve from them. Do not forsake wisdom, and she will protect you; love her, and she will watch over you. Wisdom is supreme; therefore get wisdom. Though it costs all you have, get understanding.*
>
> Proverbs 4:5-7

The command of Jesus is to seek first—make the Kingdom "Number One." Halfhearted pursuit is not enough to possess the Kingdom. When Jesus said "seek first the Kingdom and His righteousness," He was calling us "To make it our top priority to go after the Kingdom." Jesus was offering us an opportunity to step into His greatest need for us. In exchange, He promised to provide our needs. What an offer!

> *Blessed are those who hunger and thirst for righteousness, for they shall be satisfied.*
>
> Matthew 5:6 (NASB)

When we're hungry or thirsty, we become obsessed with fulfilling our desire. Our priority and preoccupation are to satisfy our need for food and drink. This type of pursuit will produce an unveiling and unfolding of the Kingdom to us. It is our responsibility to engage our Wills towards this end. When we do, God provides the substance that brings satisfaction. The principles of the Kingdom were not given to all of the followers of Jesus, only the inner circle He called Disciples— those that listened to Jesus when He said: "seek first the Kingdom" (Matthew16:9, Luke 8:10).

Q/A: What is the key to our authority in the Kingdom?

_____

_____

Kingdom Citizen Authority

The key to our authority is the knowledge of our adoption into Kingdom family. The key to fulfilling the Lord's purpose for our lives on earth is knowing, understanding, and applying Kingdom concepts.

A wise man studies his rights and puts demands on his country to enforce those rights when they are being violated. Under all governments, the wisest of citizens are always the politicians and lawyers. God established His Kingdom on earth in the very beginning (Genesis 1:26). In order to enforce His rights on earth, we need to know and understand them. Taking back what the devil has stolen demands embracing a new way of thinking. This new way of thinking is precisely what the Lord uses to "take back" what's been stolen.

A citizen of the United States gets his rights from the Constitution. To the citizen of the Kingdom of Heaven, the Bible is "the Constitution." Kingdom has to do with a country. Citizenship has to do with status and authority has to do with rights. This understanding is a key that reveals where a citizen gets his power (Kingdom Citizenship Authority).

 Q/A: Why is understanding the responsibility of citizenship so important?

_____

_____

_____

_____

Understanding the Responsibility of Citizenship

"Citizenship" is important because:

- Every nation possesses it. Once we understand we become integrated into our country and can effectively implement our government's systems. Additionally, our government begins the conditioning and pattern process it inherently is designed to do, ultimately placing us under its influence.

- Citizenship is about power, authority, and rights. When a government gives a person citizenship they are not handing something out that is trivial. They are granting power, authority, rights, and responsibilities. As citizens of Heaven, we are privileged to take the good news about our country to a territory (our delegated sphere of influence), offering a new way of life to whoever is willing to listen.

- A person, once granted citizenship within a country is given authority to uphold, propagate and spread the country's system of ruling. The citizen takes on the essence of the country and becomes unified on many levels with it. In the Kingdom, citizens work from a place of effortless rest. Yielding our lives to Christ, we enter into a place where self-effort dies and "Christ in us" becomes our source of strength. "I have been crucified with Christ and I no longer live, but Christ lives in me. The life I now live in the body, I live by faith in the Son of God, who loved me and gave himself for me" (Galatians 2:20).

- Every human needs citizenship. If we don't have it, we can't function in the country where we reside because we have no legal rights. We have no access to the influence, power, and authority that comes from the rights of citizenship. We have no legal right to act in a country or on behalf of a country. This is shown in Heavenly terms by an example from Acts 19.

Some Jews who went around driving out evil spirits tried to invoke the name of the Lord Jesus over those who were demon-possessed. They would say, "In the name of Jesus, whom Paul preaches, I command you to come out." Seven sons of Sceva, a Jewish chief priest, were doing this. One day the evil spirit answered them, "Jesus I know, and I know about Paul, but who are you?" Then the man who had the evil spirit jumped on them and overpowered them all. He gave them such a beating that they ran out of the house naked and bleeding. When this became known to the Jews and Greeks living in Ephesus, they were all seized with fear, and the name of the Lord Jesus was held in high honor. Many of those who believed now came and openly confessed their evil deeds. A number who had practiced sorcery brought their scrolls together and burned them publicly. When they calculated the value of the scrolls, the total came to fifty thousand drachmas. In this way, the word of the Lord spread widely and grew in power.

Acts 19:13-20

• Without citizenship we are powerless. With citizenship we have the influence and authority to even convince the most powerful within the kingdom of darkness. Kingdom expansion takes place as Kingdom citizens begin enforcing their government policy onto a territory.

Now for some time a man named Simon had practiced sorcery in the city and amazed all the people of Samaria. He boasted that he was someone great, and all the people, both high and low, gave him their attention and exclaimed, "This man is the divine power known as the Great Power." They followed him because he had amazed them for a long time with his magic. But when they believed Philip as he preached the good news of the kingdom of God and the name of Jesus Christ, they were baptized, both men and women. Simon himself believed and was baptized. And he followed Philip everywhere, astonished by the great signs and miracles he saw. When the apostles in Jerusalem heard that Samaria had accepted the word of God, they sent Peter and John to them. When they arrived, they prayed for them that they might receive the Holy Spirit, because the Holy Spirit had not yet come upon any of them; they had simply been baptized into the name of the Lord Jesus. Then Peter and John placed their hands on them, and they received the Holy Spirit. When Simon saw that the Spirit was given at the laying on of the apostles' hands, he offered them money and said, "Give me also this ability so that everyone on whom I lay my hands may receive the Holy Spirit." Peter answered: "May your money perish with you because you thought you could buy the gift of God with money! You have no part or share in this ministry because your heart is not right before God. Repent of this wickedness and pray to the Lord. Perhaps he will forgive you for having such a thought in your heart. For I see that you are full of bitterness and captive to sin." Then Simon answered, "Pray to the Lord for me so that nothing you have said may happen to me."

Acts 8:9-24

- The most influential authority an individual can possess is citizenship. Once we receive it, we become powerful because citizenship is the most valuable privilege a government can extend to an individual. With it comes great privilege and responsibility. The key to receiving the influence and authority that comes from our citizenship in Heaven is seeking first the Kingdom and our relationships with it as citizens.

- Study the constitution of Heaven (the Bible). Begin looking for rights and responsibilities as a citizen of Heaven. As you find them engage in dialog with the Lord as to how He wants you to respond to your new found discoveries.

- A citizen becomes so powerful that he can put demands on his government as long as the demands are within the confines of the law. As representatives sent to a land yet to be conformed to our government, it becomes paramount we learn to put demands on our government for our government's sake. It's important to make sure our motives are directed towards the furtherance of our government's agenda and not our own.

It is the citizen's responsibility to intercede if a law is being broken or rights are being violated. The greatest weapon earthly politicians have over a citizen is ignorance. Ignorance creates powerlessness. What we don't know is killing us. Under the Kingdom of Heaven, Abraham persuaded God to change His mind (Genesis 18:23-33) because he knew his constitutional rights of having dominion over what happens in the earth. The key to citizenship is knowing and understanding. With knowledge and understanding, our rights as citizens become responsibilities.

Remember, we have been crucified with Christ.
We no longer live for ourselves but for Him.

I have been crucified with Christ and I no longer live, but Christ lives in me. The life I live in the body, I live by faith in the Son of God, who loved me and gave himself for me.

Galatians 2:20

Then Jesus said to his disciples, "Whoever wants to be my disciple must deny themselves and take up their cross and follow me.

Matthew16:24

Effects of Citizenship

1. Citizenship is a key to empowerment.

2. Citizenship provides legitimate access to all the rights and privileges of the country.

3. Citizenship activates a transformational process on our bodies so that they become like Jesus' body. Philippians 3:20 says "But our citizenship is in Heaven and we eagerly await a Savior from there, the Lord Jesus Christ, who, by the power that enables Him to bring everything under His control, will transform our lowly bodies so that they will be like His glorious body."

4. Citizenship is the source of the individual's personal authority. Citizenship is the essence of nationhood.

5. Citizenship is the manifestation of the contract between the government and the people of a nation.

6. Citizenship makes the government our servant. "I will give my angels charge over you" (Psalms 91:11, Matthew16:9, 18:18-19). As king to the King, He has given us rulership authority on earth with the full backing of His government at our disposal. The more we find ourselves walking in godly character anchored to the Will of our King, the greater the Lord will entrust authority to us.

7. Citizenship makes government our master. Jesus being King of kings and Lord of lords, we subject ourselves to Him as a good servant would his master.

8. Citizenship makes the Constitution your bond from Heaven and personal covenant from the King.

9. Citizenship is the legal covenant between the individual and the government.

10. Citizenship makes us legal creatures with rights we enforce and establish. Religion makes you an emotional creature following a leader.

11. Only nations have citizenship. A wise man studies his rights and puts demands on his country to enforce and implement those rights when needed.

12. Citizen's don't beg, they insist through legal rights.

13. In Ephesians 2:19, the Greek word for citizen is *polites*. It means "chief citizen, politician." Believers are fellow politicians in God's country. A politician is a person who makes, enforces, and maintains laws. Politicians steer culture and provide framework and boundaries for society on behalf of the country they represent. They mold and shape the systems that create culture.

The same faith that moved the Lord to give us righteousness will be the same faith that moves the Lord to bring Heaven on earth. Kingdom politicians don't work to bring Heaven on earth, we rest in faith and wait.

14. Luke 18:1-8 is the parable of the persistent widow. This story is an example of a citizen who knows her rights. The reason why this woman kept going to the judge was she knew her rights.

15. Paul knew his rights in Acts 22 and was spared undue suffering and pain.

16. In a kingdom, a king's word becomes law. Consider the benefits of us who are citizens of God's Kingdom. His Word is full of laws benefiting us, our communities, cities, and nations. Also, consider entering His courts, spending time in prayer listening for His instruction. Then in full faith and assurance that His Word is law, set out to fulfill it.

17. A king's reputation is determined by the standard of living and status of his citizens. This fact requires us to keep in mind we do not pursue or even give a thought to "things". Those who are exalted in the Kingdom must be brought low. Only dead men are granted resurrected life in the Kingdom of Heaven.

18. When we become Kingdom citizens, the King takes over our lives personally. In a democracy, we become enslaved to the economic system where we are required to work for things and pay taxes.

19. In the Kingdom of Heaven, a citizen has no ownership but gains access to all the country possesses, entrusting the King to provide as He sees fit.

20. In the Kingdom of Heaven, when the King speaks to His citizens publicly, His word becomes national law. When a king speaks to a citizen personally, His word becomes favor. They both are laws. A

law is more than a set of rules a particular country lives under. A statement of fact in a kingdom is law. The constitution of Heaven is filled with statements of fact waiting to be appropriated on earth. Heaven is waiting for its citizens to awaken to their identity and begin representing the mind and Will of the King of kings.

21. The Bible is called a covenant. A covenant is a legal document with effects. The Bible is the Constitution of Heaven on earth, not a religious document.

It is the plan of the devil to create a religion with "members" to keep the people of God from becoming citizens. "Members" have no rights, just "privileges." Citizens have rights. The Apostle Paul declared "our citizenship is in Heaven" (Philippians 3:20). Paul is declaring that our form of government, the government we live under and the rules of that government, come from the country of Heaven. Paul's witness, testimony, and demonstration of this fact can be a catalyst for us to enter into this great and precious honor. Additionally, our citizenship in Heaven places every believer in a position of dual citizenship. The question arises then which government and laws are we going to live from?

I pray this day you choose to serve the Will and interest of the government of the Kingdom of Heaven with everything that is in you! I pray this day you declare yourself a citizen of Heaven and begin discovering your citizenship in the greatest country on earth, the Kingdom of Heaven! "And giving joyful thanks to the Father, who has qualified you to share in the inheritance of His holy people in the Kingdom of light. For he has rescued us from the dominion of darkness and brought us into the Kingdom of the Son He loves" (Colossians 1:12, 13).

 Application: Acknowledge your rights, responsibilities, and privileges as a citizen of Heaven on earth. Learn and study them so that you may walk in them everyday. Make the commitment to live as a member of the family of God, enjoying the fellowship that comes from being part of the greatest community ever assembled on earth, the community of Heaven.

Your name	Date

Chapter Five

Ambassador

An "ambassador" is someone sent from their country to a foreign land to represent their government. An ambassador is a country's legal representative. They carry legal rights from the government and possess "diplomatic immunity." This means even in wartime they are granted safe passage in the territory of the host government. We are in no way to ever engage in war. All governments assemble armies to fight on their behalf. Heaven is no different. The purpose of an ambassador is diplomacy, the art and practice of conducting negotiations between representatives of states. It's good for us to win a soul to Jesus. In the Kingdom, it becomes natural for us to win a whole country to Jesus. One is a religious act producing fruit; the other is a "Kingdom" act producing fruit trees. Read the following:

Pray also for me, that whenever I open my mouth, words may be given me so that I will fearlessly make known the mystery of the gospel, for which I am an ambassador in chains. Pray that I may declare it fearlessly, as I should.
Ephesians 6:19-20

Consequently, you are no longer foreigners and aliens, but fellow-citizens with God's people and members of God's household ....
Ephesians 2:19

Because you are born from above, you are no longer foreigners (illegal immigrants) and strangers, but fellow citizens with God's people and members of His household. We are willing servants in the form of ambassadors, affectionately representing our Father and His country.

All this is from God, who reconciled us to himself through Christ and gave us the ministry of reconciliation: that God was reconciling the world to himself in Christ, not counting men's sins against them. And he has committed to us the message of reconciliation. We are therefore Christ's ambassadors, as though God were making his appeal through us. We implore you on Christ's behalf: Be reconciled to God.
2 Corinthians 5:18-20

In 2 Corinthians 5:18-20 we read that we are Christ's ambassadors, as though God were making His appeal through us. We implore others on Christ's behalf: *Be reconciled to God.* This appeal is done most effectively as we introduce the Kingdom, offering citizenship status. As new citizens enter the Kingdom we are charged with the responsibility of equipping the citizen with understanding their identity as Kingdom citizens.

Jesus gave them this answer, "I tell you the truth, the Son can do nothing by himself; He can do only what He sees his Father doing, because whatever the Father does the Son also does ....

John 5:19

Jesus, the Son of Man, said, "I only do what I have seen my Father doing." The word "see" can also mean "to see with the mind." Think about how often you say in conversation, "Oh, I see." Jesus was saying, "I only do what I have understood My Father, the King of My Country to do. As an ambassador, I represent My country and even embody it."

E. Stanley Jones in his masterpiece The Unshakable Kingdom and the Unchanging Person said "I saw that I had discovered two absolutes; the Unshakable Kingdom, the absolute order; and the Unchanging Person, the absolute Person. There were two absolutes then, now they have coalesced and have become one. He used interchangeably "for the Kingdom of Heaven's sake and for My name's sake" (Matthew 19:12, 29). Was Jesus the Kingdom of God, embodied? Yes, and this was necessary and all-important. For without the embodiment of the Kingdom in a person, we would have read into the term "kingdom of God" our preconceptions of the Kingdom, which would all be wrong or inadequate. It had to be made concrete or it could not be conceived. Jesus is the Kingdom of God taking sandals and walking."

As "Ambassadors of Heaven," we are called to disciple nations. This will only be accomplished through diplomacy as we come to discover the Kingdom of God within, settling once and for all our identity as Kingdom embodiment representatives. The awareness of the Kingdom of God within opens the door for the spirit of revelation to expand our wakefulness of this most important truth. The religious church attempts to make disciples of individuals by joining them to a religion.

The Kingdom makes disciples of entire nations through the Church. When Jesus builds, nations get saved and entire societies come under the influence of Heaven. The more we come to know the essence of our nature to be the Kingdom, the greater the effect we will have on earth. "The Kingdom of Heaven is within you." The more you pursue the Kingdom the more it possesses you.

The intrinsic nature of an ambassador is that he embodies the nation he represents. The nation is placed inside the ambassador causing him to become a tangible and visible expression of the nation. In the same way, Jesus embodied the Kingdom, so too have we been entrusted with the responsibility to make room for the essence of our nature to be that of the Kingdom. May we discover the measure of the fullness of the influence of the Kingdom of Heaven within us!

As Kingdom representatives, it is not our responsibility to appoint leaders. We seek first the Kingdom, yield to the Lordship of Christ and allow Him to establish His Kingdom within us. This establishing of His Kingdom within takes place as greater measures of Kingdom awareness and understanding are given to us through revelation. In His time, He will raise you up in the position of His choosing, (which by the way is "servant of all"—Mark 9:35). Focusing on anything other than seeking to understand the Kingdom places us in danger of building our own Kingdom.

Moses practiced diplomacy with the leaders of Egypt as did Jesus and the apostles with the leaders of their day. All through scripture we see diplomacy in action. Whenever God asked someone to represent Him and His Will, He was offering an opportunity to step into the role of an "ambassador."

The inherent features of citizenship in Heaven contain the qualities of ambassadorship and diplomatic authority. As we discover our citizenship these inherent features will be made available to us, empowering us once again in likeness with the Saints of old.

An ambassador is the highest representative of a government in a foreign land. We represent the highest form of government on earth. Therefore, a human who has been given ambassadorship of the Kingdom of Heaven is the most influential and powerful being on earth. All New Testament Saints have, as part of their inheritance, the privilege, and responsibility of ambassadorship.

It was said of the prophet Samuel that none of his words fell to the ground. Likewise, Jesus did nothing except what He understood to be His Father's Will. These are examples of the pinnacle of ambassadorship. Let them become for us a catalyst to press onto the high calling of God in Christ.

> *On the evening of that first day of the week, when the disciples were together, with the doors locked for fear of the Jews, Jesus came and stood among them and said, "Peace be with you!" After he said this, he showed them his hands and side. The disciples were overjoyed when they saw the Lord. Again Jesus said, "Peace be with you! As the Father has sent me, I am sending you." And with that he breathed on them and said, "Receive the Holy Spirit. If you forgive anyone his sins, they are forgiven; if you do not forgive them, they are not forgiven."*
>
> John 20:19-23

In the Kingdom of Heaven, an ambassador is appointed by the government. This position comes with great authority, even the authority to forgive sins, one of the greatest powers bestowed on man.

When Jesus sent out His disciples, He was acting as the "Head of State" for the government He brought, the Kingdom of Heaven. He commissioned the 12 as ambassadors and gave the orders from the headquarters. Those instructions were to proclaim a very specific message, the good news of the Kingdom. As is the custom of Heaven, power and authority were given to confirm and validate the message. The disciples gave witness to their ambassadorship by expressing the nature of the government that embodied them. "Jesus called His disciples and gave them authority to drive out impure spirits and heal every sickness and disease" (Matthew 10:10). Essentially, Jesus sent them out with power to authenticate the message of the Kingdom. Jesus knew the message of an invisible government would be difficult to accept so He gave tangible power from that invisible government as proof of its existence. The most effective way to accomplish this is to place the country inside a person by taking the nature of ambassadorship and placing it in the identity of the person.

In the Kingdom of Heaven, an ambassador represents the government that appointed him, he never represents himself. To represent himself is to forfeit the gift of ambassadorship. This is an age-old temptation we all must overcome. The broader our understanding of the nature and essence of ambassadorship, the less likely we will represent ourselves. After receiving ample revelation of the Kingdom we have been entrusted with, no one in their right mind would choose to forfeit that for selfish ambition. However, we must always guard against the age old temptation to build our own kingdoms. The disciples were appointed with a specific message and empowered with Heaven's authority to accomplish a specific purpose. All but Judas remained true to their assignment as evidenced by their message, signs, and wonders.

Another example of Jesus sending out disciples as ambassadors is found in Luke 10:

After this the Lord appointed seventy-two others and sent them two by two ahead of him to every town and place where he was about to go. He told them, "The harvest is plentiful, but the workers are few. Ask the Lord of the harvest, therefore, to send out workers into his harvest field. Go! I am sending you out like lambs among wolves. Do not take a purse or bag or sandals, and do not greet anyone on the road. When you enter a house, first say, 'Peace to this house.' If a man of peace is there, your peace will rest on him; if not, it will return to you. Stay in that house, eating and drinking whatever they give you, for the worker deserves his wages. Do not move around from house to house. When you enter a town and are welcomed, eat what is set before you. Heal the sick who are there and tell them, the kingdom of God is near you. But when you enter a town and are not welcomed, go into its streets and say, 'Even the dust of your town that sticks to our feet we wipe off against you. Yet be sure of this: The kingdom of God is near.' I tell you, it will be more bearable on that day for Sodom than for that town. Woe to you, Korazin! Woe to you, Bethsaida! For if the miracles that were performed in you had been performed in Tyre and Sidon, they would have repented long ago, sitting in sackcloth and ashes. But it will be more bearable for Tyre and Sidon at the judgment than for you. And you, Capernaum, will you be lifted up to the skies? No, you will go down to the depths. He who listens to you listens to me; he who rejects you rejects me; but he who rejects me rejects him who sent me." The seventy-two returned with joy and said, "Lord, even the demons submit to us in your name." He replied, "I saw Satan fall like lightning from Heaven. I have given you authority to trample on snakes and scorpions and to overcome all the power of the enemy; nothing will harm you. However, do not rejoice that the spirits submit to you, but rejoice that your names are written in Heaven."

Luke 10:1-19

The disciples were given the same Heavenly means of accomplishing the same goals: proclaiming the Kingdom of Heaven has arrived, healing the sick, and casting out demons. They were using substance from the home country to authenticate the message that an invisible government is here. When the seventy returned, the Bible says they marveled at their power. Jesus told them not to get excited about the power. That became commonplace once they became established in His country and His country became established in them (Book of Acts). Jesus was saying, "Change your mind and I will change the fruit of your actions!" Instead of becoming excited about the power that is natural in the Kingdom, He told them to rejoice in their citizenship in His Father's country.

Suppose someone came to your door with legitimate credentials to bestow upon you a Ph.D. in psychology. He hands you the letter of recognition congratulating you on being awarded doctor status in the field of psychology.

 Q/A: What is the first thing we should do?

Go study to understand what it was we were given. Then, as quickly as possible, begin establishing yourself in the gift, using it to bring about change within your sphere of influence.

Jesus Christ, a King whose Word becomes law, bestowed upon us His Kingdom and has declared us to be "ambassadors." As fellow ambassadors, it is our responsibility to understand the essence and nature of ambassadorship and what it is God wants to do through us. We must study to show ourselves approved and ready for our roles as ambassadors.

 In the Kingdom the King doesn't give us a title but empowers us to accomplish a purpose. Identifying ourselves as ambassadors, for example, doesn't entitle us, it identifies a function we're capable of carrying out in Christ. As we discover our purpose in the Kingdom, we train ourselves to accept the different facet's of our identity as function, not title. This will help guard against pride, elitism and entitlement.

An ambassador is committed only to his government's interests. He only speaks the government's position. He rarely, if ever, gives his opinion. In the case of the Kingdom of Heaven's ambassadors, the words they speak become law. We will know we have been released by Heaven to function in the role of ambassador when we begin experiencing "whatever you bind on earth will be bound in Heaven, and whatever you loose on earth will be loosed in Heaven" (Matthew 18:18). Until then let's commit to allowing Holy Spirit to prepare us for such a transformational role. Let's purpose in our hearts to seek first the Kingdom long enough to know and understand the Will of our government and our identity in ambassadorship. Then we will become entrusted with the authority and influence of an ambassador.

Jesus lived His life a perfect example of an ambassador. That's why we can't find a single instance where the Bible said Jesus did not heal someone He purposed to heal. The Bible record always states Jesus healed all who were sick. Jesus' words became law. His words accomplished their meaning precisely. He opened up and displayed the substance contained in His words. What He bound was bound and what He loosed was loosed. Jesus was our perfect model. When He told Mary not to worry about Lazarus being dead, Jesus had full faith in Lazarus' return to life because He understood His role as ambassador. He knew His word would become law because He had perceptive capacity to see it was His governments Will.

As ambassadors for Christ, we can rest assured that our words have power, and soberly seek the Will of God, making sure our words are precisely what He wants. Peter and Paul not only understood their role as ambassadors but soberly sought to accurately represent the office.

Pray also for me, that whenever I open my mouth, words may be given me so that I will fearlessly make known the mystery of the gospel, for which I am an ambassador in chains.

Ephesians 6:19-20

If anyone speaks, they should do so as one who speaks the very words of God.

1 Peter 4:11

Although we leave room for God's grace to cover our shortcomings, we nevertheless press into the high calling of ambassadorship, desiring to only do and say what we understand our Father's Will to be. Jesus understood and acted in perfect union with His government. A key to His success I believe was His understanding of the nature of ambassadorship. The greater revelation and understanding of the intrinsic, inherent nature of ambassadorship, the more we will see its qualities come to life.

When the role of ambassadorship was bestowed upon us, the nation itself was placed in us. We do more than represent the nation, we became the nation. When we truly discover the Kingdom of Heaven is within us, then we will take on the nature of an ambassador and represent more accurately the Kingdom. There is no greater witness of the Kingdom, no better testimony of its authenticity than when a representative illustrates the Kingdom which they embody. To be an expression of or give tangible and visible form to the Kingdom is evidence we have become aware of the essence of your new nature in Christ. The Kingdom of Heaven within us was not placed in us to become part of us but rather to become who we are. Our humanity is our appearance and the Kingdom is who we are—our essence and nature.

The ambassador's government takes responsibility for all living expenses and expunges any debt in order for the ambassador to focus on his government's wishes, never thinking about anything else. The ambassador is not supposed to be worrying where he's going to get his clothes, car, house payment, children's expenses, retirement or anything. His mind is given over to his government. The function of an ambassador contains the gift of taking NO THOUGHT of things.

That's why Jesus said don't worry about what you will eat, drink or what you will wear. Just get in the Kingdom and all these things come with the position (Matthew 6:31-33 paraphrase). This does not assure you that debt, in a practical sense, will instantly be removed. It does, however, make room for a new way of perceiving debt. Moving from a mindset of "my debt" to "God's debt" is as liberating as the practical removal of the debt itself. This is a benefit of understanding ambassadorship and Kingdom living.

An ambassador is protected by his government and never engages in warfare. In the Kingdom of Heaven, the angels are the military, God is the "Lord of Hosts." The angels do our bidding. No weapon formed against us will prosper not because our ability to "fight for the Kingdom" but because the Lord of Hosts is in charge (Isaiah 54:17). You can be sure weapons will be formed against you, but you can be equally sure they will not prosper no matter what it feels like at the moment.

> *Pilate then went back inside the palace, summoned Jesus and asked him, "Are you the king of the Jews?" "Is that your own idea," Jesus asked, "or did others talk to you about me?" "Am I a Jew?" Pilate replied. "It was your people and your chief priests who handed you over to me. What is it you have done?" Jesus said, "My kingdom is not of this world. If it were, my servants would fight to prevent my arrest by the Jews. But now my kingdom is from another place." "You are a king, then!" said Pilate. Jesus answered, "You are right in saying I am a king. In fact, for this reason, I was born, and for this I came into the world, to testify to the truth. Everyone on the side of truth listens to me."*
>
> John 18:33-37

Jesus stood before Pilate and said, "I am a king. My Kingdom is not of this world. If it was I would have my followers fight for me. Even now I could call my angelic military right here to fight for me." See also Luke 4:10 and Psalms 91:11-12. These verses show that He has given his angels charge concerning us. We must learn to trust God in the midst of trouble, resting on His power to distinguish any and all weapons formed against us. Let's leave the fighting to the Lord of Hosts and give ourselves over completely to seeking the Kingdom.

God told David the battle is the Lord's! (1 Samuel 17:34, 47). Jesus said if you offend one of these little kids his angel will get you (Matthew 18:10). These two passages alone provide sufficient evidence God takes responsibility for any fighting. The church must cast down her present mindset towards "fighting against the kingdom of darkness" and understand it's the Lords battle. We have lost too many Kingdom Saints on a battlefield they were never commissioned to enter. The only fighting we are to engage in is the battle in the realm of the mind. Fight the good fight of establishing a belief system in line with Christ's (1Timothy 6:12) and leave all other battles to the Lord.

These are Kingdom truths as well as realities of existence that liberate the child of God from unnecessary fighting. The enemy will not lay down and quit attacking, but instead of fighting him, we petition our government to defend us, trusting the outcome to our King. We were not created to defeat every attack against us. Only God knows when to defeat an enemy and when to proclaim over you, "My grace is sufficient for you, for my power is made perfect in weakness" (2 Cor. 12:9).

As an ambassador, a key to establishing Jesus' rule on earth, is to possess understanding of His government and how to approach the King in times of need. We train our minds to remember that our Father is the Judge, the Holy Spirit is our counselor and Jesus is our witness. In doing so, we will live life knowing we have been set up to win! Even in a situation that appears to be a loss, victory is assured. Keep in mind we have been crucified with Christ. It is no longer us who lives but Christ who lives in us.

We no longer let ambition, selfish desire, impatience, carnal zeal or any attribute of the old nature take up life within us. We learn to accept suffering as a means to learn obedience. Instead of a conditioned response of rebuking the enemy, we entrust the fight to the Lord and rest assured that obedience is a reward for our suffering and a means of obtaining a better resurrection (Hebrews 11:35).

We are ambassadors of Heaven and so, therefore, we live on earth. We are in the world but not of it. Our location is earth but our citizenship is in Heaven (Philippians 3:20). We are on the earth but functioning from Heaven. We are in Heaven projecting our substance on earth. That's what makes us ambassadors.

Diplomacy

Diplomatic immunity is a form of legal immunity that ensures diplomats safe passage and not susceptible to lawsuit or prosecution under the host country's laws. Because Jesus has imputed His righteousness to us we can rest assured we are given safe passage on earth. Right standing with our government ensures nothing formed against us will prosper and every accusation that rises against us will be condemned. We have this promise in our constitution and need to learn to rest in our governments laws.

An ambassador is as wealthy as the country he represents and trusts his government to provide all their needs (Philippians 4:19). He has given himself over to the purposes of his government so totally that he thinks no thought of "things" (Matthew 6:33). When something is given he receives it with thankfulness and continues on with the mission, seeking opportunity for diplomacy. When something is taken from him, the same posture of thankfulness surfaces from within his heart. An ambassador understands, "Naked I came from my mother's womb, and naked I will depart. The LORD gave and the LORD has taken away; may the name of the LORD be praised" (Job 1:21).

Consider this: a business owner has two options in establishing a business on earth or in Heaven. If he chooses earth he's limited to its resources. If he chooses Heaven he's unlimited in resources as he trusts the Lord to give and take away as He sees fit. On earth, the resources are the banks' lending practices which put him in bondage to this world's system. In Heaven, an all-knowing benevolent King freely gives as He sees fit. If the business is established in Heaven the Lord takes ownership. He is responsible for everything. We simply become a steward of the business, willingly handing all responsibility over to the rightful owner, King Jesus.

An ambassador is not given authority and jurisdiction by the host government, but are regulated by the government from which they are sent. As long as we remain in right standing with Heaven through the righteousness of God in Christ we exist on earth under the directive and ruling order of Heaven. To the degree we intently seek the Kingdom and His righteousness is the degree we will understand the government of Heaven. To the degree we understand the government of Heaven largely determines the expression of the Kingdom we demonstrate.

Hindrances to Ambassadorship

The greatest hindrance to stepping into our role as ambassadors from Heaven is:

1. Not seeking first the Kingdom of God and His righteousness.

2. Not understanding the role or its power.

3. Not understanding and seeing the intrinsic, inherent nature of ambassadorship.

4. Not knowing what to say. This requires cultivating an intimate relationship with the Father, and King Jesus, as well as moving beyond a rudimentary understanding of the Kingdom and His righteousness.

5. Limited understanding and knowledge of scripture. Our words matter because as an ambassador, our words become law.

6. Not carrying the message of the Kingdom. Look at the three hindrances to receiving the Kingdom in the parable of the sower (Matthew 13:1-23): a) not having understanding of the Kingdom; b) the inability to properly handle trouble and persecution; and c) worry and the deceitfulness of riches in your pursuit of the Kingdom. Overcoming these obstacles is necessary to your participation as ambassadors of the Kingdom.

7. Not allowing patience to transform knowledge into understanding. Without this process we become prideful (1 Corinthians 8:1).

8. Being part of the world. When we are appointed ambassadors, we are at once pulled out of the system we're in and placed in the governmental system that appointed us (John 15:19). This results in a lifestyle where your time and energy is diverted from worldly things to that which pertains to the Kingdom. Removing yourself from the activities of the world is essential to awakening the function of an ambassador.

Understanding Ambassadorship

1. Once appointed, an Ambassador can only be recalled by the ruler/king. You can rest in the loving arms of your Father knowing you are safe in His acceptance of you.

2. Ambassadors have access to all their nation's wealth and power, trusting their government fully for daily provision. Whether an ambassador has plenty or is in need, he trusts his government has provided what's necessary. If the resources are not provided to accomplish a particular task then it's not time to fulfill the task. Hold onto your vision. Pray for it to come to pass but don't try to accomplish it on your own. Introducing and establishing a supernatural Kingdom requires supernatural provision.

3. The goal of the Ambassador is to influence the territory where he is, for his nation. Knowledge, understanding, revelation, wisdom, humility, and daily taking up your cross are keys to bringing into existence the function and qualities of an ambassador.

4. All the Ambassador's needs are met by their own country. This liberates the ambassador from pursuing needs within the foreign country. We cannot experience this reality without a renewing of the mind. Seeking first the Kingdom of God and His righteousness will bring this renewal and open awareness of God's supernatural provision for us.

5. The Ambassador is totally protected by both governments. He has "extra-territoriality status" in his host country; he is exempt from most of its laws and has the power of his own nation behind him for protection. Any insult or crime against him is a matter for nations. Though we are not under the laws of the host nation we do however abide by them. We are in the host nation but under the laws and system of rulership of our government. Therefore "Render to Caesar the things that are Caesar's, and to God the things that are God's" (Mark 12:17).

6. He must remain in constant contact with both nations. The nation which is hosting him expects him to be in communication with his own nation and its government. Cultivating a lifestyle where we remain in constant contact with Heaven is what Paul called praying without ceasing.

7. The essence of ambassadorship contains specific qualities essential to our understanding. A key quality to grasp with increasing understanding is a government's power to place itself within the ambassador. Once this foundational truth is opened to us, then King Jesus can develop further truth relating to the out-workings of the qualities of ambassadorship. "The Kingdom of Heaven is within you."

John 15:15 says that you have been appointed by the King of Heaven to be an ambassador. The Romans used to give a special ring to their ambassadors and governors that certified them as a "Friend of Caesar" (John 19:12). We have been sought out by the King of Heaven. He is looking for "Friends of Jesus" to represent Him on earth just like it is in Heaven.

I have much more to say to you, more than you can now bear. But when he, the Spirit of truth, comes, he will guide you into all the truth. He will not speak on his own; he will speak only what he hears, and he will tell you what is yet to come. He will glorify me because it is from me that he will receive what he will make known to you. All that belongs to the Father is mine. That is why I said the Spirit will receive from me what he will make known to you.

John 16:12-15

This is a beautiful statement regarding communications at the ambassadorial level. King Jesus gives Holy Spirit information that He subsequently makes known to us. Understanding this protocol is critical to every ambassador because the ambassador can only speak what his government directs him to say. Once we understand this "chain of command" and cultivate a listening ear, then we acquire confidence and boldness as we speak on behalf of Heaven, effortlessly bringing Kingdom substance to earth. The same way the Father has sent Jesus He has appointed Him to send us as His ambassadors. Our goal is to represent the Kingdom of Heaven, in the same way Jesus did (John 20:21).

Also a dispute arose among them as to which of them was considered to be greatest. Jesus said to them, "The kings of the Gentiles lord it over them; and those who exercise authority over them call themselves Benefactors. But you are not to be like that. Instead, the greatest among you should be like the youngest, and the one who rules like the one who serves. For who is greater, the one who is at the table or the one who serves? Is it not the one who is at the table? But I am among you as one who serves. You are those who have stood by me in my trials. And I confer on you a kingdom, just as my Father conferred one on me."

Luke 22:24-29

This passage proves our legal standing as ambassadors. Our proof of credentials is the powers that we carry. In the same way an ambassador of the USA has the powers of America wherever he is, we have the powers of the Kingdom wherever we are. Jesus said He has conferred on us the Kingdom, therefore, we prove our credentials by our demonstration of the power of our government in and on our own life, and the lives of those around us. We become a witness to the message of our King by manifesting the Kingdom He preached.

Although the Children of Israel were never "conferred" their new lands, we can still get a picture of what's encapsulated in the idea.

I will give you every place where you set your foot, as I promised Moses.

Joshua 1:3

Every place where you set your foot will be yours: Your territory will extend from the desert to Lebanon, and from the Euphrates River to the western sea.

Deuteronomy 11:24

 Q/A: What does "confer" mean?

It means to grant or bestow. "Confer" is a legal term with covenant bonds. It is something to be Willed. The modern term would be that "something is awarded as a result of a legal process." Jesus is telling us He has made a legal covenant to transfer responsibility of His Kingdom to us. His disciples have been entrusted with His Kingdom—not merely followers, but disciples. We will discuss this important difference in the chapter on disciples. For now, consider the gravity of this transfer and imagine the magnitude of responsibility Jesus entrusted to us.

> *No one can serve two masters. Either he will hate the one and love the other, or he will be devoted to the one and despise the other. You cannot serve both God and Money.*
>
> Matthew 6:24

One cannot be an ambassador of two countries. We will either represent the government of Heaven or by default represent the government of this world. We are known by our fruits (Matthew 7:16-20) and demonstrate which kingdom we serve. As the Kingdom age emerges it is incumbent upon us to seek first the Kingdom. Then we are given the opportunity to demonstrate the Kingdom of Heaven. We cannot demonstrate what we don't possess and we only possess what we seek first.

 Q/A: Are you representing the government of Heaven or are you just a member of a church?

Are you a religious creature or a legal creature?

Are you involved in diplomacy or the pursuit of bill paying?

Are you representing a government or a religious institution?

Are you influencing a territory with the precepts and principles of your government or going to work to get a check to pay for things?

> *"Tell us then, what is your opinion? Is it right to pay taxes to Caesar or not?" But Jesus, knowing their evil intent, said, "You hypocrites, why are you trying to trap me? Show me the coin used for paying the tax." They brought him a denarius, and he asked them, "Whose portrait is this? And whose inscription?" "Caesar's," they replied. Then he said to them, "Give to Caesar what is Caesar's, and to God what is God's." When they heard this, they were amazed. So they left*

him and went away.

Matthew 22:17-22

Jesus was very clear regarding international (inter-national) diplomacy. If you are a professional communicator but your information is wrong, you have been successful in communicating error and contaminating truth. Nothing is more dangerous than an effective communicator who communicates error. There are many examples in history of this, of which Adolf Hitler is the best known. He was a very effective communicator, however, he was communicating lies and World War II was the result. We have become so well educated in contaminated truth that when "truth" shows up we frequently conclude it's "error." I know this is an extreme example but the argument could be made that if you are a leader in the church and not seeking first the Kingdom everything you speak on comes from a wrong foundation. Because you are in disobedience to Jesus' command to seek first the Kingdom, you are receiving information different than you would if you were obeying Jesus' command. All material not from seeking first the Kingdom becomes faulty substance used to build upon shifting sand.

An ambassador embodies the country they represent. A fruitful activity within the Kingdom of God is seeking for the King's "kairos." "Kairos" is a Greek word for time. It's not linear time that we find when we look at a clock but rather a favorable moment in time. An opportune time. It's a place in time when one apprehends the Lord's Will and becomes empowered to fulfill it on His behalf.

As an ambassador, when we receive God's (*kairos*) Word we hold creative power containing substance from Heaven. Possessing creative power effectively manifests the qualities of our invisible government. This opens the door for us to bring understanding to the minds of those witnessing the creative/supernatural expression of Heaven on earth. It could be said that when God's time (*kairos*) meets man's time (*chronos*) Heaven on earth is experienced.

Here are some Scriptural examples of ambassadors in action:

- The life of Jesus. Everything Jesus did, He did as if He were an ambassador of Heaven.

- Acts3:6. Peter used Heaven's healthcare system, which is supernatural healing, to represent Heaven on earth. Any time a supernatural event took place by one of God's people, it was done in an ambassadorial role.

- Each time Jesus sent out the disciples, whether in word or deed, they were functioning in an "ambassador of Heaven" role.

- Studying the life of Paul will reveal many things he said and did in the role of an ambassador for Christ.

- In the life of Moses, we see him continually taking orders from the home country and speaking them into existence.

- Samuel's life was lived as a remarkably effective ambassador. It was said of him: "The LORD was with Samuel as he grew up, and he let none of Samuel's words fall to the ground" (1 Samuel 3:19).

- From Genesis through Revelation the Bible records examples of Heaven's representatives on earth. The more we understand the role and function of an ambassador, the more we will see scriptural accounts of ambassadors speaking on behalf of Heaven.

The position of ambassador carries great power and influence. The more we understand our role of ambassadorship to the Kingdom of Heaven, the more influence we will have on earth. The more influence we exert, the greater the revolution. Look for examples in scripture of God's people representing Jesus, the Father, and the government of Heaven. Ask for the spirit of wisdom and revelation to open this precious truth to you in increasing measure.

Application: Receive your commission to be a Kingdom Ambassador and act as God's representative on earth today! Begin by seeking to understand your identity as an ambassador of Heaven as you seek first the Kingdom.

Your name   Date

Chapter Six

Prayer

"Ah, Sovereign Lord," I said, "I do not know how to speak; I am only a child." But the Lord said to me, "Do not say, 'I am only a child.' You must go to everyone I send you to and say whatever I command you. Do not be afraid of them, for I am with you and will rescue you," declares the Lord. Then the Lord reached out his hand and touched my mouth and said to me, "Now, I have put my words in your mouth. See, today I appoint you over nations and kingdoms to uproot and tear down, to destroy and overthrow, to build and to plant." The word of the Lord came to me: "What do you see, Jeremiah?" "I see the branch of an almond tree," I replied. The Lord said to me, "You have seen correctly, for I am watching to see that my word is fulfilled."

Jeremiah 1:6-12

Ask of me, and I will make the nations your inheritance, the ends of the earth your possession. You will rule them with an iron scepter; you will dash them to pieces like pottery.

Psalms 2:8-9

In his book, *A Plain Account of Christian Perfection*, John Wesley wrote, "God does nothing except in answer to prayer." This giant in the faith new something about prayer that has been buried for a long time. It is my desire to dig up this hidden treasure and bring to light a key to prayer that reconnects the people of God to Heaven like the days of old. The most important activity on earth is prayer. God's Word elevates prayer to the point He says to do it without ceasing.

Now we exhort you, brethren, warn those who are unruly, comfort the fainthearted, uphold the weak, be patient with all. See that no one renders evil for evil to anyone, but always pursue what is good both for yourselves and for all. Rejoice always, pray without ceasing, in everything give thanks; for this is the will of God in Christ Jesus for you.

1 Thessalonians 5:14-18 (NKJV)

No other activity of man is held in such high esteem. God wants us to pray constantly. A Kingdom perspective of prayer evokes interest and demands attention. In fact, it's the most exhilarating activity on earth. In the Kingdom of God, investment in prayer yields the greatest return. Far greater than worship, evangelism, and all other activities within the church. Once we discover God's mind and purpose behind prayer you will see what I'm talking about.

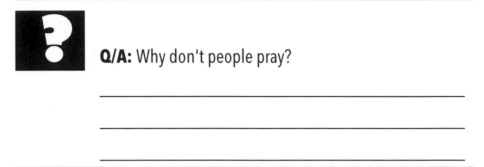

Q/A: Why don't people pray?

_____

_____

_____

Religion has made prayer boring, mundane and largely unproductive. Most Christians, if they were honest would say "prayer doesn't work." They would have to admit their prayer life is limited to "thank yous" and talks with God related to things pertaining to wants and worries. This form of prayer has its foundation in religious activity. Jesus specifically told us not to give any thought towards our needs and wants. This one statement wipes away most activity we call prayer and narrows the road leading to what God's idea of prayer is.

> *And when you pray, do not be like the hypocrites, for they love to pray standing in the synagogues and on the street corners to be seen by men. I tell you the truth, they have received their reward in full. But when you pray, go into your room, close the door and pray to your Father, who is unseen. Then your Father, who sees what is done in secret, will reward you. And when you pray, do not keep on babbling like pagans, for they think they will be heard because of their many words. Do not be like them, for your Father knows what you need before you ask him.*
> Matthew 6:5-8

No one can serve two masters. Either he will hate the one and love the other, or he will be devoted to the one and despise the other. You cannot serve both God and Money. Therefore I tell you, do not worry about your life, what you will eat or drink; or about your body, what you will wear. Is not life more important than food, and the body more important than clothes? Look at the birds of the air; they do not sow or reap or store away in barns, and yet your Heavenly Father feeds them. Are you not much more valuable than they? Who of you by worrying can add a single hour to his life? And why do you worry about clothes? See how the lilies of the field grow. They do not labor or spin. Yet I tell you that not even Solomon in all his splendor was dressed like one of these. If that is how God clothes the grass of the field, which is here today and tomorrow is thrown into the fire, will he not much more clothe you, O you of little faith? So do not worry, saying, What shall we eat? or What shall we drink? or What shall we wear? For the pagans run after all these things, and your Heavenly Father knows that you need them. But seek first his kingdom and his righteousness, and all these things will be given to you as well. Therefore do not worry about tomorrow, for tomorrow will worry about itself. Each day has enough trouble of its own.

Matthew 6:24-34 (See also Luke 12:22-32)

Jesus commanded us not to worry and taught us specific principles relating to prayer. Once discovered and implemented, these principles become keys unlocking the influence of Heaven on earth.

Prayer was so far from boring and unproductive to the disciples that they asked Jesus to teach them how to do it. They saw Jesus' devotion to it and realized there's something attractive about prayer. It becomes important the church get a glimpse of the connection between prayer and the expression of the culture of Heaven on earth.

Prayer is inherent in humanity. Everyone prays but few understand how. Every race and all religions do it but most don't believe it works and even less see results. Despite God's desire that all men ought to pray without ceasing, prayer meetings have been mostly delegated to a few faithful souls. We have largely given up out of lack of results. This chapter is designed to awaken the church to God's model, design, and intent for prayer. With a fresh insight into the purpose and power of prayer, I trust you will discover a new passion to pray like never before.

Prayer is a Key of the Kingdom

The secret to the Keys of the Kingdom is not in possessing them but knowing how to use them.

I will give you the keys of the kingdom of Heaven; whatever you bind on earth will be bound in Heaven, and whatever you loose on earth will be loosed in Heaven.

Matthew 16:19

"Keys" imply "principles." When Jesus gave us the "Keys of the Kingdom," (not the keys "to" the Kingdom) He gave us principles to unlock His country's way of doing things, empowering us to fulfill His command to pray, "thy kingdom come, thy will be done on earth."

Keys are given to grant us access, authority, power, stewardship, authorization, permission, and rulership of something. If I give you keys to my home, you have access to my home. If I give you keys to my car, you have dominion over my car. If I give you keys to my bank account, you have power. When Jesus says I give you the Keys of the Kingdom, He's saying I'm giving you principles pertaining to My country. They are principles of authority and influence I want you to put in practice on earth. It's our responsibility to humble ourselves before the Lord and allow Him to mold us into His image. As we do, He will teach us these principles which will grant us access to Heaven's power to influence what happens on earth.

Religious prayer is ritualistic and unfruitful. It goes through the motions of a form of manmade prayer but has little effect. Most religious people believe prayer to be "talking to God." If that were true almost everyone would be doing it. We are beaten down and frustrated with the lack of fruit and many have given up on prayer. Kingdom prayer is different. Kingdom prayer is an activity that has impact. It's a relationship that produces change and gives rise to the establishment of the governing influence of the Kingdom on earth.

"Have faith in God," Jesus answered. "I tell you the truth, if anyone says to this mountain, 'Go, throw yourself into the sea,' and does not doubt in his heart but believes that what he says will happen, it will be done for him. Therefore, I tell you, whatever you ask for in prayer, believe that you have received it, and it will be yours."

Mark 11:22-24

 Q/A:

What is Kingdom prayer?

_____

_____

The key to using keys is employing the right one. Before we begin to understand Kingdom prayer, let's look at a working definition.

- Prayer is mankind giving God legal permission to interfere in earthly affairs. "The highest heavens belong to the LORD, but the earth he has given to mankind" (Psalm 115:16).

- Prayer is a transaction between a government and its representatives.

- Prayer is earthly license for Heavenly intervention.

- Prayer becomes a primary system to build Kingdom rulership on earth.

- Prayer is meant to effect and impact earth with Heaven's influence.

- Prayer is influencing earth on God's behalf.

God gave us this power in the form of keys. Remember "keys" are "principles." All kingdom governments exercise authority over their citizens even when they are away from the home country. As a citizen of Heaven, our responsibility is to understand the Constitution (the Bible).

As colonial people, we let our government know when the Constitution is being violated and ask for assistance when needed. This is prayer.

The greatest privilege and perhaps most important pillar in the discipline of prayer is knowing the King. Cultivating a relationship with the Head of our government takes time, devotion and a willingness to lay down our own agendas. Developing the craft of listening is as important to effective prayer as righteousness and understanding.

Understanding the Reason for Prayer

If God is sovereign why pray?
If God can do whatever He wants, why pray?
If God can't be affected by humanity, why pray?
Prayer can affect God. Therefore, God can be influenced. God is sovereign, however, He is only as sovereign as His Word. He has chosen to esteem His word above His character (Psalms 138:2-3). When God said "I place My word above My name" what He said was "I place My Word above Myself." "I come under My Word." When God speaks His Word becomes Law. Therefore, God chose to limit Himself to His Word. God chose never to violate His Word. When He speaks His Word becomes Law.

I often played basketball with my kids. At times they would comment something like, "Dad, don't make so many shots, let us win sometimes." I would respond, "Okay, I will." Vowing to limit my abilities was not a reduction in my abilities but rather a commitment to honor my word above my abilities. I chose to make an agreement, a covenant with my kids to limit my abilities in order to keep my word. Put another way, in order to honor my word I needed to withhold part of my abilities.

Heaven and earth will pass away, but my words will never pass away.
Matthew 24:35

The fear and terror of you will be in every living creature on the earth, every bird of the sky, every creature that crawls on the ground, and all fish of the sea. They are placed under your authority.
Genesis 9:2 (HCSB)

Therefore, God chose to become only as sovereign as His Word. Please take a moment and consider the confidence the Lord must have had towards us. In order to limit Himself on earth, He must have known we would rise to a level that would empower Him to fulfill all He has promised to the earth. Let this encourage you and motivate you to step into your identity as a Kingdom representative on earth.

Because God is Spirit, He made Himself illegal in the earth.

You made him ruler over the works of your hands; you put everything under his feet: all flocks and herds, and the beasts of the field, the birds of the air, and the fish of the sea, all that swim the paths of the seas.

Psalms 8:6-8

*Then God said, "Let Us make man in Our image, according to Our likeness; let **them** have dominion over the fish of the sea, over the birds of the air, and over the cattle, over all the earth and over every creeping thing that creeps on the earth." So God created man in His own image; in the image of God He created him; male and female He created them. Then God blessed them, and God said to them, "Be fruitful and multiply; fill the earth and subdue it; have dominion over the fish of the sea, over the birds of the air, and over every living thing that moves on the earth."*

Genesis 1:26-28 (NKJV)

In Genesis 1:26 & 28, when God said "let them have dominion," He was establishing a law; only humans have legal authority on earth. The word "human" is a grammatical construct meaning, "a dirt body with a spirit." A human therefore is a spirit in a body. This is who God chose to have rule and dominate the earth on his behalf (note: any spirit without a body is illegal on the earth). Since God is a Spirit He has made Himself illegal on the earth. Being illegal means one has no authority. The devil is also illegal, but he has usurped his authority from man. He is an illegitimate and illegal ruler who has stolen what man has forfeited. Man was created to rule. Because of his sin, he lost his power to maintain dominion over the earth. Jesus came to restore that authority to man.

God needs man to intervene in earth's affairs. The Lord has chosen to work through men on earth by His own law. Prayer is God's resolution to this law. Consider:

> *If my people, who are called by my name, will humble themselves and pray and seek my face and turn from their wicked ways, then will I hear from Heaven and will forgive their sin and will heal their land. Now my eyes will be open and my ears attentive to the prayers offered in this place.*
>
> 2 Chronicles 7:14-15

 Q/A: So why doesn't God just come and heal the land?

_____

_____

Why does He place a condition needing people to put themselves in a position where He can work through them in order to heal the land? Because He gave dominion rulership on earth to humans. He appointed and authorized humans to rule and govern on His behalf. God had so much confidence in man's ability to rule earth, He limited His abilities and chose to work with us.

> *I tell you the truth, whatever you bind on earth will be bound in Heaven, and whatever you loose on earth will be loosed in Heaven. Again, I tell you that if two of you on earth agree about anything you ask for, it will be done for you by my Father in Heaven. For where two or three come together in my name, there am I with them.*
>
> Matthew 18:18-20

Jesus said that "Whatever you bind on earth will be bound in Heaven." At the same time, He said, "whenever two or more agree concerning earth it will be done." The implication is that Heaven is waiting for earth to give permission to interfere. God will not break His Word. Until we learn to pray, the earth will be lacking substance necessary to transform the present world system into the Kingdom of Heaven's ruler ship.

In Scripture, every act of God had to have human cooperation in order for Him to not violate His Word. When God wanted to destroy Sodom and Gomorrah, why didn't He just do it from Heaven? He couldn't. He needed a human in order to act on earth, otherwise, He violates his own word.

When the men got up to leave, they looked down toward Sodom, and Abraham walked along with them to see them on their way. Then the Lord said, "Shall I hide from Abraham what I am about to do? Abraham will surely become a great and powerful nation, and all nations on earth will be blessed through him. For I have chosen him so that he will direct his children and his household after him to keep the way of the Lord by doing what is right and just so that the Lord will bring about for Abraham what he has promised him." Then the Lord said, "The outcry against Sodom and Gomorrah is so great and their sin so grievous that I will go down and see if what they have done is as bad as the outcry that has reached me. If not, I will know." The men turned away and went toward Sodom, but Abraham remained standing before the Lord. Then Abraham approached him and said: "Will you sweep away the righteous with the wicked? What if there are fifty righteous people in the city? Will you really sweep it away and not spare the place for the sake of the fifty righteous people in it? Far be it from you to do such a thing—to kill the righteous with the wicked, treating the righteous and the wicked alike. Far be it from you! Will not the Judge of all the earth do right?" The Lord said, "If I find fifty righteous people in the city of Sodom, I will spare the whole place for their sake." Then Abraham spoke up again: "Now that I have been so bold as to speak to the Lord though I am nothing but dust and ashes, what if the number of the righteous is five less than fifty? Will you destroy the whole city because of five people? If I find forty-five there," he said, "I will not destroy it." Once again he spoke to him, "What if only forty are found there?" He said, "For the sake of forty, I will not do it." Then he said, "May the Lord not be angry, but let me speak. What if only thirty can be found there?" He answered, "I will not do it if I find thirty there." Abraham said, "Now that I have been so bold as to speak to the Lord, what if only twenty can be found there?" He said, "For the sake of twenty, I will not destroy it." Then he said, "May the Lord not be angry, but let me speak just once more.

What if only ten can be found there?" He answered, "For the sake of ten, I will not destroy it." When the Lord had finished speaking with Abraham, he left, and Abraham returned home.

Genesis 18:16-33

God bargained with Abraham because He gave earth to humans and won't violate His Word. Abraham had so much influence with God because the Lord requires a body to perform His Will on earth. The more we're able to see the impact and influence we are called to have through prayer, the greater the effect our prayers will have. We have been conditioned to perceive the great acts of God throughout the Bible as mere stories when in fact they were real events that took place largely due to praying Saints. Saints that discovered the keys of the Kingdom and through an intimate relationship with the King and an understanding of His mind enacted His Will on earth.

When God said in Genesis 1:26 "let them have dominion." He established a law that mankind would be the only creatures to have legal authority on earth to dominate. He delegated this responsibility to man alone. In Ezekiel chapter 4 we see another example of man's authority on the earth as God allowed the prophet to alter His plans.

Take wheat and barley, beans and lentils, millet and spelt; put them in a storage jar and use them to make bread for yourself. You are to eat it during the 390 days you lie on your side. Weigh out twenty shekels of food to eat each day and eat it at set times. Also, measure out a sixth of a hin of water and drink it at set times. Eat the food as you would a loaf of barley bread; bake it in the sight of the people, using human excrement for fuel." The Lord said, "In this way the people of Israel will eat defiled food among the nations where I will drive them." Then I said, "Not so, Sovereign Lord! I have never defiled myself. From my youth until now I have never eaten anything found dead or torn by wild animals. No impure meat has never entered my mouth." "Very well," he said, "I will let you bake your bread over cow dung instead of human excrement."

Ezekiel 4:9-15

Ezekiel had such authority on earth he was able to make a declaration that not only caused the Lord to change His mind but honored the prophets word and brought it to pass.

The highest Heavens belong to the Lord, but the earth he has given to man.

Psalms 115:16

Throughout history God has been cooperating with man, doing what He can to establish His Will on earth. Jesus discovered the means to cooperating with God. When God cooperates with man the result is our present condition. When man cooperates with God the effects of the life of Jesus become the outcome. God needs a body to exercise His Will on earth. As a representative of the church I pray we begin cooperating with God and His plans rather than asking Him to cooperate with ours.

Therefore, the Lord himself will give you a sign: The virgin will be with child and will give birth to a son, and will call him Immanuel.

Isaiah 7:14

 Q/A: Why did God send us Immanuel?

_____

_____

God sent us "Immanuel" which means "God in a body." Immanuel allowed God to come to earth while protecting the integrity of His Word.

For to us a child is born, to us a son is given, and the government will be on his shoulders. And he will be called Wonderful Counselor, Mighty God, Everlasting Father, Prince of Peace. Of the increase of his government and peace, there will be no end. He will reign on David's throne and over his kingdom, establishing and upholding it with justice and righteousness from that time on and forever. The zeal of the Lord Almighty will accomplish this.

Isaiah 9:6-7

The child was the body, the Son was the spirit. The body made the Son legal on earth. Jesus is the body, Christ is the Spirit. Jesus made Christ the Son legal. Once again we see God preserving His integrity by keeping His Word. Jesus, therefore, could only do what He did on earth not because He was the Son of God (Matthew 14:33, Mark 3:11-12, Luke 22:66-70, John 5:24-27) but because He was the Son of Man (Matthew 9:1-8, Mark 10:42-45, Luke 21:24, John 6:61-63). It was Jesus' body that made Him legal to use authority on earth.

God gave humans legal authority to do business for Him on earth. This legal authority once enacted brings to life a higher law through which to govern the earth and its systems of rulership. This law flows from the Kingdom within and is authenticated as we make visible this Kingdom authority on earth. In reading the passage below, pay close attention to whom God entrusts "judgment."

Jesus gave them this answer: "I tell you the truth, the Son can do nothing by himself; he can do only what he sees his Father doing, because whatever the Father does the Son also does. For the Father loves the Son and shows him all he does. Yes, to your amazement he will show him even greater things than these. For just as the Father raises the dead and gives them life, even so the Son gives life to whom he is pleased to give it. Moreover, the Father judges no one but has entrusted all judgment to the Son, that all may honor the Son just as they honor the Father. He who does not honor the Son does not honor the Father, who sent him. "I tell you the truth, whoever hears my word and believes him who sent me has eternal life and will not be condemned; he has crossed over from death to life. I tell you the truth, a time is coming and has now come when the dead will hear the voice of the Son of God and those who hear will live. For as the Father has life in himself, so he has granted the Son to have life in himself. **And he has given him authority to judge because He is the Son of Man.***"*

John 5:19-27

Jesus identified where He got His authority to do miracles when He answered: "for the father judges no one, but has entrusted all judgment to the son" (v.22).

The word "judge" here means "to give rights." So the Father gives no rights on earth but has given that responsibility to the Son. Jesus concludes by saying the Father "has given authority to execute judgment {rights} also, because he is the Son of man." (John 5:27) Jesus is saying I have authority not because I'm the Son of God (the Christ) but because I'm the Son of Man, a human with a body. In the same way, God needs us to use our authority to exercise power on earth on His behalf. We are needed to get God's culture and influence out of Heaven and established on earth.

The Lord said, "I have indeed seen the misery of my people in Egypt. I have heard them crying out because of their slave drivers, and I am concerned about their suffering. So I have come down to rescue them from the hand of the Egyptians and to bring them up out of that land into a good and spacious land, a land flowing with milk and honey— the home of the Canaanites, Hittites, Amorites, Perizzites, Hivites, and Jebusites. And now the cry of the Israelites has reached me, and I have seen the way the Egyptians are oppressing them. So now, go. I am sending you to Pharaoh to bring my people the Israelites out of Egypt."

Exodus 3:7-10

Here we see the Lord saying, "I have come down to deliver the Israelites." Then He says "Now Moses you go and do it." When Moses announced it to Pharaoh, God provided. Once again we see God wanting to do something and using a human to accomplish it!

Everything is permissible for me but not everything is beneficial. Everything is permissible for me but I will not be mastered by anything. Food for the stomach and the stomach for food but God will destroy them both. The body is not meant for sexual immorality, but for the Lord, and the Lord for the body. By his power God raised the Lord from the dead, and he will raise us also. Do you not know that your bodies are members of Christ himself?

1 Corinthians 6:12-15

The body was made for the Lord so He could have legal access to influence earth. An important component to the Christian life is establishing ourselves as a living sacrifice. Stilling our minds and emotions and disengaging from our own Wills, let's cultivate the discipline of prayer and anticipate Heaven's appearance on earth. As we enter into a cooperative relationship with the Lord of Heaven and earth we will begin seeing the power and influence prayer inherently contains.

It was necessary for the Holy Spirit to make His abode in man, for outside of a human, He would be illegal. Inside however He invites us into union with Him, empowering human life and bringing awareness to our authority. This new life, lived out of the Kingdom, is what begins to tip the scales in favor of the re-establishing of the Kingdom on earth.

We are called the Body of Christ and we are making God legal through us on earth.

 Q/A: What does Jesus teach us in the Lord's Prayer?

_____

_____

Jesus teaches us that we must ask the Father to interfere in earthly affairs when He said, "Thy kingdom come, Thy will be done on earth ...."

Prayer is the most powerful and influential activity on earth. Jesus' statement "I only do what I see my Father doing" implies He was in constant contact with the Father, praying without ceasing. Therefore, we would be correct in concluding that every time Heaven invaded earth through Jesus it was a direct result of prayer. Prayer is man giving God permission to interfere in the affairs of earth. In order to anchor ourselves more firmly in Christ let's root ourselves in this fact: When Jesus said "Thy Kingdom come, Thy Will be done" He placed the Kingdom in the Will of God making both His Kingdom and His Will equal.

In Luke 11:1 the disciples asked Jesus to teach them how to pray. After all they had witnessed with Jesus, why would they ask Him to do this? They saw Him walk on water, heal the sick, open blind eyes and do many great miracles yet they asked Him to teach them to pray. It's interesting to consider why they asked such a question. Maybe Jesus spent more time praying than anything. The Bible says He would get up early in the morning and pray for quite some time. Perhaps three hours according to some scholars. He would come down from prayer and take such little time to heal the sick, cast out demons, give sight to the blind, and perform other miracles. Perhaps the disciples considered that if Jesus takes that little time to heal and three hours to pray then prayer must be that much more important. Perhaps the three-hour activity is making it possible for Him to do the two-minute miracle.

Prayer is earthly license for Heavenly interference. The greater our understanding of our inheritance as kings and priests the greater the interference Heaven will have on earth. Knowing the relationship between King of kings and Lord of lords opens the door to effectual prayer by awakening the substance within righteousness.

It is man's legal responsibility to petition Heaven's influence on earth. Have you ever wondered how and why "The prayer of a righteous person has great power" (James 5:16, ESV)? Righteousness is right standing with government. The greatest expression of righteousness comes through the relationship between King of kings and Lord of lords.

Q/A: How is prayer a transaction?

Prayer is man giving God permission to work in the earthly realm, the realm He has given us as kings. Prayer is a transaction of Kingdom activity between a King and his citizens. Only in the Kingdom of Heaven will you find the King bestowing kingship—ruling authority—to all citizens. What an inheritance we have been given!

The Model of Israel

Consider, when God wanted to set the Children of Israel free why didn't He just do it Himself? He couldn't because God's a Spirit and would have violated His own Word so He found a man. He negotiated with Moses for days. Everything God wanted to do He needed Moses to say and do first.

Moses answered the people, "Do not be afraid. Stand firm and you will see the deliverance the Lord will bring you today. The Egyptians you see today you will never see again. The Lord will fight for you; you need only to be still." Then the Lord said to Moses, "Why are you crying out to me? Tell the Israelites to move on. Raise your staff and stretch out your hand over the sea to divide the water so that the Israelites can go through the sea on dry ground. I will harden the hearts of the Egyptians so that they will go in after them. And I will gain glory through Pharaoh and all his army, through his chariots and his horsemen. The Egyptians will know that I am the Lord when I gain glory through Pharaoh, his chariots, and his horsemen." Then the angel of God, who had been traveling in front of Israel's army, withdrew and went behind them. The pillar of cloud also moved from in front and stood behind them, coming between the armies of Egypt and Israel. Throughout the night, the cloud brought darkness to the one side and light to the other side; so neither went near the other all night long. Then Moses stretched out his hand over the sea, and all that night the Lord drove the sea back with a strong east wind and turned it into dry land. The waters were divided, and the Israelites went through the sea on dry ground, with a wall of water on their right and on their left. The Egyptians pursued them, and all Pharaoh's horses and chariots and horsemen followed them into the sea. During the last watch of the night, the Lord looked down from the pillar of fire and cloud at the Egyptian army and threw it into confusion. He made the wheels of their chariots come off so that they had difficulty driving. And the Egyptians said, "Let's get away from the Israelites! The Lord is fighting for them against Egypt." Then the Lord said to Moses, "Stretch out your hand over the sea so that the waters may flow back over the Egyptians and their chariots and horsemen." Moses stretched out his hand over the sea, and at daybreak, the sea went back to its place. The Egyptians were fleeing toward it, and the Lord swept them into the sea. The water flowed back and covered the chariots and horsemen—the entire army of Pharaoh that had followed the

Israelites into the sea. Not one of them survived. But the Israelites went through the sea on dry ground, with a wall of water on their right and on their left. That day the Lord saved Israel from the hands of the Egyptians, and Israel saw the Egyptians lying dead on the shore. And when the Israelites saw the great power the Lord displayed against the Egyptians, the people feared the Lord and put their trust in him and in Moses his servant.

Exodus 14:13-31

Moses is speaking to the people, proclaiming the death of their enemies. After he finished speaking, he went to a quiet place and said, "Lord did you hear what I just said?"

The Lord answered him, "Why do you come to me? Go and do what you told them." In other words, I have the power and you have the authority. You have the license and I have the ability. You give me permission and I will activate the power. Step into your identity as king and lord and go take care of our enemies."

So Moses stretched out his hand over the waters and they rolled back, allowing the Israelites to cross. When the Egyptians chased them, the Lord said to Moses, "Stretch out your hand over the sea that the water may come back upon the Egyptians, upon their chariots, and upon their horsemen." So Moses stretched out his hand over the sea, and the sea returned to its normal course.

It seems God couldn't even roll back the waters without Moses' activity on the earth. The waters remained unchanged until Moses acted. So God destroyed Moses' enemies only through the cooperation and direct activity of a body legally able to execute God's power on earth. When God wants to do something on earth He seeks a man to gain access in order to influence earth and execute His Will.

Four Laws of Prayer

1. The legal authority on earth is in the hands of a human, a spirit in a body.

2. God will never violate the laws of His Word. He needs His children

to accomplish His purposes on earth.

3. Nothing will happen on earth without mankind. As noted before, John Wesley said, "When it comes to activity on earth without man, God will not, and without God, man cannot." The earth depends on Heaven and Heaven depends on earth.

4. God cannot interfere on earth without the co-operation of mankind. We must know the Will of God and become firmly rooted in righteousness before cooperation between Heaven and earth takes place. The perfect Will of God is discovered only through the seeking first of the Kingdom of God and His righteousness.

 Q/A: Why is prayer mandatory?

_____

_____

Prayer is not only important, it's mandatory to fulfill Jesus' model prayer "Your kingdom come, on earth just like in Heaven." Prayer is the river through which Heavenly activity flows onto the earth.

In order to execute God's Will on earth, we must study the Bible and learn to hear His voice. It's important for us to see the gravity of Jesus' statement "seek first the Kingdom". We must come to understand why Jesus established this as humanities top priority. Without this foundational understanding, we cannot enter into our identity as praying Kingdom Saints.

The Bible is a legal document. It is the Constitution of Heaven for earth. It contains within it the Will of our King. With the foundation of seeking first the Kingdom in place, knowing scripture gives us confidence we are executing our Father's Will and that empowers us in times of petition.

Principles to Effective Prayer

- Seek first the Kingdom.
- Be born from above (born again).
- Understand righteousness.
- Understand our identity as a king of the earth under the Lordship of the King of Heaven.
- Cultivate a lifestyle of stillness and quietness before the Lord while developing a listening ear.
- Learn to deny ourselves and pick up our cross daily. Learn to die to self-will daily.
- Look for God to add to your faith as you grow in your understanding of the Kingdom.
- Keep praying: "Cry out to Him day and night". Adopt "the persistent widow" mindset of Luke18:1-8.
- Keep close to God. Be aware of His presence by fertilizing a lifestyle of conscious contact with His presence. Be quick to confess sins and repent when needed.
- Make "supplication." "Supplication" means "to earnestly contend for that which you are praying."
- Develop the legal side of our natures while diminishing and decreasing our emotional side.
- Through an intimate relationship with the Lord, be prepared to discover what God wants and tell Him so He can have legal access.

 Note: A "petition" is "a legal request requiring evidence as back up proof." It is not an emotional plea. A petition requires specific details laid out in a particular manner, not vague statements. When we're dealing with a government we must study the Constitution and its laws before petitioning. The Bible is our Constitution. The rights, responsibilities, and privileges of our citizenship are found in it as well as the Will, heart, and mind of our government. When we come before God keep in mind we're not coming before a religious leader but a King. God is not here to do what we suggest but what He promised. Pray His Will and have confidence that He hears us.

This is the confidence we have in approaching God: that if we ask anything according to his will, he hears us. And if we know that he hears us—whatever we ask—we know that we have what we asked of him.

1 John 5:14-15

 Note: Answered prayer has been so scarce largely because we have been praying outside of the Kingdom. In the Kingdom-age we are brought into the Kingdom which is situated in Heaven. Once this happens we no longer live in this world-system on earth. We "come up here" and begin living from the place of Heaven. Therefore, we become transported into Heaven through a shift in our mind, resulting in the renewed mind of the Spirit. We enter the Kingdom, the place of the Lord's Will for us. It's precisely this transformation that will remove the lack of answered prayers and bring about an eruption of prayers answered.

The Operation of Prayer

"For my thoughts are not your thoughts, neither are your ways my ways," declares the Lord. "As the Heavens are higher than the earth, so are my ways higher than your ways and my thoughts than your thoughts. As the rain and the snow come down from Heaven, and do not return to it without watering the earth and making it bud and flourish so that it yields seed for the sower and bread for the eater, so is my word that goes out from my mouth: It will not return to me empty, but will accomplish what I desire and achieve the purpose for which I sent it.

Isaiah 55:8-11

The Lord begins by letting us know we do not possess His thoughts and ways. They were given over to deception in the garden. This places a need in humanity. Then He gives us the answer how to fulfill this need. Herein lies the model of prayer, which is understood when we discover that God is talking about the "Water Cycle." The Water Cycle is the scientific name for the process of water coming down from Heaven, being received by the earth and then the earth giving it back to Heaven. This is the model for prayer.

- We are to wait for Heaven's Word coming down to us as "rain."
- Then we receive it and send it back in the form of prayer, which is the "evaporation" part of the water cycle. Prayer therefore has two parts: receiving and giving. Receiving the Lords Will through revelation then presenting the revelation back to Him.
- God says when we enter into a life of prayer modeled after the water cycle then, "It will not return to us empty, but will accomplish what He desires and achieve the purpose for which He sent it" (Isa. 55:11).
- Revelation is an invitation to pray what was revealed to you. In practical terms, still yourself before the Lord. Wait in quiet expectation for revelation. As He speaks to you, receive it and send it back to Him through prayer. A fruitful principle to live by is "revelation is meant to be prayed back to the Lord." The end result of cultivating a discipline of prayer is constant contact with our King. This produces a lifestyle on earth as it is in Heaven as we learn to do what we perceive our Heavenly Father doing. The more we learn to wait upon the Lord, engaged in active stillness before Him, the more our prayer life will take on new levels of effectualness.

Hindrances to Effective Kingdom Praying

1. Not seeking first the Kingdom.
2. We must understand what prayer is and its purpose.
3. We must daily deny ourselves, pick up our cross and follow the Jesus way of servanthood and sacrifice.
4. We must step into a relationship with God that reverentially demands things we hear from Him.
5. Don't just read His Word. Absorb it. Memorize it. Study it, develop intentionality and focus during your time with the Lord.
6. Don't pray for faith, pray in faith. You create faith (it comes to you) in part by what you study. Faith is belief that produces a response.

When Eve was being tempted to eat the fruit why didn't God come and stop her? He couldn't violate His own eternal Word. But He had a plan and prayer was and is an important part in fulfilling it.

In summary, the purpose of prayer is to grant Heaven access to earth.

- Petition literally means, "approaching the king." Black's Law Dictionary defines it as "a formal written request to some governmental authority."
- Pray means to "exchange."
- Intercession means to make petition.

These definitions are political and legal terms not religious. They are terms designed to help us understand our role and function as representatives of the Kingdom on earth. They are terms that bring us into a relationship with our King to the degree that we become a conduit through which He expresses His Will on earth as it is in Heaven. When the church finds her identity as a "house of prayer" the Lord will have awakened the primary character trait of the church used for expressing and establishing Heaven on earth.

A **Application:** Commit to become a Kingdom pray-er. Commit to understand your identity as a king and lord of the earth. Begin cultivating a lifestyle of stillness before the Lord with the intent of receiving revelation you can pray back to Him.

_____
Your name   Date

Chapter Seven

Original Purpose for the Church

A key to discovering the contents found in seeking the Kingdom is removing and diligently guarding against the three obstacles inhibiting Kingdom seed from taking root and bearing fruit. All three are found in the parable of the sower.

That same day Jesus went out of the house and sat by the lake. Such large crowds gathered around him that he got into a boat and sat in it, while all the people stood on the shore. Then he told them many things in parables, saying: "A farmer went out to sow his seed. As he was scattering the seed, some fell along the path, and the birds came and ate it up. Some fell on rocky places, where it did not have much soil. It sprang up quickly, because the soil was shallow. But when the sun came up, the plants were scorched, and they withered because they had no root. Other seed fell among thorns, which grew up and choked the plants. Still other seed fell on good soil, where it produced a crop—a hundred, sixty or thirty times what was sown. He who has ears, let him hear."

Matthew 13:1-9

Listen then to what the parable of the sower means: When anyone hears the message about the kingdom and does not understand it, the evil one comes and snatches away what was sown in his heart. This is the seed sown along the path. The one who received the seed that fell on rocky places is the man who hears the word and at once receives it with joy. But since he has no root, he lasts only a short time. When trouble or persecution comes because of the word, he quickly falls away. The one who received the seed that fell among the thorns is the man who hears the word, but the worries of this life and the deceitfulness of wealth choke it, making it unfruitful. But the one who received the seed that fell on good soil is the man who hears the word and understands it. He produces a crop, yielding a hundred, sixty or thirty times what was sown."

Matthew 13:18-23

The three hindrances to the Kingdom seed producing a crop are:

1. Lack of understanding (vs. 19).

2. Having some understanding but an inability to properly handle trouble and persecution (vs. 21).

3. Worry and the pursuit of money (vs. 22).

The gospel of Mark sheds light on two important purposes for the church: its intent to become a place of prayer and its design to be for the nations. "My house will be called a house of prayer for all nations" (Mark 11:17). We must discover these two essential attributes before we will see Jesus' church begin influencing the earth in the manner in which He designed. The prayers of the church will become the means to implement Jesus' influence over the nations. As we continue, let's keep this key of Kingdom influence in mind.

The church is to be God's representative on the earth. The church is an agency through which God wants to administer from Heaven onto earth. We, the church must find ourselves in the Kingdom before we can administer Heaven on earth. Our identity is not found on earth but in Heaven. The earth is our delegated sphere of influence crowned on us by the King of kings. One requirement for His success is our cooperation. The church exists not for Heaven but for the nations. The church was not to "establish a religion" but instead "be a governing influence in a nation." Having a willingness to understand the Kingdom and the fortitude to persevere through Satan's "seed snatching" strategies is essential to becoming influential.

It's important for us to acknowledge the importance of understanding the process of multiplying Kingdom seed. This most unique of all seeds is the first thing Satan attacks when we pursue the Kingdom, and the last thing he wants a child of God to receive. Understanding the Kingdom is the foundational component necessary to ensuring Kingdom seed is planted. Understanding is the soil through which the seed is planted and takes roots. Understanding is also the container of revelation. Kingdom understanding is Heaven's primary conduit through which transformation flows. As Kingdom understanding is received revelation becomes available which empowers change. It's no wonder Satan's remaining hindrances are designed to distract us from receiving Kingdom understanding. It might just be the most influential information the Lord has ever given humanity.

Until recently, Satan has succeeded in removing the understanding of the Kingdom within the body of Christ at large. John the Baptist was to Jesus what understanding the Kingdom is to the church expressing the Kingdom. Jesus will not and cannot build His church apart from the incorruptible seed of the message of the Kingdom taking root in His church. The Kingdom becomes rooted and begins growing as we enter into obedience to Jesus' highest priority of seeking first His Kingdom and His righteousness.

In the New Testament, the word "church" is not a religious word but rather a political one. Jesus coined the word from the Roman Government who developed it from the Greeks. The word was "*ekklesia*" which means in Greek "assembly, congregation, council or convocation." The term is used to describe what we today would have called the meeting of the "Roman Senate." There was no such thing as "separation of church and state" in the Roman Empire. The two worked together to establish the influence of the culture of the king. Additionally, in Latin, the "*ecclesia*" was the assembly of the Senate. These are two blueprints laid out before us showing how the Lord plans to re-establish His rule and reign on earth as it is in Heaven. Once we enter a lifestyle of seeking first the Kingdom, God begins growing us into a house of prayer by awakening the relational qualities of prayer mentioned in the chapter on prayer. A dominating character trait of the Kingdom church is her dynamic prayer life and the effects from such a lifestyle. Jesus said, "Is it not written: "My house will be called a house of prayer for all nations ..." (Mark 11:17).

Note: The church should not rush into the present political system in attempts to establish the Kingdom. We cannot pour "new wine into old wineskins. If they do, the skins will burst; the wine will run out and the wineskins will be ruined. No, they pour new wine into new wineskins ..." (Matthew 9:17). The church needs a dramatic change in thinking before we can see her designated influence flourish.

Jesus builds His church by first establishing His Kingdom within us. Then He joins us together and begins His outward expression of the Kingdom He established within us. This is Jesus' blueprint for building His church.

- The church, as God planned it, is a family of ambassadors representing a government that's not of this world, but has its headquarters in Heaven. "Our Father who is in Heaven." There is a tipping point in our search for the Kingdom where we discover ourselves in Heaven (Ephesians 2:6). This discovery through revelation will awaken a cry in our spirits of longing and anticipation. No longer in the world, we begin living out of a supremely higher form of government, one humanity at large is ready to embrace.
- The church is to stay in touch with the government of Heaven and is so passionately in love with her King they have committed themselves completely to His desires.
- Heavenly government sends down its ruling directives to the church through the outworking of prayer.
- The church is then to implement heaven's instructions on the earth as a legal representative through proclamation, petition, intercession and/or waiting in faith for Heaven to respond.
- The church rooted in the Kingdom has no affiliation with earthly political parties and pays its allegiance wholly to the King of Heaven, Jesus.
- The church uses Heaven's governmental principles for establishing the Kingdom, not earthly. For example, the church uses prayer to initiate change, trusting in Heaven to bring it about. We NEVER resort to physical violence or pushing our government's agenda down people's throats. The Church is not an agent of change, but rather a conduit through which change comes.

A principle of primary importance whenever studying the Kingdom is knowing that the government of Heaven must first be established within the individual before it can be represented accurately on earth. We must pursue the King's reign within us, then we will be equipped to function as the church Jesus is building.

The church is a training school for ruling and reigning on behalf of our King. Before Adam fell he reigned. Since he fell, humanity has become slaves to another kingdom's way of doing things, the kingdom of darkness. We need to be re-trained on how to reign. The church who commits to bringing understanding of the Kingdom will plant the seeds that will produce the end time harvesters. These harvesters will reseed themselves until the whole earth is filled with the Kingdom of God.

After John was put in prison, Jesus went into Galilee, proclaiming the good news of God. "The time has come," he said. "The kingdom of God is near. Repent and believe the good news!"

Mark 1:14-15

That's why Jesus' first words in public ministry were change your way of thinking. Repent because the government through which we will reign again has arrived. "Your present way of thinking will not work." The present condition of our mind has kept us from entering the Kingdom and blinded us from seeing it. In effect, He was saying, "You must ascend your thought life to My thoughts. In order to do this, you must begin making it your top priority to understand My Kingdom." The church's mandate is to restore mankind back to God's original plan. The most effective and efficient way of doing this is establishing His Kingdom on earth.

Jesus said to him, "Today salvation has come to this house, because this man, too, is a son of Abraham. For the Son of Man came to seek and to save what was lost."

Luke 19:9-10

By the church collectively seeking first the Kingdom we prepare ourselves for Jesus to act through us to accomplish His Will fully. He came to seek and save "something" knowing it's the means of redeeming all things to Himself. That "something" being the Kingdom of Heaven's systems of rulership re-established on earth. Jesus began this task with His entrance into the world. His life was a model of how the Father was going to restore the earth and its inhabitance back under the domain of Heaven. His message became the information that would bring about the transformation necessary to fulfill His Will. He then passed this message on to a group called disciples who continued establishing and furthering the influence of Heaven on earth. The Book of Acts is the evidence of this and is filled with insight into how the church effectively carries out Jesus' mandate.

Then the King will say to those on his right, "Come, you who are blessed by my Father; take your inheritance, the kingdom prepared for you since the creation of the world. For I was hungry and you gave me something to eat, I was thirsty and you gave me something to drink, I was a stranger and you invited me in, I needed clothes and you clothed me, I was sick and you looked after me, I was in prison and you came to visit me." Then the righteous will answer him, "Lord, when did we see you hungry and feed you, or thirsty and give you something to drink? When did we see you a stranger and invite you in, or needing clothes and clothe you? When did we see you sick or in prison and go to visit you?" The King will reply, "I tell you the truth, whatever you did for one of the least of these brothers of mine, you did for me." Then he will say to those on his left, "Depart from me, you who are cursed, into the eternal fire prepared for the devil and his angels. For I was hungry and you gave me nothing to eat, I was thirsty and you gave me nothing to drink, I was a stranger and you did not invite me in, I needed clothes and you did not clothe me, I was sick and in prison and you did not look after me." They also will answer, "Lord, when did we see you hungry or thirsty or a stranger or needing clothes or sick or in prison, and did not help you?" He will reply, "I tell you the truth, whatever you did not do for one of the least of these, you did not do for me." Then they will go away to eternal punishment, but the righteous to eternal life.

Matthew 25:34-46

In Verse 34 we plainly see that the Kingdom is not the church and the church is not the Kingdom. The church is a part of the Kingdom which is the whole. The Kingdom has been here from the foundation of the world. We lost the right and responsibility to reign on earth through the "Original Sin" of the man and woman in the garden. But Jesus brought back the reign of His Kingdom. It is the church which God has chosen to use to re-establish his rule and reign (Matthew 16:18). As the church moves from a religious institution to a Kingdom community we will once again witness the substance of Heaven on earth. Until we come out from the oppression of the religious system the Lord will not reveal, equip and empower His church to function in Kingdom authority.

A primary vehicle through which this exodus will take place is the decision to make the Kingdom of God number one in our lives.

 Q/A: What is the church's role and responsibility?

The Church as Equipping Center

The church is designed to equip believers with the information received while walking out Jesus' command to seek first the Kingdom. The atmosphere of the church is that of a loving community made up of a royal family. The church's job and responsibility is to discover each individual's God-given gifts and train them to become leaders under Christ while cultivating a family environment. You may be confident in having identified your gift but only in the Kingdom will you find additional substance within the gift: Kingdom substance!

We are called the head, not the tail (Deuteronomy 28:13). We are called to become kings who follow only Christ (Ephesians. 4:11-13). The purpose of the Church is to equip the citizens of Heaven to do the work of ministry—the ministry from a governmental office, not religious. We are called to minister to a government and for a government. The Church is called to make students, "disciples" of the good news of the Kingdom. As the Church equips the Saints it is essential we lay the foundation of Kingdom understanding before we consider gifting—substance that brings to life the nature and character of Heaven!

We fail in our attempts to represent the Kingdom when we take and use our gifts out of the Kingdom. We must understand the Kingdom and function out of it. We must cry out for revelation of the Kingdom as a whole.

Jesus manifested Heaven while under the oppression of the Roman Empire and the local religious authorities. In spite of great resistance, Jesus brought the proof of Heaven's existence everywhere. He understood the government He brought to earth. This understanding, along with the proclamation of the message of the Kingdom became the channel through which He became empowered with Heavenly substance.

- His message on the Kingdom was always backed up with a demonstration of its existence.
- He never departed from the Will of the Father.
- His words brought storms at sea, and water and wine, and fig trees under His commands.
- His Kingdom compassion, coupled with understanding of His governments ways, brought sickness and disease under the Kingdom's healing influence.
- Angels responded to His commands and aided Him in times of need.
- Fish went where He told them as He effortlessly rested in His dominion mandate to rule.
- He had money to pay taxes when needed.
- Children's lunches enabled Him to feed thousands.
- His influence and fame spread rapidly. Multitudes followed Him as He pointed the way to this most beautiful life, Kingdom living.
- Jesus was never oppressed despite being under oppression.
- Jesus established His identity in the Kingdom and brought forth all words and activity out of this place which produced the substance He demonstrated and brought into existence. This introduced humanity to a place where the nature, character, and essence were very different from anything known to that point.

Jesus lived under a different government rule with different laws and different principles from everyone around Him. Jesus lived in Heaven but was on earth. He ministered from Heaven to earth. In order to be conformed to the image of Jesus, we must act the same as He did, and that starts by studying the Kingdom He operated out of, which is the same Kingdom He has given us. The change in our mind from our thoughts to His is foundational to the transformational process. The purpose of the church is to keep us on earth developing and serving with our gifts from the location of Heaven until it looks like Jesus is doing it. Let's commit to seeking the Kingdom with the intent of receiving revelation of the Kingdom. As we do we become equipped to teach others and begin active participation in the greatest idea ever introduced to humanity: The Kingdom coming to earth as it is in Heaven!

The Kingdom Comes to Make Us Witnesses

In addition to being an equipping center, the role of the church is to be Jesus' witness. The purpose of a witness is to confirm, verify and authenticate that which is in question. The nature of a witness expands awareness of the thing under investigation adding credibility, plausibility, and believability to those questioning. In a courtroom if we want to test and see if someone is telling the truth we bring in witnesses. The human heart is a courtroom waiting for witnesses to arise, bringing substance from the Kingdom as proof of its existence.

> *After his suffering, he showed himself to these men and gave many convincing proofs that he was alive. He appeared to them over a period of forty days and spoke about the kingdom of God. On one occasion, while he was eating with them, he gave them this command: "Do not leave Jerusalem, but wait for the gift my Father promised, which you have heard me speak about. For John baptized with water, but in a few days, you will be baptized with the Holy Spirit." So when they met together, they asked him, "Lord, are you at this time going to restore the kingdom to Israel?" He said to them: "It is not for you to know the times or dates the Father has set by his own authority. But you will receive power when the Holy Spirit comes on you, and you will be my witnesses in Jerusalem, and in all Judea and Samaria, and to the ends of the earth."*
>
> Acts 1:3-8

Jesus told His disciples that He was going to give them power in order to demonstrate His authenticity. To prove that He spoke the truth regarding His message of the Kingdom. In effect, He said, "I'm giving you My message and power to prove that My Kingdom is here on earth and that I'm Lord of all." This template for Heaven's activity on earth remains to this day. As the church finds herself once again under the teaching of the Kingdom, signs and wonders will be given to once again authenticate the teaching. The church carrying Heaven's message with Heaven's character will demonstrate Heaven's power.

Then Jesus came to them and said, "All authority in Heaven and on earth has been given to me. Therefore go and make disciples of all nations, baptizing them in the name of the Father and of the Son and of the Holy Spirit, and teaching them to obey everything I have commanded you. And surely I am with you always, to the very end of the age.

Matthew 28:18-20

Jesus left the world in the hands of the church. He said all power and authority has been given to Him. The incubation of Kingdom expression, the "all power and authority" is fostered and developed in the gathering of information found in the discipline of seeking first the Kingdom. As Kingdom expression materializes in word and deed, we are to go and disciple the nations. In other words, make the entire world our "classroom" and everyone in our nation a "student." The church is responsible for the condition of the nation. The condition of a nation is determined by the state of the church. The sooner we take up our primary assignment to seek first the Kingdom the sooner Jesus will make us witnesses, authenticating our message with signs and wonders.

 Q/A: If there are so many churches in our nation why is there so much darkness? Why is there so much violence, drugs, gang warfare, killings, domestic violence, divorce, addiction, etc. Why aren't Kingdom attributes like love, joy, peace, kindness, forgiveness, health, and wholeness the dominant traits in culture?

The Original Message and Assignment of the Church

Almost every king has a counsel just like every prime minister and president have a cabinet. The most important assignment a king can give is to spread His thoughts. In doing so He assures His Will to be understood, His culture to spread and His mind to be duplicated. The result? Influence and colonization. The fall in the garden was the King's cabinet declaring independence. A major consequence was we lost not only our relationship with the King but His message and method of implementing His Will on earth. God has restored His cabinet and is waiting for us to realize it and begin growing in our understanding of our assignment: seek first the Kingdom and teach others to do the same. But Jesus' "*ecclesia*" is not voted in. He chooses them.

> *You are my friends if you do what I command. I no longer call you servants, because a servant does not know his master's business. Instead, I have called you friends, for everything that I learned from my Father I have made known to you. You did not choose me, but I chose you and appointed you to go and bear fruit—fruit that will last.*
>
> John 15:14-16

The church is an embassy located in a colonized state. It is an extension of the Kingdom of Heaven with its existence in Heaven while manifesting its nature and essence on earth.

> *Pilate then went back inside the palace, summoned Jesus and asked him, "Are you the king of the Jews?" "Is that your own idea," Jesus asked, "or did others talk to you about me?" "Am I a Jew?" Pilate replied. "It was your people and your chief priests who handed you over to me. What is it you have done?" Jesus said, "My kingdom is not of this world. If it were, my servants would fight to prevent my arrest by the Jews. But now my kingdom is from another place." "You are a king, then!" said Pilate. Jesus answered, "You are right in saying I am a king. In fact, for this reason, I was born, and for this I came into the world, to testify to the truth."*
>
> John 18:33-37

When Pontius Pilate asked Jesus if He was a king, Jesus replied that He was. Note that He didn't say He was "a priest," because He didn't come to introduce a religion, but a government. The church is a family of political appointees who are chosen and appointed by the King. The mission of the church is to represent the government of God on earth and to serve as ambassadors of Heaven recruiting citizens for the Kingdom of God.

> *"I tell you that you are Peter, and on this rock I will build my church,
> and the gates of Hades will not overcome it."*
>
> Matthew 16:18

Jesus basically said "I will build My cabinet, those that will represent My government. Ceasar has his council and representative and I will have mine." Notice Jesus didn't say I will build THE church. He couldn't because there were many "churches."

In Jesus' post-resurrection ministry He did not get away from His original message.

> *I wrote about all that Jesus began to do and to teach until the day he
> was taken up to Heaven, after giving instructions through the Holy
> Spirit to the apostles he had chosen. After his suffering, he showed
> himself to these men and gave many convincing proofs that he was
> alive. He appeared to them over a period of forty days and spoke about
> the kingdom of God.*
>
> Acts 1:1-3

Jesus continued teaching on things pertaining to the Kingdom. We see just prior to the birth of the church that Jesus spoke to its founders for 40 days about "the Kingdom of God." Could this be a piece of the puzzle needed in order for Jesus to build His first century like church once again? As the head of the church, Jesus led by example. He gathered followers, turned them into students of the message of the Kingdom and commissioned them to do likewise. The Church once again needs to become students of the message of the Kingdom in order to follow in His footsteps.

The church is an agent of transformation (Romans 12:2). The more we teach and preach things pertaining to the Kingdom the more transformation will result. This world's way of doing things is according to the representatives of the kingdom of darkness, (earthly mindsets established in government, media, education, and religion). In order to be transformed into His image, we need to make it our top priority to seek His way of thinking and doing things which are found as we seek

His Kingdom. Whichever one you give the most effort and time to is the one you belong. The church is called to present "renewing of the mind" material to all those being equipped for the purpose of transformation. This "material" is unwrapped as we present understanding of the Kingdom.

No matter what our wishes are, we are known by our fruits (Matthew 7:16-20). The more we think and talk about the Kingdom, the more it will renew our minds. The more our minds become renewed, the greater the transformation we experience. The more we devote ourselves to things related to the Kingdom, the more it becomes a part of us. When you eat something long enough your body takes a liking to it. There is a biological adjustment that takes place where your physical makeup craves the food you have begun eating. So it is as we begin taking in things pertaining to the Kingdom of Heaven, leaving behind the things pertaining to the kingdom of darkness.

Repetitiveness in education is a key to allowing the information to become a particular characteristic of your identity. If I want to become a psychologist I must get "psychology" in me. This is only accomplished through making the study of things pertaining to psychology my top priority. This is mandatory for all Masters and Doctoral level students. Jesus requires the same devotion in order to enter His field of study and practice, the Kingdom. To the degree we devote ourselves, will be the degree of our "expertise." The church who commits to the message of the Kingdom will be the church who possesses the keys of the Kingdom and makes known the secrets of Heaven!

Colonization is the original assignment and the Kingdom is the original message of the church. Colonization is a king's way of expanding his rule and reign over a territory. God invented colonization. The Romans were the first major government to have a formal structure of colonialism. That's why God waited so long to send Jesus ("in the fullness of time God sent his son into the world"). The phrase "fullness of time" means at the right time. If Jesus came before the Roman model of colonialism, He would have had no representation to present and the people would have remained in darkness. You cannot effectively communicate without a mutual understanding of the meanings of terms.

Suppose I'm looking for bread to eat. I ask a teenager and because in his language "bread" means "money," would I be communicating effectively? If I tell someone I'm "cool," depending who I'm talking to they will think I'm chilly or an "all right guy." Your terms and my terms need to have the same meaning in order to communicate effectively. God waited for man to set up a model of His government and sent His Son into it in order to communicate effectively. In order to reintroduce the Kingdom, we must clarify important terms to students prior to discipleship. The Church is a family of political appointees equipped with Kingdom material to impart to any and all who become willing to receive. You are a cabinet minister, not a religious minister. Therefore, the mission of the church is to represent the government of God on earth and serve as ambassadors of Heaven inviting citizens into the Kingdom of God.

 Q/A: Once a person is born from above, as a new citizen what is their first responsibility?

Study the constitution in order to know the mind of the government, along with the rights and responsibilities of the citizens. Jesus put it this way: "seek first the Kingdom of God and His righteousness."

When an individual or a nation's leaders submit to the Lord, it is the church's responsibility to make disciples of the new citizens. A "disciple" is a "learner" or "student." A disciple of Jesus is a student whose top priority is to understand the Kingdom. The more we devote ourselves to learning about the Kingdom the greater our awareness becomes of the Kingdom. Someone who is learning his rights as a citizen and responsibilities as a cabinet member and ambassador are positioned before the government of Heaven to be used. Paul was so committed to ambassadorship he said: "I am an ambassador in chains." He was in prison to his ambassadorship, that's all he could do. He concluded asking for prayer that his words may not be different from his governments.

Pray also for me, that whenever I open my mouth, words may be given me so that I will fearlessly make known the mystery of the gospel, for which I am an ambassador in chains. Pray that I may declare it fearlessly, as I should.
Ephesians 6:19-20

Consequently, you are no longer foreigners and aliens, but fellow-citizens with God's people and members of God's household....

Ephesians 2:19

We are no longer illegal immigrants, but citizens and family members—"members of a political body." We are fellow politicians in God's kingdom. It is important to understand God is not desiring for us to align ourselves with an earthly political party so He can begin working. Quite the opposite, it is when we realize that earthly politicians represent earthly governments that we can more accurately begin representing Heaven. Heaven's Kingdom politicians could never work with earthly governments and their politicians, they diametrically oppose one another.

His intent was that now, through the church, the manifold wisdom of God should be made known to the rulers and authorities in the Heavenly realms, according to his eternal purpose which he accomplished in Christ Jesus our Lord.

Ephesians 3:10-11

"His intent" implies purpose. It was God's original intent that through the church (the called-out group of cabinet members chosen by God) He might reveal His manifold wisdom (applied knowledge) to the heavenly realm. Don't be impressed if you impress men. It's none of our business what others think of us. Instead, humbly seek to impress angels. Angels are our servants following us around looking for those representing God. When we represent God accurately, in mind and deed, it opens the door for activity in the heavenly realm. This activity collapses one kingdom making way for the Kingdom of Heaven.

Are not all angels ministering spirits sent to serve those who will inherit salvation?

Hebrews 1:14

Angels are supposed to help us dominate the earth. When Jesus was in the wilderness 40 days, the Bible says He overcame hunger and the devil himself three times. Jesus is both God and man. He laid aside His divine attributes while on earth and like us was dependent on God the

Holy Spirit for His constant direction and communication with His Father. Jesus was a man with God inside. When He was finished angels came running over as if to say, "We found a human who looks like God." There is God manifested. And they went to minister to Him (Matthew 4:11). Not just angels but the whole of creation is waiting for us to manifest as sons of God (Romans 8:19).

Initially, we must allow the Lord to establish His rulership within us. No Saint will ever be endowed with Kingdom expressing power until Christ be first formed in him. Once the Lord is ruling in the temple of man, He will spread His influence out. The result will culminate in the kingdom of this world becoming the Kingdom of the Lord's. Note that further discussion of this is found in Chapter Eleven, "World Systems." As cabinet members, we cannot publicly speak our own opinion. We must speak only what the King says. This requires cultivating a listening ear as we spend quiet time with the Lord. We don't have our own opinions; we only have the expressed thoughts of our King. The art of union with Christ takes time and patience to develop. "Be still and know that I am God" is the prerequisite for effective representation of the Kingdom. This is a worthy endeavor to embrace and one that ensures you will walk in humility.

 Q/A: What are some examples of us having dominion on earth? How does the church manifest God on the earth?

The fall of man was the cabinet declaring independence from the King. We must reconnect the cabinet back to the King. That was Jesus' mission. He came to seek and to save THAT which was lost by turning the heart of the Father back to the Son and the Son to the Father. Since man would not come back to God, He came and got us. The coming of Christ was a family matter producing political action.

How does God strengthen a political cabinet member? By revealing specific agendas. In the case of an ambassador, He adds power and authority to His representative's words, with healing, signs, and wonders. In the case of citizens, He teaches them their rights and responsibilities. The more we are shown our identity in Christ the more we are strengthened with divine empowerment. The moment we become "born again" we lose the right to our own opinion. We become citizens of a Kingdom who demands our allegiance. We no longer ought to live under the mindset of our old nature which is entrenched in democracy and the tenants of this world system. We no longer represent ourselves; we represent Christ and His Kingdom. We desperately need the spirit of wisdom and revelation to enlighten our hearts to this and all things Kingdom related. We must ask the Lord for a hunger and thirst to seek first the Kingdom and prepare ourselves for transformation. The church is coming out from under this world system and aligning herself with the Kingdom. This shift will be propelled and gain momentum as more and more Saints enter into the commitment to seek first the Kingdom of God and His righteousness.

The reason the pagans in Corinth called the disciples "Christians" was because they were accurately representing Christ. They knew Jesus was crucified, yet He was all over the city. A president goes to a foreign nation without ever leaving home. He sends a representative. The representative never speaks his own words and opinion, only his government's. He embodies the government he represents. Colonization is a king using his counsel (church) to establish his reign in a foreign territory. The counsel has the full backing of the government and not only represents the mind of the king but the country itself. Everything the representative does and says becomes an expression of the government. In the same way "the Son is the radiance of God's glory and the exact representation of His being" (Hebrews 1:3a), so too ought the Kingdom church pursue such likeness.

The ministry of the church as a group does not go to the world but exists to train the saints to go. As we discover our training manual to be information received from seeking first the Kingdom we will discover a unity birthed out of a belief system directly deposited to us from Heaven. Additionally, this Kingdom training manual will transform us into the image of Christ through information producing revelation that results in Kingdom substance found in the "knowledge of the Son of God."

It was he who gave some to be apostles, some to be prophets, some to be evangelists, and some to be pastors and teachers, to prepare God's people for works of service, so that the body of Christ may be built up until we all reach unity in the faith and in the knowledge of the Son of God and become mature, attaining to the whole measure of the fullness of Christ."

Ephesians 4:11-13

This is how it should work in the church. The people go out to invite citizens to come to the embassy. The embassy trains those that come in to become diplomats in order to represent the Government of God. If we're a part of the church, our mindset ought to be to take charge of the earth for Christ and to steward all that is in it for the continued influence of God.

The word "colonization" is where we get the word "colon" which means to connect. What goes in the mouth comes out the end. Whatever happens in the headquarters happens in the territory. What is going on in Heaven ought to be happening on earth. Jesus said, "I only do what I see my Father doing" (John 5:19). He modeled this perfectly.

In order to become an effective church, we must consider Jesus as our model. Jesus came to earth carrying a government (Isaiah 9:6). He brought us a government. He spent His ministry life attempting to bring people under the influence of that government. He desired to bring societal transformation one person at a time primarily through a renewing of the mind. He did this in three primary ways: prayer, teaching and demonstrating the superiority of His government on earth.

1) Prayer: Jesus spent much time making room for Heaven to do its business on earth. As a legal representative granting Heaven access on earth, Jesus prayed. Our mindset towards prayer and the way we approach prayer greatly determines Heaven's response. Refer to prayer section for more details.

2) Teaching: Jesus only had one message, the Kingdom. He taught the Kingdom and its principles. He was hoping to introduce and impart another way of thinking. He wanted to transform their way of thinking from the way they were taught to the things He was teaching. If Kingdom information is received by a heart diligently seeking it,

Kingdom revelation will sooner or later spring forth. This is a Kingdom principle on earth and one that is sure to capture all who come under it. In 1 Peter 2:9, the church is a nation. All nations are made up of government which is their primary means of influence. In Acts 1:6-8, we are called into the world to infect it with the Kingdom (government) of Heaven.

3) Demonstrating the superiority of His Government: The whole earth is filled with the influence of the Lord as the waters cover the earth (Isaiah 9:11, Habakkuk 2:14). The Kingdom is not limited to the inner man. All creation is waiting for the manifestation of the sons of God (Romans 8:19). One manifestation of a Son of God is rulership (Genasis1:26). We can't limit the Kingdom's influence to our hearts, rather we must first let it dominate us. It must permeate our character, way of thinking, behavior, and the like. Then we will be entrusted to release Kingdom power and demonstrate it on the earth.

The Kingdom and the Great Commission

The more territory a kingdom gains, the more influence the king has. Jesus said the Kingdom of Heaven is like a mustard seed and yeast (Mark 4:30-32, Luke 13:20-21). In other words, the Kingdom of Heaven is about influence. Expansion is the key. That's what the Great Commission is about—Kingdom influence and expansion. It serves not only to gain citizens but territory. The church is Christ's means to Kingdom influence and expansion. The spread of His Kingdom begins with a change of mind. Repentance towards the direction of understanding the Kingdom. This takes place most effectively as we seek first the Kingdom of God and His righteousness.

At the end of Jesus' mission on earth, He established His program for global restoration and redemption through the church. He called men to complete what He had begun. Jesus left the world in the hands of the church He founded, not in the hands of the devil nor political powers. His commission was clear:

Then Jesus came to them and said, "All authority in Heaven and on earth has been given to me. Therefore go and make disciples of all nations, baptizing them in the name of the Father and of the Son and of the Holy Spirit, and teaching them to obey everything I have commanded you. And surely I am with you always, to the very end of the age."

Matthew 28:18-20

The assignment of the church is not to go to Heaven. Jesus redeemed us in order for us to go to the nations and make disciples—make "students of the Kingdom." The assignment of the church is to influence and restore the world back to God through the teaching of the message of the Kingdom and demonstrating its existence through signs, and wonders, and prayer.

The Difference Between the Church and Kingdom

1. The Kingdom existed before the church. The Kingdom was before the earth was created (Matthew 25:34). The influence of the Kingdom on earth was lost in Genesis 3. Jesus brought the Kingdom back to earth and when He left He put the church in charge of influencing the earth with His Kingdom.

2. When we go to work we don't bring our church. People are not looking for church, they are looking for things found only in the Kingdom.

3. The key to the Kingdom is the influence of Heaven on earth by the Holy Spirit through the agency of the Church.

4. The fall of man caused the departure of the Holy Spirit from the spirit of man, thus, the Kingdom influence of Heaven on earth was lost.

5. God wants to influence the earth with His image and nature through the Church which is to become an expressed image of the Kingdom.

Q/A: What are we supposed to be sharing at our job or with our friends?

_____

_____

Don't talk about the church; talk about the Kingdom. People are seeking answers found only in the Kingdom, not a church. Religion is hollow and deceptive and draws the carnal man. The Kingdom deals with the original purpose and plan of God and awakens what man was created for. Since God created a purpose and plan for mankind then certainly He created us with the desire to fulfill it. Therefore, if mankind can connect with God's purpose and plan he will find ultimate fulfillment. The DNA of man contains within it a desire for the Kingdom. When man discovers the Kingdom, it's only a matter of time before he becomes consumed with it.

God's Purpose and Plan for the Church

1. The Church is to be the extension and expression of His Heavenly Kingdom on earth.
2. The destiny of mankind is for God to have a family of sons and daughters that would influence and govern the earth for Him.
3. He planned for humans representing Him to have dominion over the earth.
4. The redemptive purpose of God is to restore mankind back to Himself, which means recovering a right relationship with Him and rulership over the earth through Heaven's governing systems.

In Matthew. 24:14, why did Jesus say "this" gospel not "the" gospel? Jesus declared that a very specific message—the message of the Kingdom—will be preached to the entire world. Luke 4:43 was the purpose of Jesus: "I must preach the Kingdom .... Since Jesus is the head of the church, we must conclude that it's the church's purpose as well. In

Matthew 10:7 Jesus commanded His disciples to preach a very specific message—the Kingdom. Additionally, Jesus' final words command us to teach what He taught us which is the Kingdom (Matthew. 28:18-20).

The church is not an army. We must cast down this stronghold of the mind and erect the truth. Until then we will be expending energy in a war we were never created to fight. Whenever God wanted to fight He sent "the Hosts of Heaven." He never called His ambassadors and citizens to fight anything except the good fight of faith. In fact, once Peter began fighting and Jesus told him immediately to stop (Matthew 26:51-56). When the Israelites were under the Kingdom Lordship of God He promised to fight for them. Nowhere were they expected to engage in battle. As long as they remained in His Kingdom, they were free from fighting. The moment they asked Samuel for another king that changed. The first curse of leaving the Kingdom of God was the need to fight our own battles (1Samuel 8:10-12). As soon as the church commits herself under the Lordship of King Jesus we enter a rest of which warfare is part of it.

In order to partake in the divine destiny of the church, we must understand that God's thoughts are not ours. We must repent and begin stepping into His thoughts. Then we will be transformed into His image, empowered to fulfill our destiny on earth. "Thy kingdom come ... on earth just like it is in Heaven."

> *But you are a chosen people, a royal priesthood, a holy nation ....*
>
> 1 Peter 2:9

> *... and has made us to be a kingdom and priests ....*
>
> Revelation 1:6

> *You will be for me a kingdom of priests and a holy nation ....*
>
> Exodus 19:6

These are examples of God's word proclaiming us to be both spiritual and political creatures.

Royal=political.
Priesthood=spiritual.

Holy=spiritual.
Nation=governmental.

A kingdom is a form of government and priests are spiritual servants. The two-edged sword of the Kingdom is political and spiritual. The original mission of the church was and still is to restore man to relationship with God once she is restored. The Church is to do this by preaching the "good news" that there is a new ruler in town. He is Jesus! He has come to take over and return creation to its perfect order. God has chosen to do this by means of the Church. His plan was and is to empower transformed people to represent Him with power in the earth by capturing hearts who will turn to Jesus and demonstrate the power of God over the evil in this world. We have been called to rule in His stead. Let's get on with it.

Application: Recognize your purpose for being—to become a witness of the Kingdom. Receive your calling and release yourself to be all that the Father has created, gifted, and purposed you to be. Commit today to be His witness of Heaven on earth. Anticipate the Lord bringing revelation to you as you seek first the Kingdom of God and His righteousness!

Your name	Date

Chapter Eight

Economics

Mankind is motivated, driven, and preoccupied with the pursuit of possessions. Western culture has been conditioned to pursue possessions and save money for more possessions. Everything we do in life is to amass possessions. We go to work to pay for possessions and save up money for more possessions. Our homes are full of possessions. Our prayers are typically focused on possessions. Advertising conditions us to focus on possessions. Our faith is focused on possessions. Religion itself is built on the promise of possessions. The "ownership" mindset deeply rooted in man demands we preoccupy our thoughts with possessions.

For most of humanity, life is defined as the pursuit of things, both necessary and wanted. Things have become our top priority. This misfortune is the source of mankind's problems. Crime, sickness, stress, depression, jealousy, covetousness, malice, envy, strife: all have their foundations in the preoccupation with things.

The love of money is birthed out of a pursuit of things and is a root of all kinds of evil (1 Timothy 6:10). Money is Satan's great distraction to the Kingdom and a snare that enslaves all who pursue it. "He who loves money never has enough" (Ecclesiastes 5:10). The Church's preoccupation with things is the greatest obstacle keeping us from seeing the Kingdom. Once we get our minds off things long enough to seek first the Kingdom then we will experience change and become agents of transformation. Shifting our mindset from ownership to Lordship is the first step in a long list of benefits for both the individual and society.

God's number one priority is the Kingdom of God and His Righteousness. The Kingdom of God is the governing influence of Heaven on earth. This is the governing influence of the King and His culture and lifestyle over a territory impacting it with His Will and purpose. The first place the Lord wants to establish His Kingdom is in our hearts. Then and only then can he expand outward. In order for the Kingdom to become rooted in us, we must confront this inner clash between seeking things and seeking the Kingdom. Making the decision to direct our thoughts towards seeking the Kingdom brings revelation and will eventually collapse the stronghold of amassing possessions.

"Righteousness" is "right standing with government authority" or "right positioning and alignment with the governing authority." In Matthew 6 it appears Jesus identified two categories of people: those who seek things and those who seek the Kingdom and righteousness. Both are means to provision, one is God's way and one is the way of the world. One awakens the divine nature within us and the other keeps awake the carnal nature. One is rooted in freedom and the other in enslavement and chasing after the wind. One mindset produces a turning to the Lord while the other causes us to look to the economy and our ability to get paid.

The Way of the kingdom

No one can serve two masters. Either he will hate the one and love the other, or he will be devoted to the one and despise the other. You cannot serve both God and Money. Therefore I tell you, do not worry about your life, what you will eat or drink; or about your body, what you will wear. Is not life more important than food, and the body more important than clothes? Look at the birds of the air; they do not sow or reap or store away in barns, and yet your Heavenly Father feeds them. Are you not much more valuable than they? Who of you by worrying can add a single hour to his life? And why do you worry about clothes? See how the lilies of the field grow. They do not labor or spin. Yet I tell you that not even Solomon in all his splendor was dressed like one of these. If that is how God clothes the grass of the field, which is here today and tomorrow is thrown into the fire, will he not much more clothe you, O you of little faith? So do not worry, saying, 'What shall we eat? or What shall we drink? or What shall we wear? For the pagans run after all these things, and your Heavenly Father knows that you need them. But seek first his kingdom and his righteousness, and all these things will be given to you as well. Therefore do not worry about tomorrow, for tomorrow will worry about itself. Each day has enough trouble of its own.

Matthew 6:24-34

Jesus invites us to take our focus off things, and cancel our priorities in exchange for His. He introduced an entirely different way of life; a higher way. He summoned us to lay down the world's way of living and step into His Kingdom thinking. In order to step into this new dependence on God for our provision, we must receive a revelation of His power of provision through the act of seeking first the Kingdom. He who is found diligent in his commitment to seeking first the Kingdom can rest assured a revelation is forthcoming.

Kingdom thinking always produces Kingdom living. Fleshly thinking always produces fleshly living. "Flesh gives birth to flesh, but the Spirit gives birth to spirit" (John 3:6). In fact, Jesus called those who run after things "pagans" and went so far as to say "take no thought" of the things they sought. In God's Kingdom, "things" are a bi-product to those who pursue His priority of seeking first His Kingdom. They are given freely as the King sees fit. As a King who owns everything, He can not only make that claim legally, but the integrity of His Word ensures He will do it.

 Q/A: Why did God give us jobs?

God never gave us jobs to make a living, He gave us jobs:

1. To use our talents for His Pleasure and Purpose.
2. To bring the Kingdom culture and influence to our fellow workers.
3. To bring the Kingdom to our workplace and business.
4. To teach us about the Kingdom and prepare us for our destiny.
5. To bring fulfillment and satisfaction to our souls.
6. As an instrument to test us and allow us to examine ourselves during hard times.

All humans are motivated by needs; getting needed things in their lives. The Kingdom is the ultimate response to mankind's needs. Nothing fulfills our needs more completely and satisfactorily than the Kingdom. We haven't experienced the Kingdom's ability to fulfill us because the Kingdom has not been our priority. To make the Kingdom our priority is to set in motion the process of the Kingdom providing for us in ways only the King can.

> *The kingdom of Heaven is like treasure hid in a field. When a man found it, he hid it again, and then in his joy went and sold all he had and bought that field. Again, the kingdom of Heaven is like a merchant looking for fine pearls. When he found one of great value, he went away and sold everything he had and bought it.*
>
> Matthew 13:44-46

This magnificent Kingdom is so fulfilling for us that when we find it, we willingly lay down everything in which we have previously found fulfillment. The initial sighting of the Kingdom provokes such a powerful conversion into it. One revelation has the force to shift your mindset completely away from the things of the world. Can you see this? Look at the parable again closely and see if that's not what Jesus is portraying and declaring. Jesus could make that claim because He knows everything humans seek for is found in the Kingdom of God. Those who cry out for such a revelation are sure to receive it in due time.

We have been conditioned to depend on an economic system put in place by man. The world's economy has become our source, instead of our "Father." Remember, "father" means "source." This is a difficult mental obstacle to overcome. We have been conditioned deeply by the economic system of the world to rely upon a paycheck and our skills. We go to work to get a check to pay our bills and put food on the table. We depend on this system to sustain and provide us with things. To remove the economy as our source we must begin thinking with a Kingdom frame of mind. Through seeking first the Kingdom we begin the transition by understanding a new source. As we continue, more and more awareness of our Father being our source is made available to us. Eventually, all earthly ties are broken and we find ourselves resting in the unfailing love and provision of our Heavenly Father. Seeking first the Kingdom is a gateway to revolutionary revelation, something the Lord is waiting to share with you and the church at large.

Note: One exercise that benefited me in this transition was, as I read scripture I replaced the word "Father" with "source" and the word "Lord" with "owner". This discipline, over time seemed to awaken to me the attributes of God as my source and owner in a personal and life changing way.

My wife is owner and director of a psychological clinic. She's in charge of it all. Recently she came home energetically exclaiming, "I got it! Baby, I finally got it! I had a shift in my thinking and suddenly all stress, anxiety, and worry are gone! I no longer look at the clinic as "my business" but rather I now have stepped into my God-ordained role as a steward of a Kingdom business owned by our Father!" In a moment, in a blink of an eye, the Lord brought revelation to my wife that instantly changed the way she thinks. This has had a profound effect on her emotional health and lifted her countenance in a special way. There is a way of life that awaits all those who diligently pursue the mind of Christ. An existence where peace, rest, and joy rule the inner life! Where strife is gone forever and worry, fear, stress and anxiety come to an end, having no influence over you.

 Q/A: Why did Jesus ask us to make it our top priority to seek the Kingdom?

Because He knows where the treasure lies, in the field of seeking first the Kingdom. As we make a decision, like the man in the parable of the treasure, to buy the field, we discover the treasure. Buy the field, make a decision to begin seeking first the Kingdom.

God created us to depend on Him; to make Him our source. In a kingdom the king owns everything. Because our Father is the King, He invites us to make Him our source by accepting His terms and trusting His Way of doing things. He invites us to lay down the world's heavy yoke and take up His light one. Transformation begins as we enter into a commitment to foster a way of thinking in line with Christ the King through the seeking first of His Kingdom.

Come to me, all you who are weary and burdened, and I will give you rest. Take my yoke upon you and learn from me, for I am gentle and humble in heart, and you will find rest for your souls. For my yoke is easy and my burden is light.

Matthew 11:28-30

Our Father's Kingdom is the ultimate fulfillment of human desires and needs. Consider the obvious deterioration of the systems of this world. These systems are falling apart, unreliable and opposite the Kingdom system. The four basic tenets democracy is built on are in contradiction to everything God's Kingdom stands for.

1. The power of the people and their rights. Government authority flows from the people.
2. The power of private ownership. Individual rights of ownership.
3. The power of personal pursuit.
4. Government of the people by the people.

According to Winston Churchill, "Democracy is the worst form of government, except for all the others." Churchill was implying democracy is the best form of government man has created. Of course, like anything man has created, it's failing much the same as all the other forms of human government. The church must see this, rise up with a resoluteness to seek first the Kingdom and trust our Father to collapse man's government and replace it with His.

Abraham shifted his dependency from the world's system to the Lord (Gen.15:6-21). Job lived his life under the Kingdom tenants of government, as evidenced in his statement:

At this, Job got up and tore his robe and shaved his head. Then he fell to the ground in worship and said: "Naked I came from my mother's womb, and naked I will depart. The Lord gave and the Lord has taken away; may the name of the Lord be praised." In all this, Job did not sin by charging God with wrongdoing.

Job 1:20-22

What a Kingdom mindset! Job got it! He understood the Lord as King. He received his identity as a Kingdom citizen. He fully trusted in the Lord's provision. He embraced the goodness of his Lord, the "owner" whether or not something was given or taken away! While those surrounding Job were in chaos and turmoil he remained anchored to attributes only found in a Kingdom citizen who knows his King as Source. We become transformed into the Kingdom life as we renew our minds through a laying down of earthly thinking and picking up the mindset of Christ the King.

We need to stop working for a living and let Jesus add all things to us as we commit to His priority of pursuing, above all, His Kingdom. The greatest motivation of all humans is self-preservation, so we sell ourselves to gain "things." The greatest fear of all humans is scarcity. Nation fights against nation for the commodities of the world. The principle source of all criminal behavior is the combination of both the drive for self-preservation and the fear of scarcity. The desire to secure and accumulate goods is a curse on humanity. We spend an entire lifetime pursuing things we cannot take into eternity. Their value is fleeting at best. The "spirit of ownership" is a dangerous concept full of consequences. The spirit of ownership creates limitations, frustrations, depression, contention, lack, stealing, poverty, stress, sickness, disease, jealousy and envy.

It's hard for a rich man to enter the Kingdom because he has to turn from "I own" to "He owns" (Matthew 19:23-24). He has to turn from this world system being his source to the Lord being his source. Those who step out in faith and endeavor the Kingdom way have a future as secure as an unshakable, all powerful government.

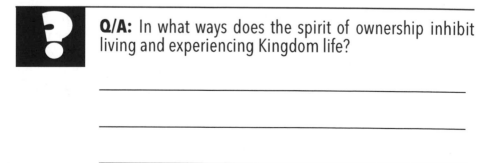

Q/A: In what ways does the spirit of ownership inhibit living and experiencing Kingdom life?

_____

_____

_____

Whoever loves money never has money enough; whoever loves wealth is never satisfied with his income. This too is meaningless. As goods increase, so do those who consume them. And what benefit are they to the owner except to feast his eyes on them? The sleep of a laborer is sweet, whether he eats little or much, but the abundance of a rich man permits him no sleep. I have seen a grievous evil under the sun: wealth hoarded to the harm of its owner, or wealth lost through some misfortune, so that when he has a son there is nothing left for him. Naked a man comes from his mother's womb, and as he comes, so he departs. He takes nothing from his labor that he can carry in his hand. This too is a grievous evil: As a man comes, so he departs and what does he gain, since he toils for the wind? All his days he eats in darkness, with great frustration, affliction and anger.

Ecclesiastes 5:10-17

The Curve of Ownership

"Currency" is the legal form of money that a country uses, whether paper or any other form, but Heaven's currency is different.

Let's look at the two. Money is defined as a fungible proxy for man's ability to reason, labor, create and produce. Money is your humanity turned into a fungible proxy that we use for exchange. For example, suppose you want some milk. The problem is you drive a truck. How do you change what you do into milk? You can't go to the farmer and drive for the farmer to earn the milk. It isn't worth a day's work on your part. But the farmer needs something in exchange for his labor. So the person who hires you gives you currency for your labor, and you exchange some of it for milk from the farmer. "Proxy" means "a substitution or representative agent." "Fungible" means "completely interchangeable." Money, therefore, is a representative of your humanity. Money is a substitute for our ability to labor. Money is a completely interchangeable substitute.

He who has been stealing must steal no longer, but must work, doing something useful with his own hands, that he may have something to share with those in need.

Ephesians 4:28

The purpose of work in the Kingdom is not to provide for your needs. God does this. Instead, we are to be having excess in order to share with others in need. Under the Kingdom economic model not only does the King provide your needs but gives in abundance so that you may participate in expressing His heart of giving.

 Application: Give all that you are and all that you own to the Father today. Declare your dependence on Him and allow Him to show you both the folly of the world's economic system and the sufficiency of His Kingdom.

Your name   Date

Chapter Nine

The Commonwealth

A commonwealth is the opposite of democracy. The Kingdom Commonwealth began in Genesis when God said: "you are free to eat from any tree in the garden." At that moment, the Lord established His wealth to be communal. God's wealth became common to those under His Lordship. God, our Father and Owner, made His wealth available to all under His care. The Kingdom commonwealth way of thinking releases the individual from the curses that exist in the ownership mindset.

Prince Charles of England has never had to work for money. All he had to do was be born because in a kingdom the royal family owns the country. When the children of royalty are born, they are automatically heirs of all their father owns. Of course, Prince Charles can never sell Buckingham Palace because it's owned by royalty, but he has complete access to it. Prince Charles has nothing to take and everything to receive. Trusting the King to provide for us is key to entering the quality of life designed for us.

The Bible is about a King, His Kingdom, and royal family. Accepting our identity as royal children opens up a new way of life. The more we discover what this new identity holds for us the freer we are to become what we were created to be. Identity predetermines behavior. As we identify ourselves in Christ and His Kingdom we take upon ourselves behaviors found in our new identity. Leaving the ownership mindset opens a new identity to us, the one we were created to live out of.

An immense source of human poverty and pain flows out of the adoption of the concept of ownership. Pharaoh was a big problem for the earth and its inhabitants. When reading about his life we see God dealing with him continually.

The Lord told Moses to tell Pharaoh various things, including, "I will send locusts to devour the land in order that you may know I am the Lord, (the "Owner") ... I will send frogs ... so that you might know that I am the owner ... I will send blood in the water ... so that you might know that I am the owner ... I own everything Pharaoh and there shall be no other owners as long as I have a representative of My government doing My bidding in the earth."

Pharaoh was trying to establish himself as owner and God made a point to show us what a curse that idea really is. God destroyed Pharaoh's army, ruined Egypt, and overthrew Pharaoh and his army in the Red Sea (Exodus 14:1-15:21). Since the fall of man Satan has conditioned the minds of man to think ownership. Nothing short of a revelation of the commonwealth heart of God will set us free from the enslavement mindset of ownership and its consequences.

Governments have set up systems and are ruling their perspective societies in an ungodly manner. They have constrained and driven the minds of man towards ownership and created a consumer mentality. In fact, the governments of this world have become the representatives of the kingdom of darkness. The peoples of the earth are enslaved to the kings governing these systems no different than Pharaoh's relationship to Israel. The more "Moses'" God finds to represent Him the more liberation we will experience, both as individuals and as a nation. This Moses-anointing must begin with the basic principle of Kingdom understanding: The Lord is owner of all!

An ungodly system will remain in power until the church takes its God-ordained position of legal stewardship of God's Kingdom on earth and begins educating Heaven's citizens to this end. The Bible says the influence (glory) of the Lord fills the earth. It's up to us to make manifest this reality. There is no greater bondage breaker than receiving revelation through the pursuit of seeking first Kingdom knowledge and understanding.

 Q/A: What is the glory of kings? Who are God's legal representatives on the earth?

Territory and influence are the glory of kings. Humans born into Christ's Kingdom who possess knowledge, understanding, and wisdom of right Kingdom concepts become God's legal representatives on the earth. It is precisely this knowledge that sets the foundation for Kingdom influence. Look at Habakkuk's prophecy closely: "For the earth will be filled with the knowledge of the glory of the LORD as the waters cover the sea." Jesus knew that by finding a group of disciples willing to seek first His Kingdom He would use them to unlock the influence of the Kingdom on the earth to the degree the waters cover the sea. The key to such influence is knowledge and understanding of the Kingdom which is received when we seek first the Kingdom. This specific knowledge and understanding contain the revelation necessary to influence earth with Heaven permanently.

The Spirit of Ownership

The spirit of ownership is the source of:

1. *Fear* – "I'm going to lose my things."
2. *Suspicion* – "Someone's trying to take my things."
3. *Competition* - For limited resources that you believe to be yours.
4. *Greed, poverty and covetousness, worry, jealousy, envy, strife, discrimination, racism, malice, deceit.*

The curse of ownership is broken by coming under the Lordship of King Jesus: In His Kingdom, these curses crumble under the weight of the mindset and mentality of the commonwealth Lordship of Jesus. As revealed in the book of Acts, a group of disciples living out this way of life receives supernatural provision both for the church and its immediate surroundings. The more groups that step into this revelation the broader the Kingdom influence.

 Q/A: How are these curses canceled in the Kingdom?

_____

_____

_____

These curses are canceled in the Kingdom by accepting the King's role as owner of everything and understanding our role as stewards working with Him. This decision sets in motion a response from Heaven and we begin seeing the very thing we set our hearts and mind to. We can rest assured a new existence awaits us. Anxiety, fear and all emotions connected to this world system collapse under the weight of quiet assurance and peaceful trust as the awareness of our Source becomes awakened. Imagine with me for a moment what it would look like if a group, city or nation clothed themselves with this way of thinking.

> *They devoted themselves to the apostles' teaching and to the fellowship, to the breaking of bread and to prayer. Everyone was filled with awe, and many wonders and miraculous signs were done by the apostles. All the believers were together and had everything in common. Selling their possessions and goods, they gave to anyone as he had need. Every day they continued to meet together in the temple courts. They broke bread in their homes and ate together with glad and sincere hearts, praising God and enjoying the favor of all the people. And the Lord added to their number daily those who were being saved.*
>
> Acts 2:42-3:1

What a beautiful picture of a group of followers of the Jesus way, living out this concept of commonwealth on earth! What materializes is an inward transformation resulting in righteousness, joy and peace. Put another way, the awakening of the Kingdom both within the individual, church, and its surroundings ends in expansion of Heaven's culture. "They broke bread in their homes and ate together with glad and sincere hearts, praising God and enjoying the favor of all the people. And the Lord added to their number daily those who were being saved"(Acts 2:46-47).

God's solution to man's problem of ownership is Lordship. The source of Lordship is the Kingdom. This is why we can have absolute confidence in the parable of the treasure. Truly when we find the Kingdom operated by a wealthy, loving Ruler who happens to be our Father, we've found EVERYTHING. Once discovered there remains but one question: Am I willing to take on the role of a child and submit to the Will of my Father? Am I willing to lay down my own agenda and ambition, no matter how noble and pick up my cross of self-denial, choosing the Will of my Father over mine? Making a decision to detach from our mindset of ownership opens the door for the Lordship paradigm to take root. What you don't receive by revelation you can take in through right thinking. Think Lordship not ownership. Think stewardship not possession. Become aware of patterned thoughts by thinking about what you're thinking about. Cast down those thoughts not in line with the Kingdom and sooner than later you will experience a collapse of a way of thinking conditioned after this world. This will make room for Kingdom thoughts to surface and remain, creating a transformation through the renewal of the mind. I pray what we initially count a loss will be realized as a gain.

Doing things under the yoke of this present system will quickly become repulsive as we find the only response to such a benevolent and loving King is ever increasing submission. The more we conform to our King's way of thinking the more revelation we will receive. "For whoever has will be given more, and they will have an abundance" (Matthew 25:29). It is my hope and earnest desire, we discover the only right response to such realization is acceptance and surrender to a benevolent King's way of doing things. A child of God is never safer than at home in the arms of his Heavenly Father.

The Kingdom Commonwealth Concept of Lordship

1. The key to all kingdoms is the king.
2. The glory of all kingdoms is influence through territory expansion. The glory of the Lord will fill the earth (Psalms 57:5, 11).
3. The power of all kings is personal ownership of territory.
4. The word "owner" is "*adon*" and it means "Lordship." The king automatically owns the country. All true kings are automatically the Lord or owner of the country and everything in it.
5. In true kingdoms, there is no private ownership. "The earth is the Lords and all that it contains" (Psalms 24:1, 1 Corinthians 10:26).

"Commonwealth" is the definition of a kingdom economic system.

*On their release, Peter and John went back to their own people and reported all that the chief priests and elders had said to them. When they heard this, they raised their voices together in prayer to God. "**Sovereign Lord**," they said, "you made the Heaven and the earth and the sea, and everything in them. You spoke by the Holy Spirit through the mouth of your servant, our father David: 'Why do the nations rage and the peoples plot in vain? The kings of the earth take their stand and the rulers gather together against the Lord and against his Anointed One.' Indeed Herod and Pontius Pilate met together with the Gentiles and the people of Israel in this city to conspire against your holy servant Jesus, whom you anointed. They did what your power and will had decided beforehand should happen. Now, Lord, consider their threats and enable your servants to speak your word with great boldness. Stretch out your hand to heal and perform miraculous signs and wonders through the name of your holy servant Jesus." After they prayed, the place where they were meeting was shaken. And they were all filled with the Holy Spirit and spoke the word of God boldly. All the believers were one in heart and mind. No one claimed that any of his possessions was his own, but they shared everything they had. With great power, the apostles continued to testify to the resurrection of the Lord Jesus, and much grace was upon them all. There were no needy persons among them. For from time to time, those who owned lands or houses sold them, brought the money from the sales and put it at the apostles' feet, and it was distributed to anyone as he had need. Joseph, a Levite from Cyprus, whom the apostles called Barnabas (which means Son of Encouragement), sold a field he owned and brought the money and put it at the apostles' feet.*

Acts 4:23-37

Here we see a kingdom commonwealth community on earth described. The believers began praying by addressing God as "Sovereign Lord" identifying their understanding and acknowledgment of Jesus as King. They knew they were addressing not a religious leader but the king of a country they were part of. Like the first century church, as we commit to becoming students of the message of the Kingdom we too will enter into relationship with the Lord of Heaven. This relationship will produce a radical change in the way the church functions on the earth and begin drawing multitudes into the Kingdom. When we begin seeing ourselves the way the first century church saw themselves, as Kingdom citizens living in Heaven on earth, then we to will experience life the way they did.

The early believers were being harassed by government and religious leaders and needed help. They asked, "Now Lord, consider their threats and enable your servants to speak your word with great boldness. Stretch out your hand to heal and perform signs and wonders" (Acts 4:29-30). God's immediate response to the disciples prayer to speak in an ambassadorial role was to extend His Kingdom to earth. He found a legal representative willing to do His bidding. Immediately God sent Heaven's chief government representative, the Holy Spirit, and they spoke the word of God boldly. After that, a manifestation of life under Kingdom Commonwealth took place as, "All the believers were one in heart and mind. No one claimed any ownership of their possessions but shared everything" (Acts 4:32). Great power was in their midst. God's grace was so powerful not one person was in need. All things were given to those in need.

This continual expression of Kingdom life did not come into existence without intentional focus on the Will and plan Jesus. We discuss this in great detail in *Chapter 13: Discipleship*. For now know this: The primary focus of the leaders of the church in the book of Acts was seeking first the Kingdom. Their obedience to Jesus' top priority for them became the foundation for Kingdom expression and a catalyst to the ever-expanding demonstration of Heaven's culture. The same model is available to us. Heaven is waiting to move in on a group of individuals seeking first the Kingdom of God and His righteousness. As these groups begin taking form within the church, Heaven will invade earth in the same manner in which it did in the book of Acts.

2 Corinthians 8 reveals further validation of Christ's commonwealth economic system that functions through a group of educated students of Jesus. Paul is addressing financial inequality amongst the churches. He acknowledged some churches as having more than others and encouraged those with plenty to give to those in need. In verses 13-15, Paul gives his reason for recommending this exchange: "Our desire is not that others might be relieved while you are hard pressed, but that there might be equality. At the present time, your plenty will supply what they

need so that in turn their plenty will supply what you need." The goal is equality, as it is written: "The one who gathered much did not have too much, and the one who gathered little did not have too little." This is a beautiful picture of Heaven's economic system of commonwealth being implemented on earth. Life under the commonwealth economic system of Heaven has security far surpassing that of any earthly system and contains a rewarding component to it that cannot be found in a system of ownership. May the revelation of Kingdom commonwealth arise in your heart and mind. As it does, I pray for faith and boldness to pioneer a group of like-minded Saints and wait on the Lord for Him to show Himself strong on your behalf.

> *Then Moses went up to God, and the Lord called to him from the mountain and said, "This is what you are to say to the house of Jacob and what you are to tell the people of Israel: 'You yourselves have seen what I did to Egypt, and how I carried you on eagles' wings and brought you to myself. Now if you obey me fully and keep my covenant, then out of all nations you will be my treasured possession. Although the whole earth is mine, you will be for me a kingdom of priests and a holy nation.' These are the words you are to speak to the Israelites."*
>
> Exodus 19:3-6

God was telling Moses, "the whole earth is mine and I will choose a group of people to display My ownership through. They will be a Kingdom of priests, not a religious organization but a fully functioning government. A spiritual government so in union with Me by the time I'm done the colony will look just like My Country." And how did God say He will fulfill this? "If you obey me fully" and "keep my covenant." To obey Him fully is to be righteous. Jesus fulfilled the first part when He gave us His righteousness. In order to keep His covenant, we must educate ourselves as to what the covenant is. This comes to pass as we take on Jesus' top priority for us, seeking His Kingdom. The covenant is not concealed but revealed in the Constitution. It is laid bare in plain sight for all who have put on the eye salve found in the field of seeking first the Kingdom. The mysteries of God are not hidden from us but rather hidden for us. "It is the glory of God to conceal a matter; to search out a matter is the glory of kings" (Proverbs 25:2).

 Note: It is the author's belief that the most important and expansive covenant Jesus contracted with us is found in His statement, "Seek first his kingdom and his righteousness, and all these things will be given to you as well–Jesus is the head of the Kingdomology department at the school of the Spirit looking to train, equip, and release Kingdomologists.

The earth is the Lord's, and everything in it, the world, and all who live in it; for he founded it upon the seas and established it upon the waters.

Psalms 24:1-2

Every creator legally owns what he creates. By the creative rights of God, He is the legal owner of the earth and all that is in it. A key to understanding the concept of commonwealth is seeing a citizen's access to everything within the Kingdom at the King's discretion. The wealth in the Kingdom is not for the King, but for every citizen. The wealth of the King is for the welfare of His citizens. All those who understand and have experienced the heart of the Father are ready to step into Heaven's commonwealth economy. This chapter provides the understanding of God's commonwealth economic system. All we need to do is make the decision to step into the renewed way of thinking and God will bring the transformation. Through revelation, faith, and patience we inherit the better way: The way of the Kingdom!

The most powerful human motivation is self-preservation. Social scientist Abraham Maslow concluded all humans are motivated by the same basic needs. These needs being water, food, shelter, protection, significance and self-actualization, which is the need to know we have purpose.

 Q/A: How do we get water, food, shelter, protection, significance and purpose?

Michael Gissibl

The answer is the economy. All these needs are met through our economy. Since all humans are motivated by self-preservation, the economy is the most powerful and influential system on earth.

Jesus understood Maslow's theory but disagreed with how to get our needs met. Our economic system says, "If you want to fulfill your needs, get a job, go to school, get a good education, work hard, earn a paycheck and buy water, get food, buy a house or rent an apartment and buy locks."

The problem with this economic system is it patterns the mind to think in terms of ownership and places the responsibility upon us to get what we want and need. We must first depend on our ability to get a good education so we can have a good job to buy enough water for our family and a nice house for us to raise them. Then we have to rely on our government to sustain the economy in order for us to continue to receive a paycheck to provide for our loved ones. This is tiresome, to say the least, yet we have embraced this system causing it to become a stronghold in our thinking, thus making it our way of life. Furthermore, the moment we receive a paycheck as something we earned we accept ownership. This concept is further conceptualized and perpetuated when we deposit it in "our bank account" and write checks from "our checking account" and buy things with "our money." This idea of ownership eventually takes root in every area of our lives and becomes a conditioned mindset producing patterned behavior.

Who has bewitched us? How have we fallen so far away from the plan and Will of God? Under the world's economic system we go to work to live. Most of the world's economic system is called "Capitalism" or a "mixed market system." The latter means "aspects of both a free market capitalism system and a government socialism system merged into a mixture of the two. Under the Kingdom's economic system we go to work to learn, develop character and bring Heaven's culture and way of life to our job. As we learn Kingdom concepts and principles we apply them to our daily lives. Under the world's system, the economy is used to "preserve" us. We get our self-worth and self-esteem largely from the economy. If we are "successful" pride and arrogance usually follows as we begin thinking of ourselves more highly than we ought. If we live below the norms set by society we often take on a low self-esteem and even resort to cheating, stealing and other unhealthy adaptive behaviors.

Heaven's invitation is to "Lay it all down! Enter the rest of the Lord through the understanding and appropriation of His Lordship over our lives." As we seek first His Kingdom, we are placed under the care of His Kingdom economic system. The most stable, reliable system ever conceived.

Some nations are presently engaged in a currency war. They are manipulating the value of currency through many unjust tactics. There is no better time than the present to invest in the most stable currency in world history, the currency of Heaven.

 Q/A: What currency does Heaven offer?

_____

_____

_____

The answer is faith. Faith is the currency of Heaven. A belief system that emerges out of the discipline of seeking first the Kingdom. Seeking first the Kingdom is to faith like the refiner is to gold. The longer you remain in the furnace of seeking first the Kingdom the more your belief system will be made pure: transfigured into the image and likeness of the King. You have been given the mind of Christ, whether or not you take it upon yourself is a matter only you can decide. When Jesus declared in Luke 11:52: "Woe to you experts in the law, because you have taken away the key to knowledge. You yourselves have not entered, and you have hindered those who were entering." Amongst other things He was sounding a warning. "If you don't take back the knowledge of the Kingdom you will lose your currency, your ability to enact business with Heaven."

Jesus counseled us to "buy from me gold refined in the fire, so you can become rich; and white clothes to wear, so you can cover your shameful nakedness; and salve to put on your eyes, so you can see" (Revelation 3:18). The headquarters of Jesus' business is Heaven where the medium of exchange is faith—belief found while seeking first the Kingdom. Is it even possible to "do business" with Jesus outside of His Kingdom? Since

Jesus is seated on the throne in Heaven I would submit we need to enter the Kingdom of Heaven before "buying" from the King.

The economy is the process by which we all seek to survive and have our needs met. The economy has become our life. When the economy fails our life fails. This is why it's important to be rooted and grounded in the right economy. Jesus promises us if we "seek first the kingdom of God …." He will become our Source, thus making Himself our economy. Make a decision today to begin anchoring yourself to the Kingdom commonwealth economy. We do this by seeking to understand the King's way of providing for us while accepting our Father as our source.

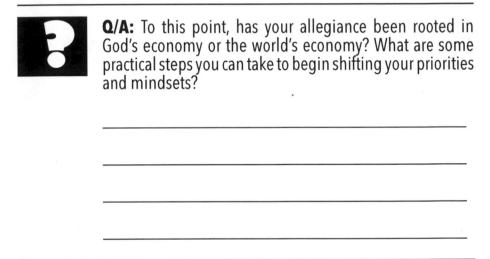

Q/A: To this point, has your allegiance been rooted in God's economy or the world's economy? What are some practical steps you can take to begin shifting your priorities and mindsets?

_____

_____

_____

_____

The economic concept of Jesus removes the earthly economy as our source of life and places the King of Heaven as our source. The difficulty with this reality is we have been conditioned by the world of substance to believe that "if you can't see it, then it's not real." If we could dare to suspend this belief long enough to give Jesus a chance, our belief system will be changed. Paul exhorted the church in Corinth to "fix our eyes not on what is seen, but on what is unseen, since what is seen is temporary, but what is unseen is eternal." This requires an intentional commitment I pray you carry out long enough to receive vision of the eternal Kingdom. The substance found in faith contains an essence that satisfies the human heart in ways the world's substance will never know.

Q/A: What is the key to the Kingdom of Heaven's economy?

Lordship

The answer is Lordship. This is a difficult concept as well for those that have been conditioned in a democracy. Nevertheless, it is of utmost importance to our economic security—and our ability to no longer conform to the pattern of this world economy. In God's country, His Lordship is the entirety of the economic system. All goods flow from His river of provision. Receiving this revelation shifts our priorities and creates more time to devote to seeking the Kingdom.

The key to economic stability and development is Lordship. This principle applies equally to the individual, church, community, city, state and nation. The word "Lord" is used more than 5000 times in the Bible. We cannot be a student of the Bible and not understand the term "Lord" any more than we can experience the Kingdom apart from accepting King Jesus as Lord. God is waiting for a community to model the Kingdom economic system in order that He might show Himself strong: first to the community, then to others willing to step out in faith.

The problem in America is we cannot live in a democracy and embrace "Lordship." We must come out from among the world's system and be separate from it. "Do not conform to the pattern of this world, but be transformed by the renewing of your mind" (Romans 12:2a). The number one claim God makes about Himself is He is "Lord." To the degree we are delivered from the worldly system which is opposite the Kingdom is the degree we will come to know the Lordship of Jesus experientially.

I am the Lord, and there is no other; apart from me there is no God.
I will strengthen you, though you have not acknowledged me, so that

from the rising of the sun to the place of its setting men may know there is none besides me. I am the Lord, and there is no other.

Isaiah 45:5-6

"Lordship" is the source of all conflict and comfort to mankind. If we surrender to His Lordship we will find comfort. As we discover His way of doing things, He proves to be a trustworthy provider. If we choose not to, we place ourselves in conflict with the Lord and His Will and purposes. As you see nations crumble and economic systems fail consider it an invitation to jump ship from earthly government into the Kingdom.

The term "**Lord**" is reserved for kings and their kingdoms. The king owns everything in his kingdom. Knowing and understanding Lordship will empower us to walk into a lion's den with peace. We'll experience the same storms as everybody else, but only what He has built will remain. As we submit to Christ, any and all shaking in our lives moves us in the direction of the Kingdom. This brings great comfort as we accept the things we "lose" as a means of God establishing us more firmly in His Kingdom. In the Kingdom, loss, persecution, suffering and the like become an agent through which we might "obtain a better resurrection" (Hebrews 11:35).

I am not saying this because I am in need, for I have learned to be content whatever the circumstances. I know what it is to be in need, and I know what it is to have plenty. I have learned the secret of being content in any and every situation, whether well-fed or hungry, whether living in plenty or in want. I can do everything through him who gives me strength.

Philippians 4:11-13

Paul understood Lordship so much he was able to live life in steady confidence with an attitude that His unfailing Father would provide for Him perfectly no matter the circumstance. Listen again to Paul's testimony: "I have learned to be content whatever the circumstances. I know what it is to be in need, and I know what it is to have plenty. I have learned the secret of being content in any and every situation, whether well-fed or hungry, whether living in plenty or in want." Paul knew everything he had was from the Lord. He knew he owned nothing and his "Source" would take care of him. He discovered a security outside of people, places, and things. He put his trust in what he came to know as a loving King able to care for him perfectly. The great Apostle Paul found the essence of life to be in an invisible world. Simply put, Paul was at rest living in the Kingdom.

Additionally, Paul discovered his place in Christ and from that place strength was provided for everything! It is the author's belief that Paul came to the realization the King and the Kingdom are one in the same. A thorough study of Paul's life has me believing he discovered the nature of King Jesus to be the Kingdom. His appearance was that of a man but His essence was indeed the Kingdom. Paul came as close as any to representing this king-Kingdom relationship partly through his understanding of Jesus' relationship to the Kingdom. This is the church's great challenge of the hour. May we too re-discover the surpassingly great revelations of the king-Kingdom relationship in order to begin functioning out of our identity in Christ.

We have democratized the church so much so that prosperity is "spiritualized capitalism." We can't bring capitalism into God's Kingdom any more than we can bring in other forms within earthly government. God says, "That's not My system. I have a system I implemented from the foundation of the world and that is the system I have blessed. I cannot and will not bless a system that has its roots in a kingdom opposing mine. Come out from amongst earthly economic and governmental ways of thinking."

When God cooperates with man the result is our present condition. When man cooperates with God the effects of the life of Jesus and the first-century church become our outcome. Seeking first the Kingdom is the first step in cooperating with Jesus and His Kingdom plan!

It's time we stop asking God to come into our system and plead for Him to adjust us to His Will. It's time for the church to move out from under the world's system into the Kingdom of Heaven's system. As we change our way of thinking we will experience life the way God designed it.

Free of worry. Free of anxiety. Free to be content in any and every situation. Free from the curses that come with ownership. Full of contentment, joy, and peace infused with a gift to persuade and influence others in the direction of the Kingdom's economic system.

God's System vs. the World's System

Therefore I tell you, do not worry about your life, what you will eat or drink; or about your body, what you will wear. Is not life more important than food, and the body more important than clothes? Look at the birds of the air; they do not sow or reap or store away in barns, and yet your Heavenly Father feeds them. Are you not much more valuable than they? Who of you by worrying can add a single hour to his life? And why do you worry about clothes? See how the lilies of the field grow. They do not labor or spin. Yet I tell you that not even Solomon in all his splendor was dressed like one of these. If that is how God clothes the grass of the field, which is here today and tomorrow is thrown into the fire, will he not much more clothe you, O you of little faith? So do not worry, saying, 'What shall we eat?' or 'What shall we drink?' or 'What shall we wear?' For the pagans run after all these things, and your Heavenly Father knows that you need them. But seek first his kingdom and his righteousness, and all these things will be given to you as well.

Matthew 6:25-33

Once again, we see in Matthew how Jesus proposes the most secure economic system ever presented to mankind. Jesus never shifted the needs of humanity. He merely shifted the source; where we get things from. He turned our attention from earth to Heaven. We suffer worry because we have the wrong source. We experience fear and anxiety because our conditioned way of thinking is anchored to something other than the understanding and revelation of the commonwealth economy of Heaven. Shift your thinking in order that times of refreshing may come (Acts 3:19).

 Q/A: How do we actually make the shift from the wrong source to the right one?

Understand, in God's economy, what pagans consider the reason for living, God considers a "bonus." What Maslow calls our "motivating needs," God says, "I'll throw in for good measure."

God's System	World's System
We go to work to LEARN. We go to work to influence territory for our country, to be yeast, salt, and light. In the Kingdom, life is experienced through the act of seeking first the Kingdom of God and His righteousness.	We go to work to EARN MONEY TO LIVE. We go to work to feed our family and to pay for needed things. Under earthly systems, we experience life as we go to work to provide for ourselves and acquire things.

Problems are not problems, they are opportunities. A problem becomes a problem only when our foundation is wrong. The Israelites under the rulership (Lordship) of God received:
- Protection (Exodus 13:21, 14:19)
- Provision to get through hardships (Exodus14:21-29)
- Financial provision (Psalms 105:37)
- Destruction of their enemies (Exodus 14:25-31)
- Water in the desert (Exodus 15:22-25 & 17:2-6)
- Food in the desert (Exodus 16:4,13-18)
- Victory over their enemies (Exodus 17:8-13)

Herein lies a great example of the results of a community giving themselves over to the mind and Will of the government of Heaven! They had everything they needed! After rejecting God's rule and choosing their own government, however, the Israelites brought hardships on themselves. 1 Samuel 8:10-18 lists all the hardships that would come upon them as a result of choosing to have a king other than the Lord as their governing influence. The moment they chose to come out of Heavenly living under the Lordship of the All Mighty, they exchanged freedom for enslavement. The Israelites ignorantly but willingly placed themselves in the hands of the kingdom of darkness and the Devil was given more power to control the systems of rulership over them. Pay close attention to how similar our government presently treats and rules over us.

> *Samuel told all the words of the Lord to the people who were asking him for a king. He said, "This is what the king who will reign over you will do: He will take your sons and make them serve with his chariots and horses, and they will run in front of his chariots. Some he will assign to be commanders of thousands and commanders of fifties, and others to plow his ground and reap his harvest, and still others to make weapons of war and equipment for his chariots. He will take your daughters to be perfumers and cooks and bakers. He will take the best of your fields and vineyards and olive groves and give them to his attendants. He will take a tenth of your grain and of your vintage and give it to his officials and attendants. Your menservants and maidservants and the best of your cattle and donkeys he will take for his own use. He will take a tenth of your flocks, and you yourselves will become his slaves. When that day comes, you will cry out for relief from the king you have chosen, and the Lord will not answer you in that day.*
>
> 1 Samuel 8:10-18

The contrast between the two governmental systems of rulership is clear. Today, we find ourselves in the same predicament as the Israelites did after choosing to rule themselves. We live under the oppression of the governments of the world largely controlled by the kingdom of darkness. This world's system is using our kids to fight their wars, taxing and taxing us more and enslaving society for their own gain. Power has been consolidated into the hands of a few. Their heavy hand is upon the whole world. They have become sold out to Satan and are committed to steal, kill, and destroy whatever is necessary to build their own kingdoms. The only power capable of tearing down this system of bondage and enslavement is the Kingdom of Heaven.

Moving forward are we going to continue allowing this, or will we surrender all to the Lordship of Jesus and begin crying out once again for the Moses' to rise up? Are we going to let the government systems of the world control our life or the Kingdom of Heaven? As members of the Church Jesus is building, we must rise up and begin understanding what needs to take place in order for us to come back under the governing influence of God. The answer will be discovered and re-instituted as we humble ourselves, pray, and turn from our own ways to seek first the Kingdom of God and His righteousness.

Are we going to continue to make our source the world economy, and our ability to provide for ourselves, or are we going to embrace the Lordship of our Father and make Him our source? Are we going to continue to pursue things or make it our top priority to pursue the Kingdom, knowing He will add all things to us? Knowledge empowers us as we understand God's ways and make a decision to come under the governing influence of Heaven. The more we seek knowledge of the Kingdom, the more empowered we become as the Lord adds understanding, revelation, and wisdom to our knowledge. May we all choose this day to serve the Lord, first, by making His top priority for us our top priority. May we all, in unity of heart confess, *as for me and my house we will choose the Lord.*

A decision to leave the ways of Egypt brings deliverance from the ways of the world. This decision becomes the moment of our deliverance from Egypt. However, in order for Egypt to leave us, we must commit to the process of renewing our minds in the direction of Kingdom thought. Seeking first the Kingdom is the Lord's instrument for removing the ways of the world first within us, then within the systems of government.

 Application: Declare today that you have no other source for life, liberty, and the pursuit of happiness than our Father in Heaven. Commit your whole being, heart, and soul to the Father and start walking in Kingdom life today. Be patient with yourself as you transition out from under the yoke of this world's economic system.

Your name   Date

Chapter Ten

Fasting

Biblical fasting is abstaining from food, and at times, drink, and other wants, needs, and pleasures. Fasting helps remind us there's a price to pay for representing Heaven on earth. There are some things you can't get done without fasting. In the days ahead the church must reach levels of humility beyond the ordinary. Fasting is a primary means to this end. The disciples loved God, followed Jesus and spent lots of time in His presence. On one occasion they learned an important lesson regarding fasting and its relationship to Heaven expressing itself on earth. A lesson that invites us into a deeper, more fulfilling life in the Spirit.

Then one of the crowd answered and said, "Teacher, I brought You my son, who has a mute spirit. And wherever it seizes him, it throws him down; he foams at the mouth, gnashes his teeth, and becomes rigid. So I spoke to Your disciples, that they should cast it out, but they could not." He answered him and said, "O faithless generation, how long shall I be with you? How long shall I bear with you? Bring him to Me." Then they brought him to Him. And when he saw Him, immediately the spirit convulsed him, and he fell on the ground and wallowed, foaming at the mouth. So He asked his father, "How long has this been happening to him?" And he said, "From childhood. And often he has thrown him both into the fire and into the water to destroy him. But if You can do anything, have compassion on us and help us." Jesus said to him, "If you can believe, all things are possible to him who believes." Immediately the father of the child cried out and said with tears, "Lord, I believe; help my unbelief!" When Jesus saw that the people came running together, He rebuked the unclean spirit, saying to it, "Deaf and dumb spirit, I command you, come out of him and enter him no more!" Then the spirit cried out, convulsed him greatly, and came out of him. And he became as one dead, so that many said, "He is dead." But Jesus took him by the hand and lifted him up, and he arose. And when He had come into the house, His disciples asked Him privately, "Why could we not cast it out?" So He said to them, "This kind can come out by nothing but prayer and fasting."

Mark 9:17-29 (NKJV)

Here we have an example of when the disciples couldn't cast out a demon. They had done it before (Matthew 10:5-8). Why didn't it work this time?

There are things we want Jesus to do that require a price we need to pay—a price more costly than our present state of existence. There are also things Jesus wants us to do but require greater measures of self-sacrifice. We must learn to overcome the power of our belly in order to fulfill God's Will on earth. When the disciples asked Jesus why they couldn't cast out the demon He answered, "this kind does not go out except by prayer and fasting" (Matthew17:21). "You're praying and you got that right," Jesus is saying. "But in some of the work I have for you fasting is required." In the Kingdom fasting is not only required for greater works, it is essential to expressing the life of Christ in and through us.

 Q/A: What does fasting accomplish?

_____

_____

The Spirit World is a Spiritual World

Fasting increases your capacity to receive spiritual power.

It's interesting to note that due to Jesus' ability to cast out the demon, He obviously had been fasting and praying. This beckons us to consider strongly the idea of incorporating fasting in our lives. If Jesus, the Son of God fasted, how important is it for us who desire to walk in His footsteps? Fasting is a God-appointed way to humbling ourselves. Fasting is one act in which we pick up our cross. It becomes an important part of the process of dying to the self-life. God never says He will humble us. He tells us to humble ourselves (Luke 14:11, James 4:10, 1 Peter 5:5-6).

Don't pray, "God humble me." Instead, figure out how to humble yourself. The first sin in the universe was pride coming from Lucifer (Isaiah 14:12-15). We are brought low or highly elevated depending whether we humble ourselves or not. John Bunyan prayed, "He that is down need fear no fall. He that is low, no pride. He that is humble ever shall have God to be his guide." We can rest assured we will be exalted if we humble ourselves. The Lord knows the proud from afar off and that's where He keeps them.

> *Though the Lord is on high, he looks upon the lowly, but the proud he knows from afar.*
>
> Psalms 138:6

To those who may think this is merely an Old Testament concept. Consider the following:

> *But he gives us more grace. That is why Scripture says: "God opposes the proud but gives grace to the humble." Submit yourselves, then, to God. Resist the devil, and he will flee from you. Come near to God and he will come near to you. Wash your hands, you sinners, and purify your hearts, you double-minded. Grieve, mourn and wail. Change your laughter to mourning and your joy to gloom. Humble yourselves before the Lord, and he will lift you up.*
>
> James 4:6-10

Fasting is One of the Most Effective Ways to Humble Ourselves

In Psalms 35:13, David humbled his soul with fasting. The soul is the arrogant, selfish part of our humanness. Until the soul becomes the servant to the spiritual man it will oppose God every time it becomes agitated. Before transformation, its carnal fleshly appetites wage war against the Will and purpose of God. Reading Leviticus 16:29-31, we see God wanted the Israelites to "afflict their souls." The Jewish people knew this to mean, "to go without food and fast." Israel was required to fast (humble their souls) in order to receive the benefit of the sacrifice offered on their behalf. In Acts 27:9 this day is called "The Fast" which is New Testament confirmation that the Old Testament phrase "afflict our souls" meant fasting. Although we can't work to earn anything from God, the act of fasting is an outward expression that we are humbling ourselves. We are acting in such a manner as to show the Lord we deny ourselves because we want to see the life of Christ possess more of our being. This moves God to draw near and exalt us for His purposes.

Consider Ezra 8:21. After the Babylonian Captivity, Ezra the priest was assigned the task of leading a group of exiles back from Babylon to Jerusalem. Ezra was on a long journey where there were many potential problems (robbers, enemies of Israel, weather issues, sickness). He not only had woman and children with him but some of the most precious vessels of the temple. The question he needed answered was "how am I going to get safe passage?" Ezra proclaimed a public fast and the hand of the Lord gave them safe passage (vs. 31). Fasting, and the humbleness it produced, moved God's hand of protection over Ezra and his people. When we think we're doing the Lord's Will, it's wise to begin fasting. This helps anchor us to humility, the position where God moves on our behalf. We can attempt to bring about God's Will, but if pride arises it positions us to be on our own, an impossible place to fulfill His Will.

Ahab was a wicked king who married Jezebel. He led Israel into wickedness.

Ahab said to Elijah, "So you have found me, my enemy!" "I have found you," he answered, "because you have sold yourself to do evil in the eyes of the Lord. I am going to bring disaster on you. I will consume your descendants and cut off from Ahab every last male in Israel—slave or free. I will make your house like that of Jeroboam son of Nebat and that of Baasha son of Ahijah, because you have provoked me to anger and have caused Israel to sin." And also concerning Jezebel the Lord says: "Dogs will devour Jezebel by the wall of Jezreel. Dogs will eat those belonging to Ahab who die in the city, and the birds of the air will feed on those who die in the country." (There was never a man like Ahab, who sold himself to do evil in the eyes of the Lord, urged on by Jezebel his wife. He behaved in the vilest manner by going after idols, like the Amorites the Lord drove out before Israel.) When Ahab heard these words, he tore his clothes, put on sackcloth and fasted. He lay in sackcloth and went around meekly. Then the word of the

Lord came to Elijah the Tishbite: "Have you noticed how Ahab has humbled himself before me? Because he has humbled himself, I will not bring this disaster in his day, but I will bring it on his house in the days of his son."

1 Kings 21:20-29

In 1 Kings 21, Elijah had a confrontation with Ahab and pronounced God's judgment (vs 22-25). In Verses 27-29 it says Ahab humbled himself by fasting. The Lord responded "See (understand) how Ahab has humbled himself before me? Because he has humbled himself before me, I will not bring the calamity in his days ...." Here is a wicked king having the Judgment of God pronounced on him. He humbles himself by fasting and God lifts the judgment from him. A key to experiencing the fruit of fasting for the sake of the Kingdom is UNDERSTANDING it was Ahab's fasting that moved God's hand for earth's sake.

 Q/A: If fasting can do this for a wicked king what's the potential for His beloved church?

Jonah, a prophet of God, walked into a wicked, violent city and pronounced judgment on it. He presented a message from God letting the people know their city would be destroyed. In Jonah chapter 3 the inhabitants of Nineveh all fasted (vs. 6). God saw their works and relented from the disaster. If fasting could do this for Nineveh what might it do for your city or nation? Remember, God is the same yesterday, today and forever. Not only does His character remain unchanged, so too do the methods laid out in scripture. Let's consider these examples of the Lord's response to fasting a prototype for the present day church. As we identify our role as Heaven's agent of change, may we clothe ourselves with humbleness that sprouts from fasting and wait in expectancy for God to move like He did in days of old.

In the book of Esther, an evil man named Haman succeeded in

bringing a plot to take down an entire nation and its people. The decree went out but there was a woman named Esther who succeeded in diverting disaster. What was her plan? "Go gather all the Jews who are present in Shushan, and fast for me: neither eat nor drink for three days, night or day. My maids and I will fast likewise" (Esther 4:16). By the end, the situation had reversed and ended in triumph for the people and their nation. The turning point was when God's people fasted.

Humbling ourselves moves God to act in unique and special ways. For those walking in the Kingdom, it might be almost impossible to exaggerate the potential fasting has on changing the course of history.

An Individual Fast

In 2 Corinthians 6:5 and 11:27 we see that twice Paul gives a list of the ways he proved himself a Minister of Christ. In both lists he mentioned fasting. Scripture also informs us Paul fasted often (2 Corinthians 11:27 & Acts 9:9). Christ's Ministers need to fast. For that matter, all those in the Kingdom need to fast in order to humble themselves in a Christlike manner. It is also important to understand an individual fast is a viable means of denying ourselves, something Jesus told us was a necessary character trait of a disciple. A fasting lifestyle, therefore, becomes a legitimate means of anchoring ourselves to self denial.

A Corporate Fast

In the church at Antioch there were prophets and teachers: Barnabas, Simeon called Niger, Lucius of Cyrene, Manaen (who had been brought up with Herod the tetrarch) and Saul. While they were worshiping the Lord and fasting, the Holy Spirit said, "Set apart for me Barnabas and Saul for the work to which I have called them." So after they had fasted and prayed, they placed their hands on them and sent them off. The two of them, sent on their way by the Holy Spirit, went down to Seleucia and sailed from there to Cyprus.

Acts 13:1-4

One of the most significant moments in the book of Acts, the sending forth of Apostles, took place in Acts 13. There were five men recognized as prophets and teachers in that local body (vs. 1). The Bible says they ministered to the Lord by fasting (vs. 2). At one of the most crucial points in the history of the church, the leaders were found fasting. Instead of forming a committee or gathering an elders meeting they vacated from all activity, fasted and waited on God. He honored this protocol and spoke His Will by identifying who was to be sent out; Barnabas and Saul. After this revelation, the church didn't send them immediately. Instead, they fasted again, waiting on the timing of God. Then the apostolic ministry was birthed (vss. 3-4). The first time the church fasted to find God's Will, the second time they fasted to commit the men to carrying out God's Will. This is a scriptural pattern for "thy will be done on earth" waiting to be picked up and implemented once again. As this puzzle piece to Kingdom expression is incorporated back into the church, we become better equipped to carry Kingdom power. Since signs and wonders are the most effective witness of the existence of the Kingdom, let's be diligent to incorporate this necessary prerequisite to manifesting Kingdom power. No amount of religious activity will ever compare to the combination of fasting and waiting on God.

As the story continues, we encounter additional insight. By Acts 14:14 Barnabas and Saul are no longer called Prophets and Teachers but Apostles. The word "apostle" means "sent one." This is another scriptural pattern initiated by God that reveals how we can establish and institute apostolic ministry today. If Prophets and Teachers wait on God fasting, praying, and seeking Him, it opens a biblical means to send forth Apostles. The early church set the pattern and established the model. If we want to receive God's Will and implement it on earth we need to gather together, fast, pray and wait. The church who applies this protocol and has the foundation of seeking first the Kingdom will become catalysts for Kingdom expression and expansion. I encourage all leaders in the church to lay a foundation of seeking first the Kingdom while adding this protocol. As you do, I believe a shift towards Kingdom manifestation will begin.

The Apostles won many to the Lord in the cities they visited. The influx of disciples caused the Apostles to begin establishing churches. An essential component of the church is governmental leadership. The Bible calls these leaders "Elders." In Acts 14:21-23 the Apostles appointed Elders with prayer and fasting. The Apostles once again found God's mind through prayer and fasting. The establishment of Apostles and Elders in the early church both came about through prayer and fasting.

Q/A: Why would we expect to do it any other way? Can we improve on God's original methods?

_____

_____

_____

Note: The 2 Chronicles 7:14 prayer may have been where the early church found its pattern of establishing the Will of God on earth.

If my people, who are called by my name, will humble themselves and pray and seek my face and turn from their wicked ways, then will I hear from Heaven and will forgive their sin and will heal their land.

2 Chronicles 7:14

The similarities between prayer and fasting are striking.

And when you pray, do not be like the hypocrites, for they love to pray standing in the synagogues and on the street corners to be seen by men. I tell you the truth, they have received their reward in full. But when you pray, go into your room, close the door and pray to your Father, who is unseen. Then your Father, who sees what is done in secret, will reward you. And when you pray, do not keep on babbling like pagans, for they think they will be heard because of their many words. Do not be like them, for your Father knows what you need before you ask him.

Matthew 6:5-8

When you fast, do not look somber as the hypocrites do, for they disfigure their faces to show men they are fasting. I tell you the truth, they have received their reward in full. But when you fast, put oil on your head and wash your face, so that it will not be obvious to men

*that you are fasting, but only to your Father, who is unseen; and your
Father, who sees what is done in secret, will reward you.*

Matthew 6:16-18

There is a close parallel between what Jesus says about prayer and
fasting. He explains first how not to pray and concludes by teaching how
to pray. He goes on telling us how not to fast and concludes by teaching
us how. The phrase "when you pray" is an indication Jesus expected
his disciples to pray. The phrase "when you fast" is an indication Jesus
expected his disciples to fast. Jesus put praying and fasting on the same
level. If Jesus expects us to pray he expects us to fast.

Q/A: Why was the first act of Jesus fasting?

_____

_____

This is how He chose to enter ministry. The leader of the church,
Jesus Himself, chose to begin earthly ministry by humbling Himself
through fasting. Could it be He was establishing and strengthening His
connection with the Father by anchoring Himself to humbleness of
heart? Could it be Jesus understood things about fasting the church is
yet to grasp? As important as fasting appears to be, we need revelation
and understanding beyond our present level. May the spirit of wisdom
and revelation enlighten us to humble ourselves through fasting and
empower us to enter greater depths of meekness. If it's true the meek
will inherit the earth, and it is, then fasting is a necessary discipline that
awakens the spirit of meekness and enables us to be clothed in such a
nature.

The disciples of John the Baptist, whom Jesus said, "was the greatest
amongst men," asked Jesus, "How is it that we and the Pharisees fast, but
your disciples do not fast?"

*Jesus answered, "How can the guests of the bridegroom mourn while
he is with them? The time will come when the bridegroom will be*

taken from them; then they will fast."

Matthew 9:15

In other words, the students of John are right to fast. Jesus' students will begin fasting once He has been taken out of the earth. Jesus prophesied that we would fast. There will come a point in time when the Lord will begin speaking to us of the importance and necessity of fasting. If we are already fasting, may it become a lifestyle. If not yet, may we be introduced to this discipline now and experience the Lord draw nearer than ever.

Increasing Spiritual Power

Food is the substance used by our physical body to provide strength and energy to the body, much like fasting provides spiritual qualities to our spiritual man. Food awakens and energizes our natural man. Fasting awakens and energizes our spiritual man. Fasting provides opportunity for the divine nature within us to exercise authority over our flesh. This elevates the spirit man to his rightful position over the natural man, silencing the demands of our fleshly nature. "He that rules his spirit is better than he that takes a city" (Proverbs16:32b).

 Q/A: If this is true, what is our influence potential?

_____

_____

_____

The mind governed by the flesh is death, but the mind governed by the Spirit is life and peace.

Romans 8:6

When we fast we are strengthening the spiritual side of our being and exercising dominion over our flesh. The broader our fasting spreads into other areas outside of food the more our spiritual man is given rulership authority over our flesh. Fasting, therefore, becomes a key to activating the principles that are found in 1 Corinthians 2:6-16:

We do, however, speak a message of wisdom among the mature, but not the wisdom of this age or of the rulers of this age, who are coming to nothing. No, we declare God's wisdom, a mystery that has been hidden and that God destined for our glory before time began. None of the rulers of this age understood it, for if they had, they would not have crucified the Lord of glory. However, as it is written: "What no eye has seen, what no ear has heard, and what no human mind has conceived the things God has prepared for those who love him, these are the things God has revealed to us by his Spirit. The Spirit searches all things, even the deep things of God. For who knows a person's thoughts except their own spirit within them? In the same way, no one knows the thoughts of God except the Spirit of God. What we have received is not the spirit of the world, but the Spirit who is from God, so that we may understand what God has freely given us. This is what we speak, not in words taught us by human wisdom but in words taught by the Spirit, explaining spiritual realities with Spirit-taught words. The person without the Spirit does not accept the things that come from the Spirit of God but considers them foolishness, and cannot understand them because they are discerned only through the Spirit. The person with the Spirit makes judgments about all things, but such a person is not subject to merely human judgments, for, "Who has known the mind of the Lord so as to instruct him? But we have the mind of Christ."

Then in Galatians 5:17, it says:

For the flesh desires what is contrary to the Spirit, and the Spirit what is contrary to the flesh. They are in conflict with each other, so that you are not to do whatever you want.

 Q/A: In light of 1 Corinthians 2:6-16 and Gal.5:17 how can fasting help?

_____

_____

_____

The spirit is willing, but the flesh is weak. Empower your spirit to victory over your flesh through fasting.

Matthew 26:41

 Q/A: In light of Matthew 26:41, how can fasting help?

_____

_____

Fasting will improve your ability to accomplish what the Spirit Wills while inhibiting fleshly appetites. Fasting builds self-control and opens our eyes to deception (Proverbs 23:1-3, Ecclesiastes 10:16). These are characteristics necessary for us to become living stones for Jesus to use to build His church.

- When we eat our body takes energy from itself and uses it to digest the food. Toxins are produced called "free radicals," as a result of eating. These responses within the body promote spiritual dullness. Fasting reduces these spiritually dulling bodily responses; opening pathways to stronger Spirit to spirit connection.
- Fasting also creates a type of stress that releases a natural chemical near the brain that is a contributor to our connect-ability to the spiritual realm called DMT. The more DMT that is naturally released the more awareness and wakefulness we have towards the Lord and His Kingdom.
- Overeating is shown to negatively affect the nerves in the brain and weakens the systems of the brain. Overeating also adds a spiritual dullness to the body, latches the senses onto the carnal man and produces a comma-like state to our spiritual senses.
- Eating too much can do more to hurt your mind and body than working too hard.

Jesus fasted 40 days. Both Moses and Elijah fasted 40 days. We can find it worth our contemplation why the only three people in the Bible who fasted 40 days also appeared on the mount of transfiguration. There is a correlation between fasting and transformation we need to understand. Revelation in this area will help us nurture and develop the fasting discipline according to the Kingdom way. May we receive the divine empowerment to both understand and apply fasting to our lives with the intent of it becoming a conduit for transformation. The Kingdom-minded individual who cultivates a lifestyle of fasting will continually express the divine nature and be a carrier of Kingdom realities.

Different Types of Fasts Found in Scripture

1. A fast of repentance - 1 Samuel 7:6, 2 Samuel 12:6
2. Fasting while mourning - 2 Samuel 1:12
3. A fast for guidance and protection - Ezra 8:21, Acts 13:2-3 Note that the Holy Spirit spoke after they fasted.
4. A supernatural fast - Exodus 34:28 Moses was sustained in the same way that the angels are sustained
5. Intercessory fast - Mark 9:28-29, Psalms 35:13, Daniel 6:18, 2 Cor. 11:27
6. Reading the Word continually followed by a prolonged time of confession - Nehemiah 9:1-3
7. Seeking knowledge - Daniel 10:2, Daniel fasted to seek understanding of a vision and God sent an angel with understanding for Daniel (vs14). Be patient, it took this angel 21 days to get in front of Daniel!
8. A fast to avert judgment - Jonah 3:5, 1 Kings 21:27-28, Joel 2:12-15 Turning back to God with fasting is a common scenario in the Bible.
9. Marital fast - 1 Corinthians 5:7
10. Simple food fast - Daniel 10:3 - No meat went into Daniel's mouth.
11. Fasting to break the bonds of wickedness - Isaiah 58:2-14
12. Fasting as a practical way to present yourself to God - Romans 12:1-2.

To those walking in the discipline of fasting, it's important to ask the Lord if He wants us to be fasting for a specific purpose. In most cases He will alert us to a particular fast. We dedicate the fast to what we were told, and that will help fulfill God's Will more precisely. Fasting may be new to some, but we are encouraged to humble ourselves and do it. Enter into this precious discipline of the Saints of old. It helps to be patient with ourselves and trust the Lord to lead us. As we encounter our flesh rising up, let it be a cue for us to begin looking for the King and His Kingdom. Seek the unseen realm of the Kingdom instead of focusing on the pain associated with denying ourselves. What we hold in front of us will manifest.

Fasting is a Key to Answered Prayer

The stomach is a terrible master but a wonderful servant. John Wesley would not ordain anyone to the ministry who would not commit to fast every Wednesday and Friday. That was a basic necessity of ordination within his ministry. At the same time we devote our lives to the discipline of fasting, we need to guard against pride and a religious spirit. Whenever we move closer in relationship with Christ and His Kingdom, which is a natural outcome of humbling ourselves, pride and the religious spirit will test our advance with hopes of stifling our progress. Knowing religion is the great enemy of the Kingdom, let us cast down thoughts not in line with Christ's and ascend the hill of the Lord with clean hands and a pure heart. Don't become entangled in thoughts related to the test. Remain focused on the Kingdom, thanking the Lord for the test. As we grow in Kingdom awareness and expression, the more we seek first the Kingdom the better off we are. Focusing on the test gives rise to awareness of the tester, while focusing on the Kingdom gives rise to the King.

Abraham Lincoln set apart a national day of fasting. He said, "It is the duty of nations as well as men to own their dependence upon the overruling power of God to confess their sins and transgressions in humble sorrow. Yet with assured hope genuine repentance will lead to mercy and pardon. It behooves us then to humble ourselves before God."

Senator James Harlan of Iowa, whose daughter later married President Lincoln's son Robert, introduced a Resolution in the Senate on March 2, 1863. It asked President Lincoln to proclaim a national day of prayer and fasting. The Resolution was adopted on March 3, and signed by Lincoln on March 30, one month before the fast day was observed.

Minnesota's governor John S. Pillsbury declared April 26, 1877, "a day of fasting, humiliation and prayer" to deliver the people from the locusts that were devouring their crops. The people participated and God sent a killer frost destroying the grasshoppers and not harming the wheat. They had a bumper crop that year.

During the Reformation, many of those who translated the Bible, Wycliffe, Luther, Tyndale, and others fasted when they were engaged in their work. This helped them stay mentally fresh longer.

The Strongest Human Drive is Eating

Sigmund Freud identified the strongest human drive to be "sex." He was mistaken. Food is the strongest, most intense human drive. That's why God responds to fasting so powerfully. Sacrificing our greatest desire and need is the deepest form of humility. In addition, fasting is a tool to employ in overcoming sin, including sexual. If we can conquer our greatest desire, food, we can conquer anything. My prayer for the church is that She take up the discipline of fasting. In humbleness of heart, as we pursue the Will of the Lord, I pray He reveal it and empower us to bring Heaven's influence for the sake of the King and His Kingdom!

Application: Commit today to sacrifice everything for the Kingdom. Begin to learn the power of sacrifice in your life and your world. As you do make it a habit to lean on the strength of the Holy Spirit. "For it is God that works in you both to Will and to do of His good pleasure" (Philippians 2:13).

Your name   Date

Chapter Eleven

World Systems

A "World System" is a group of interacting, interrelated elements forming a complex whole. A world system is a system of organized structure erected and controlled by governments. They are used to pattern thoughts, mold minds and form culture. Both the Kingdom of God and the kingdom of Satan have their own systems of rulership. We are all under the influence of Satan's kingdom until we begin seeking the Kingdom of God. A renewing of the mind away from the pattern set in motion by this world into the Kingdom of Heaven is the transformation that awaits all who commit to seek first the Kingdom. We can be delivered from Egypt, but until Egypt is delivered from us, it's not possible to enter the promised land.

The foundation of world systems is rooted in its inherent ability to create thought. The Lord told us and science has recently discovered it's not the man that creates thought but rather thought that creates the man (Proverbs 23:7). The system which controls thought manages behavior. Whichever world system you are conformed to determines who you become. As a man thinks so is he. We must make a decision to change the way we think by choosing to come out from amongst this present world system and under the government of Heaven. Seeking first the Kingdom is Jesus' narrow pathway leading to the promise land.

Like the classic movie, *The Matrix*, the Kingdom of Heaven is all around us. We are blinded to it because we do not possess the thoughts of the One responsible for granting sight into His Kingdom. In the same way Neo needed to take the red pill to see *The Matrix*, so do we need to seek first the Kingdom in order to see the Kingdom. This act alone will place us under the governing system of Heaven which will conform our thinking to the Kings. It takes an intentional commitment to come under the government of God. We begin this transfer through the seeking of His Kingdom in order to receive the thoughts of Christ.

The design of Satan is to keep humanity ignorant. He knows there is death in ignorance and therein lies his power. Both a spiritual death in humanity and a practical death of the existence of the Kingdom of Heaven ruling and reigning on earth. "My people perish for lack

Michael Gissibl

of knowledge"(Hosea 4:6a). The ignorance that Satan works tirelessly to maintain is centered on one idea. He knows that "Narrow is the way that leads to life" (Matthew 7:14). This one idea provides for humanity all that it needs. It fulfills our deepest longings and holds the true source of Life. Everything humanity was created for is found here. God chose to put all His Glory, Majesty, Power and Beauty into this one idea.

Humanity's ignorance of this idea is the only tool Satan possesses that gives him power—power to maintain the systems that have enslaved humanity since The Fall, effectively controlling language, thought and reality. While in Egypt, the Israelites were controlled by Pharaoh's government of occult powers. These powers were so effective that even Moses' leadership could not remove the mindset of the Israelites. They were delivered from Egypt but were unable to enter the promised land because they adopted no change of mind. We need to understand the importance of renewing the mind, otherwise, we will die in the wilderness under the captivity of a mindset constructed in us through the world system of Satan. Don't mistake a form of godliness with the power that comes from a renewed mind.

- The greater the knowledge and understanding you possess of the King and His Kingdom, the less power Satan has over you and the less influence he exerts on earth.

- Receiving the mind of Christ requires we enter the field of seeking first the Kingdom. This decision becomes the means through which He places us under His government and begins the flow of His thoughts to us.

 Q/A: What two results did Jesus' life perfectly model?

The life of Jesus modeled perfectly two results that come from understanding this one idea.

1. Freedom from bondage to the systems established by the rulers of the day.

2. Authority to present and establish a higher system to live in.

Although the god of this age has blinded the minds of humanity to this higher Way, Jesus brought us the knowledge and the Holy Spirit who translates us from bondage to freedom. This knowledge is none other than the information and substance contained in the single idea of the Kingdom of Heaven. The narrow path to discovering this liberating system of rulership is found in seeking first the Kingdom. As we commit to focusing our eye singly, substance only found in the Kingdom is made visible and available to us. This substance brings awareness of the bondage we thought was freedom while at the same time revealing true freedom. Inherent to being born from above, in Heaven, is eyes to see from Heaven's perspective.

- Luke 19:10 - He came to seek and save THAT which was lost—The Kingdom and its system of governing. As the church restores Heaven's system of rulership the influx of souls into the Kingdom will be as the stars in the sky.
- John 18:37 - Jesus came as a King to establish a Kingdom.
- Isaiah 6:9 - He came with a government on His shoulders, not a religion.
- Luke 4:33 - Jesus came to preach the Kingdom.
- 1 John 3:8 Jesus came to destroy the works of the devil through humanities awareness of the Kingdom of God.

A king aspires to expand his territorial rule. We call this "colonization." All kings want to colonize to expand their kingdom. The glory of a king is influence. The greater the territory the greater his influence. Kingdoms use systems of rulership to maintain and spread their governance. World systems are the single most influential structure ever assembled on earth. Satan holds the key to his system and has delegated agents to maintain control of humanity. Jesus also has delegated agents, His church, and will use us to collapse the present system as His rises. The modus operandi for Jesus' system to influence the earth once again begins with a commitment to seeking first the Kingdom of God and His righteousness.

Before Adam's sin, the earth was directly under God's Kingdom authority. His Influence was reigning supreme. When God delegated authority to humanity He was telling humanity He wanted us to maintain His Influence and Culture on the earth. The Fall of man was not only the separation between God and man relationally but the fall from superior influence over the earth. Humanity forfeited our responsibility to maintain God's design to rule planet earth and its inhabitants. Satan's tool to overthrow us is the same tool he uses to maintain his kingdom rulership: Changing our minds. Thinking differently than what God intended for us to think. "Did God really say" was enough of a push for Eve to fall away from her created mindset. Once that happened the mind was changed and humanity fell. Not until we change our minds back to the way God intended for us to think will we see the Lord's Kingdom system of rulership once again governing the hearts and affairs of man.

The moment Satan's thoughts were received by Eve he was given license to develop his influence on earth. It was a human's thought that became Satan's building material for his kingdom to rise on earth. The more he was given influence in the minds of humanity the more expansive his jurisdiction on earth became. Murder, jealousy, hatred, ownership, and strife began to dominate. The culture of Satan's kingdom invaded the inhabitants of the earth through a change of mind. Generation after generation Satan deposited his thoughts into the systems of rulership until the minds of humanity were conditioned and patterned after his likeness. In the same way the thoughts of man have empowered and perpetuated Satan's rule, once we come under the governing influence of the Kingdom, our thoughts will empower and perpetuate Christ's rule.

All territory is governed by a specific group of interrelated, interacting, interdependent elements. This is the mechanism by which both the Kingdom of Heaven and the kingdom of darkness operate. The Bible often refers to this system of ruling when you see the word "world" (*kosmos*).

This system of ruling was established by God, taken over by Satan and will be placed back under the control of Jesus once again. The vehicle through which Jesus will accomplish this is His church. Spirit-filled disciples of Jesus with understanding and wisdom of His Kingdom that will once again shake the world systems like they did in the first century. Only this time, it will end with the greatest harvest of all time, the Kingdom community reigning on earth just like it is in Heaven.

The king which controls a given territory can implement his system of rulership. That's why kings are so concerned with the continual spreading of their kingdoms. The greater the territory the greater the influence. Territory is the container that holds the means of governing. Territory is the primary instrument used to establish a king's system of influence. When a king rules territory he determines who leads and is empowered to create thought in the minds of those living in the area of land under the jurisdiction of His rulership.

When the righteous are in authority, the people rejoice; But when a wicked man rules, the people groan.

Proverbs 29:2 (NKJV)

 Q/A: How does a king expand his territory?

_____

_____

_____

A king expands territory by teaching citizens His system of rulership and sending them out to teach others. He changes the citizens minds in the direction of His system of governance. Both kingdoms operate on the model of the Great Commission. The most effective way a king establishes and expands territory is by placing his citizens in positions of power and influence. This is called subversion, referring to an attempt to transform the established social order and its structures of power and hierarchy. Satan began subversion in the garden by presenting his thoughts to humanity. Jesus began subversion by presenting His thoughts when He taught on the Kingdom and commanded us to seek it above everything. The church will complete the transformation of world systems for Christ as we populate the earth with seeking first the Kingdom of God mindsets.

Keep in mind we are citizens of Heaven. Our positions of power are found in places located in Heaven's government, not earth's. In our attempts to discover the Kingdom, the Lord places us in seats of power and authority as He sees fit. The greatest of these positions of power is found in the seat of servanthood. Our desire for power must disintegrate in the furnace of seeking first the Kingdom before God will entrust us with Heaven's authority.

A prerequisite to affecting others with the Kingdom is having it planted and bearing fruit in our own hearts. This process is more than knowledge, although it begins here. The Holy Spirit must bring understanding which is an added component to knowledge rewarded through perseverance, commitment, and grace. Those who diligently seek first the Kingdom will receive not only the knowledge of the Kingdom but understanding. "All by itself the soil produces grain—first the stalk, then the head, then the full kernel in the head" (Mark 4:28). First comes knowledge, then comes understanding, resulting in wisdom, which is "applied knowledge." God tells us, "I will give you every place where you set your foot, as I promised Moses"(Deuteronomy 11:24, Joshua1:3). A key to stepping into this promise is becoming aware of the treasure that's been placed in you: The priceless treasure of the Kingdom of God. "But we have this treasure in jars of clay to show that this all-surpassing power is from God and not from us" (2 Corinthians 4:7).

Territory is Important to God

The seventy-two returned with joy and said, "Lord, even the demons submit to us in your name." He replied, "I saw Satan fall like lightning from Heaven. I have given you authority to trample on snakes and scorpions and to overcome all the power of the enemy; nothing will harm you. However, do not rejoice that the spirits submit to you, but rejoice that your names are written in Heaven."

Luke 10:17-20

Jesus told us, "I have given you authority to trample on snakes and scorpions and to overcome all the power of the enemy; nothing will harm you" (Luke 10:19). In effect, Jesus was saying, "When you go and take territory for me you will have the authority to beat down and destroy the enemy's established rule. You will crush, deflate, overwhelm, override and overtake the enemy's territory for My Kingdom." When Satan fell so did his kingdom. Inherent within Kingdom Saints is a substance that collapses the kingdom of darkness. That same substance is responsible for building God's systems of rulership. What might that substance be? The Kingdom of God within man. Remember, as ambassadors of the Kingdom we embody the country we represent. When we talk we release the essence of Heaven. Every act is a visible demonstration of our invisible Kingdom.

 Note: Although this passage depicts a violent and graphic overthrow of demonic power it's not the means through which God accomplishes this on earth. Rather this is a picture taken out of the spiritual realm, describing violent spiritual activity. We are called to walk as sons and daughters of God, equipped with an understanding of the Kingdom, which produces substance that causes a collapse of the kingdom of darkness and a rising of the Kingdom of light. The "trampling" and "overcoming of the enemy" takes place as we repent. It's a change of mind away from this world systems thinking towards the Kingdom of Heaven's. Renewing of the mind brings about a transformation that results in the destruction of Satan's kingdom and erection of Christ's, first within the believer then spreading throughout the earth.

When Jesus spoke again to the people, he said, "I am the light of the world. Whoever follows me will never walk in darkness, but will have the light of life.

John 8:12

"Light" represents "knowledge." Whenever we have Kingdom knowledge as it relates to the systems of rulership, Christ-like life is produced in the world. As we follow Jesus, everywhere we walk we take territory back for the Kingdom of Heaven as long as we leave the place of ignorance: "darkness." The god of this age has blinded the minds of unbelievers. We are living in a computer programmed reality with Satan as the "programmer." The only way to perceive this is by changing a specific variable. The variable being perception of the Kingdom of light through revelation.

Quantum mechanics has discovered a principle called *superposition* which supposes two realities existing at once. Because our experience never views the two realities together it begs the question: "When does *superposition* end and what collapses this 'dual reality' into one possibility or the other?" The answer might surprise you: The observer's perception collapses the *superposition,* leaving only the observer's perception of which of the two realities is real. This may sound unreal but in the quantum field, this is established science. I wonder if our Creator had quantum *superposition* in mind when he said: "Be it unto you according to your belief."

 Q/A: How does the concept of *superposition* impact our discussion of the Kingdom?

Let's consider *superposition* in relation to world systems, specifically the kingdom of darkness and the Kingdom of Heaven. Suppose these two kingdoms existed at once. If the observer's perception collapsed the *superposition* what would be the determining factor of which reality remained? The observer's perception—the ability to see and become aware of one or the other kingdom. That's what determines which kingdom is made real on earth. The kingdom who succeeds in molding a nation's perception is given the stage of reality. The first three letters of "seek" are "see." In order to seek first the Kingdom, we must first **see** it. When we see it, as we become aware of it, we become co-creators of His Kingdom on earth.

This is one reason governments establish cultural norms. These norms create and establish perception which perpetuates the established reign of the particular kingdom by opening the eyes of society to itself and patterning thought within the confines of its structure. A society's beliefs, customs, and way of life determine which kingdom becomes reality by forming community and societal perception. Make a decision to remove your self-imposed limitations regarding the nature of your ability to effect earth for Heaven. Choose this day to enlarge your capacity to receive God's identity of you. As you do a continual awakening to the eternal Kingdoms rule and your part in it will become abundant.

The kingdom of darkness is presently ruling the nations because it has succeeded in entangling the collective perception of society thus ensuring its existence being maintained as reality. What if God's people re-discovered the Kingdom of Heaven? What if we became aware, once again of the existence of the Kingdom God on earth? Is it possible that if we can perceive the Kingdom of God we can create and reestablish its reality on earth? Is it possible for us to see and become aware of the Kingdom of Heaven to the point where we "collapse" the present reality of the kingdom of darkness while simultaneously "creating" the reality of the Kingdom of Heaven?

 Application: Today, denounce the influence of this world's system over you. Declare your adoption into the Family of God and begin seeking first the Kingdom of Heaven.

Your name   Date

Chapter Twelve

Faith

"Faith" means "belief." Every religion has a belief. Every country has their own faith. Faith is not isolated to Christianity; it's a universal phenomenon. All culture is formed and maintained out of a community's set of beliefs. If we are alive we have faith. Faith is also a belief system. Jesus required followers to become students (disciples) in order that they might become partakers of His Kingdom's belief system. As a teacher, Jesus wanted to transfer the disciples' thinking from the world's system to His Kingdom's. He did this by giving fresh life and substance to their minds thus empowering them as Kingdom representatives. The goal of possessing the Kingdom's belief system must be that it, in turn, possesses you. Scripture is filled with examples of the Kingdom's belief system possessing those that believe. James said, "Faith without works is dead." Belief, without it possessing you, cannot produce its desired end. We can say we believe in healing, but until the substance of healing is brought forth we may possess belief in healing, but the Kingdom expressing itself through healing has yet to possess us. As a psychologist's belief system is psychology, so too is a Kingdomologist's belief system Kingdom. In order to put in practice Kingdomology, we must first make it our top priority to seek the Kingdom.

In the same way, faith by itself, if it is not accompanied by action, is dead. But someone will say, "You have faith; I have deeds." Show me your faith without deeds, and I will show you my faith by what I do. You believe that there is one God. Good! Even the demons believe that—and shudder. You foolish man, do you want evidence that faith without deeds is useless? Was not our ancestor Abraham considered righteous for what he did when he offered his son Isaac on the altar? You see that his faith and his actions were working together, and his faith was made complete by what he did. And the scripture was fulfilled that says, 'Abraham believed God, and it was credited to him as righteousness, and he was called God's friend.' You see that a person is justified by what he does and not by faith alone. In the same way, was not even Rahab the prostitute considered righteous for what she did when she gave lodging to the spies and sent them off in a different direction? As the body without the spirit is dead, so faith without deeds is dead.

James 2:17-26

Without the manifestation of that which we believe our faith is yet to come alive. All belief must undergo a series of tests in order to be resurrected. Be patient in affliction for in due time what you know to be true will bear fruit. The church needs a perception change which starts with a belief change. In Hebrews 11, God describes Kingdom faith as being "the substance of things hoped for and the evidence of things not seen." How can we present evidence of something not in existence without manifesting it? How do we manifest something not in existence? The same way God did: through words spoken with a Kingdom mindset. The key to activating the faith of God is carrying with us Heaven's Beliefs and Heaven's Words. The Bible distinguishes between having faith in God and possessing the faith of God. Each faith carries its own distinct substance which produces its own results. Having faith in God always has as its destination the faith of God. The faith of God always produces Kingdom perception which creates the manifestation and evidence of His Kingdom on earth.

In Mark 11:22, Jesus makes a statement that most translations missed but the Greek makes clear. "And Jesus answering, saith to them, Have the faith of God" (Worrell). Most translations render this "have faith in God." If Jesus wanted to use the word "in" He would have. But He didn't, instead He said *exete pistin theo*—the "faith **of** God." If He wanted to say "faith in God" the Greek would read *exete pistin en theo* (phonetic spelling). Jesus was telling us to possess the faith of God not merely faith in God. The faith of God is securely locked up in the Kingdom of Heaven, only entrusted to disciples committed to Jesus' top priority: Seeking first His Kingdom and righteousness.

The building material of a belief system is our thoughts. Our thoughts are produced out of what we choose to place before us. Primarily what we listen to and view. It's mostly our ears and eyes that create perceptual awareness. As we replace what is presently coming into our eyes and ears with Kingdom ideas, terms, concepts, pictures thoughts, etc ... we begin the renewing of the mind which activates the transformation process. This transformation adds substance to our visual acuity and insight, bringing awareness to the existence of Kingdom realities in progressive measure. The more we look upon the Kingdom the more our belief system is changed from one degree of influence to another. Laying down our own wants in exchange for Jesus' greatest desire for us is important to the transformation process.

A key to ensuring we possess the faith of God is knowing and understanding that we are dead to ourselves and maintaining that death by picking up our cross daily. The most important area needed to surrender over to the Lord is our priorities. Dying to our present schedules in favor of Jesus' priority for us, seeking first the Kingdom, will set us on course with encounters of the Kingdom kind.

I have been crucified with Christ and I no longer live, but Christ lives in me. The life I live in the body, I live by faith in the Son of God, who loved me and gave himself for me.

Galatians 2:20

If we are crucified with Christ, then Christ lives in us. If Christ lives in us then we are joined with the faith of God. The more we disengage from our Will and attach ourselves to His, the more we see His faith arise in us. The more we understand Christ and His Kingdom in us the larger the territory He establishes within us. This ultimately equates to more of the faith of God taking up residence in us. Jesus gave us the key to expediting this rise in the faith of God: seeking first the Kingdom. Unless a kernel of wheat falls to the ground and die it bears no fruit. But if it dies it will enter into progressive levels of union with the faith of God, bearing much fruit (John 12:24).

This is where we as Kingdom Representatives and Ambassadors re-present the beliefs of God with influence. Jesus said, "If you remain in me and my words remain in you, ask whatever you wish and it will be given you" (John 15:7). In other words, "Because I'm a King my words become law, and whatever I speak manifests." We must know and understand the mind of Christ if we are to represent accurately in word and deed. If we stand in His Counsel He will teach us His beliefs and give us His Words. His Words will become ours and what we speak will be brought into existence. Jesus gave us His highest counsel when He commanded us to seek His Kingdom more than anything. By accepting and implementing His counsel we prepare ourselves to receive Kingdom power and influence. Just like an apple carries the tree in seed form, so too does the faith of God carry the substance of its origin, the Kingdom.

In the same manner, Jesus spoke and the Father manifested. So to will what we speak be manifest. "As the Father has sent me so I send you." If only we could carry our crosses long enough to get to the place of crucifixion. Then substance from the Kingdom within will resurrect in and through us. We must die to self before we engage in resurrection power and life.

In the Kingdom of God:

- A cross is designed for a crucifixion.
- A crucifixion is designed for death.
- Death is designed for resurrection.
- Resurrection is designed for Heaven and
- Heaven is designed for earth!!

"By faith the people passed through the red sea, as on dry land: but when the Egyptians tried to do so, they were drowned" (Hebrews 11:29). Put differently, by Moses' belief system, he stretched out his hand over the waters to roll them back and God brought into existence His Will through Moses. In the same way, the Egyptians drowned. Moses stretched out his hand over the waters and God said "there's a man with my beliefs" and the waters came crashing down. Two belief systems operating on earth at the same time. One producing protection and life and the other producing death.

Before Jesus calmed the storm in Matthew 4 His disciples were afraid. They woke Jesus and expressed their fear and worry. Jesus had a completely different mindset. After rebuking the storm He said to them "do you still have no faith?" That is to say, "is your belief system still rooted outside of mine? Have you yet to renew your mind in the things I've been teaching you?"

In the Bible, how does it say we conquer kingdoms? Only through a belief system that is planted in and sprouts from a superior Kingdom, the Kingdom of Heaven. Religious faith creates communication centered on begging and pleading to God for things. This faith develops the mind out of material from Satan's system of ruler ship and conditions thought in the realm of the carnal mind. This patterned way of thinking is rooted in the kingdom of darkness. Kingdom faith produces legal petitioning and interceding, resulting in God moving on our behalf. Kingdom faith gets the attention of the King. Once we understand the laws and culture of the Kingdom, when we see laws and culture in existence that are contrary to those of the Kingdom, then we petition Heaven. Once we understand our kingly role we implement law as we receive direction from Heaven. The difference between a religious Christian and Kingdom citizen is the difference between the present weak church and the dramatically powerful life of Christ in a believer as demonstrated throughout the book of Acts.

Q/A: If you are presenting the Will of a judge to the judge himself how could you be denied your petition?

Note: It's important to understand that once you see and accept a new belief you don't necessarily possess it. There is a process that takes the information you discovered and, over time fashions it into your identity. Once it is moved into your identity you become equipped and empowered. This requires the participant to continue revisiting the information. The definition of "seek" implies a continual revisiting of the information you are seeking. In Matthew 7:7 the original Greek says " Ask and keep on asking and it will be given to you; seek and keep on seeking and you will find; knock and keep on knocking and the door will be opened to you." Seek and keep on seeking first the Kingdom of God and all things will be added to you!

None of Samuel's words fell to the ground (1Samuel 3:19) because he learned the Will of the King of kings and chose his words carefully. If he didn't know what to say he said nothing. What great discipline Samuel possessed. What magnificent listening skills he acquired.

When possessing the power of God through the spoken word, it's better to be silent than wrong. The church will know she is representing the voice of God more accurately when Heaven backs up her message with great power and the church finds herself dealing with nations more than individuals. Before "the kingdom of this world will become the kingdom of Christ" the nations will come to the church seeking answers (Revelation 11:15). May we be found with oil in our lampstands ready to be the shining city on a hill (Matthew 5:14 and Matthew 25:1-13).

Kingdom Faith

One way to define Kingdom "faith" is "the substance of things hoped for and the evidence of things not seen" (Hebrews 11:1). As Kingdom representatives, our belief system produces a perception that equips and empowers us to make manifest things not seen. We bring substance where there is none. This includes healing from sickness, wholeness from brokenness, life from death, and revelation from ignorance. We make visible the invisible as the invisible is first made visible to us. We demonstrate an effect (a manifestation from Heaven) and teach about the cause (the dominion it has on earth). This becomes a powerful tool in building our case for the existence of the Kingdom we preach. It also makes room for societal change, preparing the way for nations to come under the Lordship of Jesus and His Kingdom. If I want to represent WalMart I must be in WalMart. There I acquire access to buy what I want to take out of the store and share. In order to accurately represent the existence of the substance of Heaven, we must be found in Heaven. There we will be positioned to receive from Heaven and present what is received to earth.

Even the demons believe (James 2:19). To have the faith of Christ is to manifest the belief system which is evidenced in the Gospels and Book of Acts. Throughout all of scripture most if not all demonstrations of the influence of Heaven on earth was a result of an individual possessing the right belief system. We must pursue the belief system of God in order to experience Kingdom realities on earth. But someone will say, "You have faith; I have deeds." Show me your faith without deeds, and I will show you my faith by my deeds" (James 2:18). All belief systems inherently carry the power to influence behavior according to the likeness of the substance contained within the belief. All things are possible to those who believe.

God is once again raising up a company of Saints with a belief system rooted in the information and revelation received while seeking first the Kingdom. This company will be the church Jesus uses to bring awareness of His marvelous Kingdom on earth as it is in Heaven.

Application: Declare today that you will "walk by faith and not by sight!" Begin to walk in the power of the Kingdom as you exercise your confidence (faith) in the Father. Be the Will of the Father with demonstrations of His hand on you. Begin today by setting your intentions on discovering the faith of God through the commitment of seeking first the Kingom.

Your name   Date

Chapter Thirteen

Discipleship

DISCIPLES—**God's catalyst to Kingdom establishment**.

As the essence of Jesus was the Kingdom, so too will the essence of the church be disciples.

The church has been mostly powerless and without Christ-like influence the past 1900 years. This is largely due to a scheme from the devil. He replaced "disciples" with "followers" by taking out two key conditions of discipleship. He has successfully removed Jesus' highest priority for His church:

1) Becoming a student of the Kingdom; and
2) Preaching the Gospel of the Kingdom.

It is impossible to possess perception of the Kingdom without first becoming a student of the Kingdom. This is precisely why Jesus raised up students, taught on the subject of the Kingdom and instructed them to make information relating to His Kingdom their top priority. Satan's removal of this discipline has postponed the work of Jesus and stripped the church of its Kingdom Influence. We have forfeited rulership of the earth, and God's plan with humanity, for control of one system under the devil's care, religion.

 Q/A: How have we forfeited rulership of the earth?

_____

_____

By exchanging "disciples" with "followers" and replacing the message of the gospel of the Kingdom with the message of the other gospels: healing, salvation, grace, forgiveness, born again, etc.

"This gospel of the Kingdom" is the message Jesus assigned to the church. It is the only message adequate to produce an ability to see and become aware of the Kingdom's existence on earth. We have substituted the gospel of the Kingdom for many gospels thus veiling humanity from experiencing and living in the Kingdom on earth. The re-discovery of Jesus' message is giving rise to disciples once again. We are not far from life as seen in the Book of Acts.

Jesus proclaimed a message and performed miracles. He preached and demonstrated what He brought to earth: the Kingdom.

At daybreak Jesus went out to a solitary place. The people were looking for him and when they came to where he was, they tried to keep him from leaving them. But he said, "I must preach the good news of the kingdom of God to the other towns also, because that is why I was sent." And he kept on preaching in the synagogues of Judea.

Luke 4:42-44

It was His message, supernatural power, and presence that attracted followers. Out of these followers emerged another group He called "disciples." This group Jesus separated, ultimately choosing them to continue what He began: Establishing a way of thinking in people which changed their perception and produced a culture and lifestyle on earth as it is in Heaven. "And THIS gospel ...." What gospel?

And this gospel of the kingdom will be preached in the whole world as a testimony to all nations, and then the end will come."

Matthew 24:14

The only gospel that is capable of bringing the end, which is the rule and reign of Christ over the entire earth, is the gospel of the Kingdom. Until disciples emerge the church will remain blinded to the Kingdom. As a blind man lives in a reality he is unable to see and experience, so to is the church living in the midst of Heaven's reality without seeing and experiencing it. Disciples are the eye salve bringing sight to the church and ultimately Nations.

The Book of Acts is an example of a group of students under Jesus' teaching that accepted, studied, unified, and implemented this new way of thinking. They became the disciples that continued the work of Christ, making known the existence of the invisible Kingdom through the demonstration of its qualities. It was the metamorphosis that took place in their minds that created the awareness of the Kingdom which empowered them to represent Christ authentically. These disciples walked the earth transformed and transfigured as a result of the renewing of the mind that took place while resting under and submitting to the great master teacher, Jesus.

As the message of the Kingdom is being re-discovered, it is important the church be prepared to receive Divine Power. This Divine Power is an important catalyst to bringing in harvesters for the harvest. We don't pursue power we pursue the Kingdom. As our perception changes God releases the power through us by increasing our awareness of the divine nature and reality of Christ and His Kingdom in us. Power becomes a witness to the message we preach, the message that the Kingdom of Heaven is present and available NOW! To the disciple of Jesus, divine healing is proof of the existence of the invisible Kingdom. In God's Kingdom, faith is manifesting things not seen and supernatural signs and wonders are a primary means of fulfilling this. Until we are able to see the Kingdom as being greater than signs and wonders we are not ready to possess such power.

A disciple is charged with the challenge of transforming "followers" into "disciples" (Matthew 28:19). This is no different than Jesus' mission. Disciples are important because they are God's chosen vessels to establishing His Kingdom on earth. They become the carriers of material capable of bringing to life perception of the Kingdom. They are the first "workers" hired to work the vineyard in the parable of the workers found in Matthew 20. Every time Jesus sent out a group to bring Heaven on earth they were disciples. He never sent out followers. The assignment of the Great Commission was given to disciples, not followers. A disciple is a follower of Jesus but a follower of Jesus is not automatically a disciple. A follower represents part of the Kingdom, a disciple embodies the Kingdom and discovers the essence of his being to be the Kingdom. Don't think this a strange idea, rather press into understanding and revelation of this great mystery. Christ is in us, we are in Christ, the Kingdom of Heaven is within us and we are in the Kingdom of Heaven.

Note: Everything created, whether by God or man, originated as a thought. In order to co-labor with Christ in establishing His Kingdom on earth we must pursue His thoughts. The Bible says "we have the mind of Christ." It's up to us whether or not we choose to receive and unwrap that gift which is found in the field of seeking first the Kingdom! Let's commit to renewing our minds by conforming them once again to Christ's.

Jesus told his disciples in Matthew 13:11, "The knowledge of the secrets of the kingdom of Heaven has been given to you, but not to them," meaning "those following Me." Jesus told Peter, a disciple, that He would use him to build His church (Matthew 16:15-20). In Acts 1:1-8, Jesus appeared to a group of disciples with a specific function called Apostles and spent 40 days speaking to them on the Kingdom. He then ordered these same disciples to wait for the gift of the Holy Spirit. The leaders in the Book of Acts were disciples, not followers.

A follower of Jesus sees the Kingdom as a part. A disciple is trained to see the Kingdom as the whole. Therefore, a disciple has trained both his natural and spiritual eyes to perceive another substance contained within their field of awareness. The "other substance" is found exclusively in the Kingdom and is discovered while seeking first the Kingdom as a whole. This is a major distinguishing marker between a follower and a disciple. To become a disciple requires you lay down pursuing things found in the Kingdom and give yourself over to the Kingdom itself.

A difficulty in understanding the Kingdom is overcoming fragmentation, the state of being broken into parts. From birth, we are conditioned to think in a divided way. Everything is broken up: geography, industry, education, time, rooms in a home, websites, the body; life overwhelmingly is divided. The church has fragmented the gospel of the Kingdom by taking out its parts and presenting them as individual pieces. In doing so, we have removed the nature of the Kingdom from the message of the gospel. We have removed substance from the earth that can only return through the teaching and preaching of the message of the gospel of the Kingdom. Until we rediscover the gospel parts in the Kingdom we will be unable to present the essence of the Kingdom to the earth. All information communicated outside the Kingdom lacks substance only found in the Kingdom. However, once the Kingdom is found the gospel presented from the Kingdom will once again flow with substance from the place of its origin, Heaven itself.

Disciples will be the carriers of the message of the Kingdom as a whole, once again demonstrating the substance of the eternal Kingdom.

Jesus gave us the remedy that takes us from a follower to a disciple: "Seek first the Kingdom." Stop making the Kingdom a part of your life and make it the priority! In the Kingdom a heart divided cannot stand. We must saturate ourselves in seeking the Kingdom in order that we might see that which we are seeking. The foundation of the Kingdom as a whole will be unveiled to all who seek first the Kingdom.

Jesus gathered followers and turned as many as possible into disciples. Why? Because He knew disciples were to be His Hands and Feet. He knew the necessity of a student becoming fully committed to His message was the prerequisite to seeing and experiencing the Kingdom. Those completing His Work on earth need to be disciples. A key to manifesting Heaven on earth is found in the understanding of the make-up of a disciple. Once we understand what a disciple is, we can identify them. Once we identify them we can bring them together. Once they are assembled we become positioned for the outpouring of the Holy Spirit and the Great Commission: Heaven's Power flowing through groups of disciples into regions of the earth, establishing Heaven's culture and influence.

"We are on the cusp of a rushing river of revelation on the Kingdom across the earth right now. One day when we are sufficiently ready God will bring us into the revival that will never cease because it has the only sustainable issue to revival and that's the Kingdom of God."

—Jack Taylor

The Bible enlightens us to the nature and characteristics of a disciple which are different from those of a follower. Although many followers of Jesus carry characteristics of a disciple this doesn't qualify them to become disciples. Below is a list of attributes and qualities that scripture reveals about a disciple. Keep in mind it is God who determines the moment in time we are commissioned in the function of a disciple. Also keep in mind it's Christ in us that empowers us to become who He's called us to be. Take time and study this list. Go through the Bible verses and ask the Father where your Will is committed to these qualifications and where you may need His strength to step into discipleship with Christ.

1. **A disciple believes in and follows Jesus' teaching**. - Mark 1:20, Matthew 4:22. It could be that in Luke 9:59-60 Jesus was challenging followers to become disciples by telling them to proclaim the Kingdom.

2. **A disciple remains dedicated to Jesus' teaching**. - John 8:31. Luke 4:43 tells us what this teaching is, the Kingdom.

3. **A disciple is obedient to the word**. - John 17:6. To a disciple, the word is "Go preach the Kingdom" (Matthew 10:7, Luke 9:2 & 10:1-11) and seek first the Kingdom (Matthew 6:33).

4. **A disciple loves Jesus above everything** including kids, wife, family, friends, money, etc....- Luke 14:26. "If anyone comes to me and does not hate father and mother, wife and children, brothers and sisters—yes, even their own life—such a person cannot be my disciple."

5. **A disciple lays down their own Will and desire for the sake of the Kings.** - Luke 9:23,24 & 14:27, "And whoever does not deny self, carry their cross and follow me cannot be my disciple." To the disciple, carrying burdens and suffering patiently are circumstances that carry resurrection life. Therefore, we remain under the burden until it's lifted, rejoicing by faith that the suffering's producing Heavenly life within (Matthew 16:24-25, Mark 8:34-35). "Then Jesus said to his disciples, "Whoever wants to be my disciple must deny themselves and take up their cross and follow me."

6. **A disciple gives up everything in exchange for enrollment in the school of the Kingdom.** - Luke 5:11 & 14:33, "Those of you who do not give up everything you have cannot be my disciples." The only way to give up everything is to enter a kingdom. There you own nothing because the king owns it all. The most effective way to give up everything is to receive a revelation of the all-sufficient nature of the Kingdom. God is not so much asking us to give up everything as He is asking us to receive revelation of the Kingdom: then we will gladly lay everything down.

7. **A disciple is placed in Christ and learns to abide there**, resulting in manifested fruit in your life , "showing yourselves to be my disciples." - John 15:1-8.

8. **Disciples eventually make disciples.** - Matthew 28:19-20.

9. **Disciples endure great persecution.** - John 14:14, "I have given them your word and the world has hated them" - John 15:18-20, "If the world hates you, keep in mind that it hated me first. If you belonged to the world, it would love you as its own. As it is, you do not belong to the world, but I have chosen you out of the world. That is why the world hates you. Remember what I told you: 'A servant is not greater than his master. If they persecuted me, they will persecute you also.'"

10. **A disciple takes on the discipline of fasting to one degree or another.** - Luke 5:35.

11. **A disciple is given the knowledge of the secrets of the Kingdom.** - Luke 8:9, 10.

12. **A disciple proclaims the Kingdom.** - Luke 9:60, 62.

13. **A disciple has sat under the teaching of the message of the Kingdom long enough to be entrusted with the riches of the Kingdom.** - Luke 8:1.

One day as Jesus was standing by the Lake of Gennesaret, the people were crowding around him and listening to the word of God. He saw at the water's edge two boats, left there by the fishermen, who were washing their nets. He got into one of the boats, the one belonging to Simon, and asked him to put out a little from shore. Then he sat down and taught the people from the boat. When he had finished speaking, he said to Simon, "Put out into deep water, and let down the nets for a catch." Simon answered, "Master, we've worked hard all night and haven't caught anything. But because you say so, I will let down the nets." When they had done so, they caught such a large number of fish that their nets began to break. So they signaled their partners in the other boat to come and help them, and they came and filled both boats so full that they began to sink. When Simon Peter saw this, he fell at Jesus' knees and said, "Go away from me, Lord; I am a sinful man!"

Luke 5:1-8

14. **A disciple begins listening to the Teacher (Jesus) and ends bowing to a King.** You must be a student who receives the revelation his Teacher is the King. In the passage recorded above, we see an example of Peter's process of becoming a disciple. Jesus is teaching "The Word of God" which is the message of the Kingdom as evidenced in Luke 8:10-11 and Matthew 13:19. Peter accepted Jesus as his teacher. We know this by how he acknowledged Him in verse 5. By the time Jesus demonstrated the Kingdom Peter was convinced He was King, which is evidenced by the way he acknowledged Him in verse 8. The word "Lord" is a title given to kings. When Peter called Jesus Lord he was revealing his understanding that Jesus was King. It wasn't until after this that Jesus established Peter as a disciple. The word "master" means "teacher" as used by Jewish tradition of the time. The word "Lord" means owner and king. Jesus began as Peter's teacher, and because Peter concluded right, Jesus became his King. Peter first accepted Jesus as teacher. One class under the Master caused Peter to see Him as King, transforming him from a follower to a disciple. When "come follow me" becomes "you are my disciples" the Kingdom of Heaven will be expressed in the nature and likeness Jesus intended.

15. **Jesus told his disciples they would be witnesses,** but to what? They were given power to be witnesses to the Kingdom He said was here. That's why the Holy Spirit came; to give them evidence from the country Jesus preached about as proof the Son of God was speaking the truth (Acts 1:8). That evidence was the culture of Heaven demonstrated on earth. This culture was made up of the fruit of the Spirit, supernatural power, and divine empowerment to make visible the invisible. This became commonplace to the life of a disciple and the community they were joined with.

16. **A disciple does not ascribe a title to himself other than that of a servant** (Read Matthew 23:1-11). Representatives of the Kingdom are those who become servants to all.

As we identify disciples we can establish and multiply the church by taking any newly found disciple and placing them with another disciple and sending them out (Matthew 24:14). This is the biblical model for Kingdom establishment and expansion, as mentioned in Chapter 10. Remember, it's the disciple whose mind has been taught the Kingdom resulting in the ability, through the grace of God, to see and become aware of the Kingdom. This awareness becomes the catalyst for Christ to begin building His Church and demonstrating His nature and character. Without disciples, the church is limited to the position of a spiritual nursery at best. Understanding what it means to be a disciple requires each of us to make a decision.

Q/A: Will you remain a follower or will you accept the challenge of discipleship? Step onto the road of destiny today and begin preparing to be commissioned as a disciple of Jesus.

This is not an easy decision but one worth careful consideration. Discipleship is not for everyone. Many are called but few are chosen. However, the church cannot be built without the sacrifice of those willing to walk with Jesus in a manner worthy of the call of a disciple. If we are desirous of becoming disciples, we may enter the Kingdom knowing God's faithfulness to carry us through. It is not only God that works in us both to Will and do of His good pleasure, but it is Christ in us that has begun this good work. Rest in His ability to complete it.

It's important to understand God is not looking for fully mature disciples who follow him perfectly. If we have any desire to walk the life of a disciple, we qualify. A simple prayer of "I believe Lord, help my unbelief" will catch the attention of Heaven. Acknowledging our flesh is weak and our spirit is willing invites mercy and awakens divine empowerment.

Michael Gissibl

The Book of Acts:
Our Model for Transformation and Everlasting Revival

Below is a prototype I discovered in the book of Acts which describes a Heavenly model for Kingdom revival. It's not a formula but a means God chose to use to bring transformation through revival. A revival whose DNA, when implemented effectively, will never die. A revival whose substance will convert the earth back to its original design having once again the Kingdom of Heaven ruling and reigning supreme. I believe this model still carries with it the seal of approval of Heaven and will be used to ignite a global restoration of all things. A revival that will never cease because its foundation is rooted and established in Kingdom theology. God is the same yesterday, today and forever. The models and principles discovered in scripture are timeless and impossible to improve upon. We are unearthing a treasure of timeless significance. A treasure whose material will cause todays church to explode with first century style expression and substance.

1. **We need disciples** - Disciples received Jesus' message of the Kingdom (Acts 1:3b-8). We know this because John 8:31 identifies a condition of a disciple: "If you remain faithful to my teachings you are my disciples." We also know the disciples were well-schooled in the teaching of the Kingdom because:
a. Jesus came to us for the purpose of preaching the Kingdom (Luke 4:43).
b. And no teacher, let alone a master teacher like Jesus, would send out his students without first knowing they were prepared and equipped to teach and disciple.

2. **We need disciples to enter into community/unity** (Acts 1:13-14). Unity of mind is important. This word used for unity or "one accord" means with one mind, of the same passion. The unity the disciples entered into was Jesus' commands to them: pray, fast, teach, physically gather, and wait (John 17:6-19 especially vs. 11, and Matthew 28:16-20). These activities were all rooted, grounded and firmly established in Jesus' teaching of the Kingdom. To the disciple, the centrality of all that is said and done is rooted in awareness of the Kingdom.

To the first-century church, prayer flowed out from the concept "your Kingdom come", fasting was grounded in all things Kingdom, teaching sprouted from the soil of seeking first the Kingdom and waiting was in anticipation of Heaven coming to earth.

3. **We need disciples to understand and give themselves over to prayer** (Acts 1:14). We know what the disciples were praying. They asked Jesus to teach them to pray. He taught them to pray "Your kingdom come … on earth as it is in Heaven." Because the Bible identifies disciples in the upper room and we know disciples are faithful to Jesus' teaching and obedient, we can be confident what they were praying. If Jesus were a university He would have only one major—the Kingdom of Heaven. We must understand prayer and its exclusive relationship to the Kingdom (1Cor. 14:15-Pro.4:7).

4. **We need disciples to establish leadership teams under the direction of Holy Spirit** (Acts 1:21-26).

5. **The disciples devoted themselves to the apostles' teaching, which was also Jesus' teaching—the Kingdom.** (Acts 2:42, Matthew 10:5-7, Luke 10:1 & 9, Romans 1:1, 9, 15, 2 Corinthians 2:12, Acts 8:12 & 20:24-25 & 28:30-31, Revelation 1:9). It's the "gospel of the Kingdom," not the gospel of grace or salvation or any other gospel found in the Kingdom that Jesus is looking for laborers to send out with. The church is full of all other gospels producing fruit after its kind. This fruit bears little resemblance to Jesus' ministry and the community of believers in the book of Acts. The church that is devoted (continue with intense effort) to the apostles' teaching of the Gospel of the Kingdom will produce fruit bearing resemblance to substance found in Heaven. The only lasting fruit is found in the only message that will remain forever: the message of the gospel of the everlasting Kingdom!

We can expect greater works than Pentecost to manifest with healings, casting out demons, raising the dead, making disciples, radical salvations, the demonstration of the Kingdom, etc., when we develop disciples. The first thing the disciples did was receive a message (Acts

1:3b-8). When we possess the message of the Kingdom it's only a matter of time before it possesses us. When the power from Heaven comes we are to have the message (vs. 8). The Holy Spirit always comes with Heaven's message, which is: **The Kingdom of Heaven is on earth, available and accessible to all.** This is the same message Jesus preached. The same message He commanded His twelve disciples and then the 72 to preach. It was the same message Paul, Barnabas and Phillip preached.

The church has spent 1900 years unifying under all kinds of doctrine. Every "gospel" imaginable has become central to a group of people that have in turn created a denomination or movement from it. It is the author's belief that the first community that reinstates the model presented in this chapter and chooses to unify under it will become the model church for an unending expression of the ever expanding Kingdom on earth! May this model become leaven that leavens the whole earth with the influence of the eternal Kingdom!

A key to sustaining and growing a revival is making disciples. A disciple is connected to the Source; a follower is connected to our ministry and what it does for them. A follower never gets connected to the Kingdom but a disciple does (Matthew13:11-16).

More Proof of Jesus' Teaching

In Matthew 10, Jesus instructs his disciples before He sends them out.

These twelve Jesus sent out with the following instructions: "Do not go among the Gentiles or enter any town of the Samaritans. Go rather to the lost sheep of Israel. As you go, preach this message: 'The kingdom of Heaven is near.' Heal the sick, raise the dead, cleanse those who have leprosy, drive out demons. Freely you have received, freely give. Do not take along any gold or silver or copper in your belts; take no bag for the journey, or extra tunic, or sandals or a staff; for the worker is worth his keep. Whatever town or village you enter, search for some worthy person there and stay at his house until you leave. As you enter the home, give it your greeting. If the home is deserving, let your peace rest on it; if it is not, let your peace return to you. If anyone will not welcome you or listen to your words, shake the dust off your feet when you leave that home or town. I tell you the truth, it will be more bearable for Sodom and Gomorrah on the day of judgment than for that town. I am sending you out like sheep among wolves. Therefore, be as shrewd as snakes and as innocent as doves. Be on your guard against men; they will hand you over to the local councils and flog you in their synagogues. On my account, you will be brought before governors and kings as witnesses to them and to the Gentiles. But when they arrest you, do not worry about what to say or how to say it. At that time you will be given what to say, for it will not be you speaking, but the Spirit of your Father speaking through you. Brother will betray brother to death, and a father his child; children will rebel against their parents and have them put to death. All men will hate you because of me, but he who stands firm to the end will be saved. When you are persecuted in one place, flee to another. I tell you the truth, you will not finish going through the cities of Israel before the Son of Man comes. A student is not above his teacher, nor a servant above his master. It is enough for the student to be like his teacher and the servant like his master. If the head of the house has been called Beelzebub, how much more the members of his household! So do not be afraid of them. There is nothing concealed that will not be disclosed, or hidden that will not be made known. What I tell you in the dark, speak in the daylight; what is whispered in your ear, proclaim from the roofs. Do not be afraid of those who kill the body but cannot kill the soul. Rather, be afraid of the One who can destroy both soul and body in hell. Are not two sparrows sold for a penny? Yet not one of them will fall to the ground apart from the will of your Father. And even the very hairs of your head are all numbered. So don't be afraid; you are worth more than many sparrows. Whoever acknowledges me before men, I will also acknowledge him before my Father in Heaven. But whoever disowns me before men, I will disown him before my Father in Heaven. Do not suppose that I have come to bring peace to the earth. I did not come to bring peace, but a sword. For I have come to turn a man against his father, a daughter against her mother, a daughter-in-law against her mother-in-law, a man's enemies will be the members of his own household. Anyone who loves his father or mother more than me is not worthy of me; anyone who loves his son or daughter more than me is not worthy of me; and anyone who does not take his cross and follow me is not worthy of me. Whoever finds his life will lose it, and whoever loses his life for my sake will find it."

Matthew 10:5-39

The only instruction Jesus gave on what to teach is to proclaim this message, "the kingdom of Heaven is near." From this statement, we can conclude Jesus must have been teaching the disciples about the Kingdom of Heaven. No teacher would send out students to teach without first establishing the teaching in their minds and hearts. You are not qualified to receive a diploma without first demonstrating in the classroom competency of the information related to the diploma. Once you receive your diploma, however, you graduate and become qualified to demonstrate what you have learned. What qualifies a person for a degree is the students accurate representation of the mind of the teacher as demonstrated in test competency. When a teacher sees his or her mind woven into the fabric of the students identity, there is confidence the information will bear fruit, lasting fruit.

As a student, as valuable as we are in Jesus' eyes, it's the message that the teacher has confidence in, not the student. This is both liberating and humbling. At the same time, it deflates our ego and energizes us to know we are privileged to carry and give away a message so powerful it will change the world.

In part, the power comes to make manifest the existence of our invisible Kingdom (Acts14:3,7) and enlarge the hearers capacity to receive our message. It is the Kingdom message in the heart of man, brought to the place of understanding, which makes perception of the Kingdom possible. The result? Making visible the invisible (Hebrews11:1). When you have the right belief system—the Kingdom mindset—things not seen will manifest. With or without you, the power of the message of the gospel of the Kingdom will take root in the earth bringing everlasting transformation. The choice is up to you whether or not you want to participate in God's eternal plan of redemption.

The church has come into unity regarding Jesus' death, resurrection, being born again, forgiveness of sins, adoration of Jesus and many other good truths. In fact, all Christian denominations unify around parts of the Kingdom. But it has not produced Heaven's intent on earth. It's not until a community of believers commit to unifying around seeking first the Kingdom that we will see the display of Heaven on earth like never before. It's time the Church confess we have not been doing life God's way and commit to Jesus' top priority for us: Seeking first the Kingdom of God and His righteousness.

When Jesus was resurrected and came back to earth for 40 days He spoke about the Kingdom of God. The primary purpose for the power and presence of the Holy Spirit is not to heal us or let us feel the Love of God. As good as this is, there is a higher purpose. Jesus used the power of signs and wonders to gather the people and open their hearts to receive the Kingdom message. It added credibility to His message, the Gospel of the Kingdom, and made the hearts of the listeners more receptive. Signs and wonders enlarge the capacity of the on-looker to receive the message that follows. Remember this and when Heaven's power comes upon you be quick to present the good news of the Kingdom. Always connect the demonstration of power to its source: the Kingdom of Heaven. Extend an invitation into the Kingdom and offer the solution to receiving sight in the Kingdom: seeking it above everything.

Signs, wonders, and miracles are also done as a testimony of the existence of the Kingdom. The culture of Heaven on earth contains healing, signs, and wonders. Putting them on display demonstrates the existence of the Kingdom on earth. A disciple in his ministry brings faith to the hearers by making evident things not seen. There is no greater witness to the existence of the Kingdom than signs and wonders from Heaven demonstrated on earth.

Without a voice to articulate the purpose and intent of an outpouring, we limit and cut short what God wants to do in the earth. Every outpouring since the book of Acts has ceased, with one exception: The Toronto Airport Christian Fellowship revival. To date, it's still going strong. Why? Because, to my knowledge, it's the only revival in history where the Kingdom of God has been a significant message. Toronto and the Book of Acts church esteemed the message of the gospel of the Kingdom above all else. Toronto to a much lesser degree, nevertheless, they have presented something the Lord esteems above all and their fruit has testified to God's pleasure of a group seeking the Kingdom. God will never cease to promote what He wants promoted. This generation has the opportunity to launch a never-ending revival culminating in the kingdom of this world becoming the Kingdom of our Lord, bringing in His reign forever! Becoming a disciple of Jesus places you in position and brings to life gifts to be used to this end.

No doubt the outpouring of the Holy Spirit itself has benefit. Salvation, healing, people experiencing the love of God, mind changes, life changes: The list is long but self-centered and often not lasting in its fruit. All substance experienced outside the Kingdom is lacking the Kingdom itself. Ultimately if an entire nation isn't transformed we, as stewards of the outpouring have fallen short. Until God transforms a nation's culture, social norms, educational and economic system, etc .... It is not well with Him. This is the God-centered purpose for a Holy Spirit outpouring. We no longer can be satisfied with merely an outpouring. We must pursue the transformation of nations. This begins with the simple acknowledgment that the Greater has arrived. The Kingdom has come. Everything that is not the Kingdom, including its parts must bow!

 READ: Acts 8:12, 28:23,30-31,17:6-8,19:8, 20:25, 14:22-23, Luke 9:1-2, Matthew 24:14, Mark 16:15,20, and Hebrews 12:28.

The Apostles Teachings

Paul taught that Jesus would return as King to establish the Kingdom of God. Because of this teaching, he was falsely accused of inciting his followers to overthrow the Roman government. Although this was untrue, it put Paul and his associates in serious trouble. F.F. Bruce in his commentary on Acts says: "The apostles proclaimed the Kingdom of God, a very different kingdom from any secular empire, and no doubt they gave Jesus the Greek title *basileus* ('king'), by which the Roman Emperor was described by his Greek-speaking subjects" (F.F.Bruce, *The Book of Acts: The New International Commentary on the New Testament*, 1984, pp. 344-345).

You, O king, are the king of kings. The God of Heaven has given you dominion and power and might and glory; in your hands he has placed mankind and the beasts of the field and the birds of the air. Wherever they live, he has made you ruler over them all. You are that head of gold. After you, another kingdom will rise, inferior to yours. Next, a third kingdom, one of bronze, will rule over the whole earth. Finally, there will be a fourth kingdom, strong as iron—for iron breaks and smashes everything—and as iron breaks things to pieces, so it will crush and break all the others. Just as you saw that the feet and toes were partly of baked clay and partly of iron, so this will be a divided kingdom; yet it will have some of the strength of iron in it, even as you saw iron mixed with clay. As the toes were partly iron and partly clay, so this kingdom will be partly strong and partly brittle. And just as you saw the iron mixed with baked clay, so the people will be a mixture and will not remain united, any more than iron mixes with clay. In the time of those kings, the God of Heaven will set up a kingdom that will never be destroyed, nor will it be left to another people. It will crush all those kingdoms and bring them to an end, but it will itself endure forever.

Daniel 2:37-44

The ten horns you saw are ten kings who have not yet received a kingdom, but who for one hour will receive authority as kings along with the beast. They have one purpose and will give their power and authority to the beast. They will make war against the Lamb, but the Lamb will overcome them because he is Lord of lords and King of kings—and with him will be his called, chosen and faithful followers.

Revelation 17:12-14

In the Church Jesus established (the Kingdom Church), disciples were made. Revelation calls them chosen and faithful followers. The religious church produces followers (Act 6:7). An important responsibility of leadership in the Church is to transform followers into disciples (Luke 9:57-62). When leaders teach seeking first the Kingdom and discourage seeking things, then we catch the attention of Jesus and all of Heaven. A disciple expresses the mind of God through teaching scripture (Acts 8:30-35, Acts 11:26, 13:12). A disciple is one who perceives the Kingdom through the study of it until what he sees is made known to his surroundings through a co-creating relationship with Christ (Acts 19:8-12, 23). Acts 19:8,9 defines "the Way" as boldly "arguing persuasively about the kingdom of God." The book of Acts is the implementation and the manifestation of disciples making disciples. The church is weak and powerless because we have exchanged discipleship with followers.

Salvation costs us nothing but discipleship costs us everything. Salvation is something God does for us. Discipleship is something we choose to do with God (Luke 14:25-35).

A disciple obeys Jesus at their expense. A follower doesn't need to. A disciple willingly sacrifices his/her own desires for the sake of the Will of the Master. A follower doesn't need to. A disciple has the Masters Will in mind. A follower follows Jesus partly for what He has to offer.

This same Jesus, who has been taken from you into Heaven, will come back in the same way you have seen him go into Heaven. Jesus went up in a cloud. He will return on the clouds of Heaven (Matt 24:30). These clouds of Heaven are His ministers, His disciples (Acts 1:11).

My prayer is this:

Father,
Lead us to choose to become disciples
and begin by helping us make it our top priority
to understand Your Kingdom and Your righteousness.
As we do I ask You send the Spirit of Wisdom and Revelation
to awaken us to the Kingdom. Place Your Heavenly lens on the eyes of our
hearts creating vision of Your marvelous Kingdom. Do this for the sake of
the influence of Your Kingdom on earth as it is in Heaven.
Amen.

 Application: Commit today to discipline yourself to follow Jesus. You may have done it before, but mark today as the day you began fresh to be a disciple of Jesus. Expect the Father to demonstrate His Kingdom in and through you as He did in and through His Son, Jesus Christ!

Your name   Date

Conclusion

A testimony to and prayer for you, dear reader:

The year was 2012. I had been giving myself over to seeking the Kingdom for about 7 years. I had seasons of diligent study rewarded with captivating revelation and increasing Kingdom understanding. I also had seasons of dryness where my studies were so "lifeless" and boring I laid them down. Little did I know a day would come when my pursuits would transport me into another realm. I would become aware of the Kingdom's realness in a way I never knew possible. My labors, toil, and strife would come to an abrupt end and in exchange would surface an insatiable, relentless desire to pursue the Kingdom. No longer wavering from "I can't wait to jump into my Kingdom studies" to "I have no desire to study the Kingdom" and everything in between. Years ago I had grabbed hold of the Kingdom but I was about to experience the Kingdom grabbing hold of me.

I was at my office. It was one of those days I was excited to learn. I had been studying the book of Matthew. At the time, I was captivated by the parable of the sower in Matthew 13:44-45 and was pursuing revelation pertaining to the soil of our hearts and its connection to receiving the message of the Kingdom. This morning I decided I would read the entire chapter. When I came to the parable of the hidden treasure something happened. Something profound, something radically profound. I began reading:

The kingdom of Heaven is like treasure hidden in a field. When a man found it, he hid it again, and then in his joy went and sold all he had and bought that field. Again, the kingdom of Heaven is like a merchant looking for fine pearls. When he found one of great value, he went away and sold everything he had and bought it.

As I came to the part where it says "in joy went and sold all he had and bought the field" suddenly Heaven's perspective became visible to me. Right before my eyes I saw it!! It blew my mind! For the first time in my life, I saw the Kingdom in its totality. The man sold everything he had because he found everything he needed. He saw the whole which contains ALL parts! Wow! What a discovery! This same revelation was unveiled, affording me the opportunity of seeing something so vast, so altogether lovely and consuming it would cause me to lay down all other pursuits and adopt a single eye for the Kingdom. The Kingdom I had been trying to grab hold of suddenly grabbed hold of me! I became caught, captured and consumed in a way I couldn't have imagined. Instantly I was taken into a realm of existence I have never come out of to this day. Not only did I receive insight I was taken inside—inside the greatest, self-sufficient, all powerful, governmental system imaginable.

I have studied the Kingdom, investing 1000's of hours reading and watching teachings on the Kingdom. I chose to obey Jesus' command to make it my top priority to "seek first the Kingdom". Up to now I had learned many things about this marvelous system of rulership. I enjoyed consistent revelation and wonderful communion with the Lord regarding the subject of His eternal rule and reign. I had caught the Kingdom and was loving it! But nothing as earthshaking as this had happened. All Mighty God had lifted the veil and, in a split second, revealed the massiveness of His Cosmic Kingdom by showing me everything is contained in it. All needs, all wants, all provision. Everything! Absolutely everything. And when I saw this it caused me to lay down everything else at a whole new level. Not that I had built some massive idol and was running after it. Nor was I committing any terrible sin, but something happened. Seeing the wholeness of God's Kingdom captivated me in a new way. Nothing else mattered. News, sports, entertainment and the like took an even further back seat. All stress, anxiety, worry, and fear vanished altogether. Puff! Gone! Experiencing, in that split second, in an undeniable way the fact that the Kingdom is everything if it's anything placed an all-consuming burning desire in my soul to seek it like never before. As I write this in mid-2016 I can say not only has that burning desire remained, it has grown. I am confident the flame of seeking first the Kingdom of God will never go out. I discovered the reward for seeking first the Kingdom: It in turn will seek you and consume you!

For years, I never thought to consider what happened that life changing day. I just assumed I had another one of my life changing revelations and was better off because of it. When revelation comes I don't usually stop to consider what happened I just embrace it and do my best to hold on to it, trying to use it for the glory of God and the benefit of others. But this revelation had an addendum to it that would come to me 3 years later. This "add-on" was revealed to me as I heard Philippians 3:12 read:

> *"Not that I have already reached the goal or am already fully mature, but I make every effort to take hold of it because I also have been taken hold of by Christ Jesus.* (HCSB)

For seven years I had been "taking hold" of the Kingdom but that day the Kingdom took hold of me. When you "take hold of" God's big idea, "seeking first the Kingdom", it's only a matter of time before God's big idea takes hold of you. When that happens you're branded an overcomer, a chosen and faithful disciple in the Kingdom of Heaven!

This conclusion is a prayer for you. My prayer is to be a declaration over your life. I'm going to ask you to make a commitment, as best you can to seek first the Kingdom. Make understanding the Kingdom your highest priority. You don't have to commit to doing this the rest of your life. Give it a month. One month of making the pursuit of the Kingdom your highest priority. Don't pursue the "parts." Lay down the study of all "things" pertaining to the Kingdom and seek after the Kingdom. Study the material in this book. Review it, review it again. Memorize it! Find other material that reveals the Kingdom—Its essence—and study them (there is a recommended list at the end of this book). Buy DVDs and CDs on the Kingdom. Ask the Holy Spirit to open your eyes to see the Kingdom! My spiritual father, Jack Taylor once said "To one who has seen the Kingdom, it is observed that on every page of scripture the Kingdom of God is either assumed or asserted." I promise you, once the Kingdom grabs hold of you this statement will come alive in your life.

While seeking first the Kingdom, look for subtle "Kingdom sightings." Little things that, once we become aware of them, will help propel us to continue pursuing the Kingdom. Things like revelation, a special "coincidence" we identify as God, a gentle touch from the Lord, the sudden awareness of His presence or hand working, etc. We must keep our eyes open for such sightings and know that we have ALL of Heaven cheering us on, not just the great cloud of witnesses!

Caution: Prepare for resistance from the Devil. More than anything he hates when a believer commits to seek first the Kingdom. Resist the temptation to worry, become fearful or doubt. Take your thoughts captive and refuse to embrace money in an unhealthy way. Let the message of the Kingdom find root in the soil of your heart. Always carrying with you the King's promise over your life that if you "seek first the Kingdom of God and his righteousness ALL THESE THINGS WILL BE GIVEN TO YOU."

Consider using this book as a Bible study and gather others to seek the Kingdom with you. There is strength in numbers.

My prayer for you is that as you begin practicing your commitment to seek first the Kingdom, that God All Mighty would come and capture your heart with enough revelation of the Kingdom to keep your pursuit of it top priority. And as you continue to "make every effort to take hold of the Kingdom," I pray at the appointed time the Kingdom take hold of you. Utterly and completely take hold of you. The result? You become caught, captured, and consumed with the Kingdom and the Kings rule and reign first in your heart then on earth as it is in Heaven. Amen!

 Application: Review the commitments you have made as you have read this treatise on the Kingdom. Remember them and commit today to keep your promises. Declare "I Am a Kingdom Person. I am all that He says I am. And by His grace I will become all He has predestined me to be.

Your name · Date

About the Author

Michael Gissibl is a man who wears many hats.
He has been a successful business owner for over 20
years, carrying out God's word to him to "train, equip,
and release" employees, resulting in many protégés'
also having successful businesses of their own. After
experiencing a dramatic health transformation in
2009, Michael pursued a holistic health certification. Upon completion,
he established a private practice to carry out God's word to him to
"restore My Temple." Michael has helped countless people to improve
the quality of their lives through the restoration of the body, mind, and
soul. His most recent endeavor has resulted in the publication of this
book, as well as several others in the works. As a 2005 graduate of the
Morning Star School of Ministry, Michael has held numerous teaching
and leadership positions, and has been involved in several nonprofit
organizations. His passion for the Kingdom message is deeply rooted
and far reaching. Presently Michael's main focus is to continue writing
and grow his itinerant speaking ministry. Preaching the gospel of the
Kingdom is his deepest longing.

Michael is married to Sheila, a Psychologist who is Director and
owner of a clinic in Waukesha, WI, as well as a Professor at Mount
Mary University. He is blessed with 4 children and treasures the joys
and challenges of watching them grow into adulthood. He enjoys active
involvement in their sports careers, as well as their spiritual development.
His passion for traveling God's great land is second only to pursuit of
Kingdom awareness.

You can connect with Michael at his website:

www.discoveringthekingdom.org

or contact him @

kingdomwakefulness@gmail.com